British Economic and Social History

Philip Sauvain

1700-1870

A New Certificate Approach

First published in 1987 by:
Stanley Thornes (Publishers) Ltd
Ellenborough House
Wellington Street
CHELTENHAM GL50 1YW
England

99 00 01 / 20 19 18 17 16 15 14

British Library Cataloguing in Publication Data

Sauvain, Philip
    British economic and social history.
    From 1700 to the mid-1900 century
    1. Great Britain—Social conditions
    I. Title
    941.07   HN385

    ISBN 0–85950–619–3

Typeset by Blackpool Typesetting Services Ltd, Blackpool
in 11/13 Times
Printed and bound in Great Britain at Martin's The Printers, Berwick

Contents

Acknowledgements

The author and publishers are grateful to the following for supplying and giving permission to reproduce prints and artwork:

BBC Hulton Picture Library, pp 19, 22, 24, 232, 243, 245, 246, 301; Beedle and Cooper, p 308; Fotomas Index, p 81; Greater London Council, p 299; Ironbridge Gorge Museum Trust, p 64; John R. Freeman & Co. p 276; Leicestershire County Council and Museum, p 21; Mansell Collection, pp 45, 48, 83, 97, 126, 235, 237, 254; Mary Evans Picture Library, p 319; Merseyside County Council and Walker Art Gallery, p 59; Methuen & Co. Ltd for the maps showing Population Density in England and Wales, p 188; Rex C. Russell for the maps showing Waltham Before and After Enclosure, pp 8 and 9; Science Museum Library, pp 54, 74, 107, 122; Staffordshire Pottery Industry Preservation Trust, p 69; The Institution of Civil Engineers, p 105; The National Portrait Gallery, p 106; The Post Office, p 110; The Wellcome Trust, p 313; Trade Union Congress Library, p 257; Wedgwood Museum, p 70

The author and publishers are also grateful to the following for permission to reproduce text extracts:

A. & C. Black for *Mr Gay's London* by A. P. Herbert published by Ernest Benn Ltd, p 287

Bell & Hyman for *English Economic Documents* by Bland, Brown & Tawney, p 25 and *The Diary of Samuel Pepys* Vols 6 and 7, p 242

David & Charles for *Lancashire* by Edward Baines, p 96 and *John Norton and Sons* edited by Frances Norton Mason, p 163

J. M. Dent & Sons Ltd for *Humphry Clinker* by Tobias Smollett, edited by Charles Lee, p 218

Eyre & Spottiswoode for *Torrington Diaries* edited by C. B. Andrews, p 11 and *English Historical Documents* Vols XI and XII (I), pp 267, 269 and 279

Gregg International, Godstone, Surrey for *Working Conditions in the Victorian Age*, p 277

Macmillan Publishers for *Workers and Employers* edited by J. T. Ward and W. Hamish Fraser, pp 261, 262

Oxford University Press for *Diary of a Country Parson* by James Woodforde, edited by John Beresford, p 170

Penguin Books Ltd for *A Tour Through the Whole Island of Great Britain* by Daniel Defoe, edited by Pat Rogers pp 46–7, 51, 63, 101

Every attempt has been made to contact copyright holders, but we apologise if any have been overlooked.

Notes for Students

The period between the beginning of the eighteenth century and the middle of the nineteenth century was an exciting one in British history. It was a period of prodigious expansion, in which a small and rather obscure group of islands, close to mainland Europe, swiftly acquired a huge worldwide empire.

In 1851, the Great Exhibition held in the Crystal Palace demonstrated to the world that Britain was then the world's leading industrial power and envied 'Workshop of the World'. The greatest inventions of the age were British; the steam engine was the driving force at the heart of the new technology and the railways were transforming the continents of the world. By 1870, roughly half the world's coal, cotton cloth and pig iron, and about three-quarters of its ships, came from the British Isles.

A revolution in farming techniques and methods, a vast growth in overseas trade, and a rapid expansion of banking and insurance facilities which made London the unrivalled centre of world finance, parallelled the industrial expansion.

The population of the British Isles soared, from less than 9 million in 1700, to nearly 30 million by 1870. In that same period, London grew eightfold from 500,000 to nearly 4,000,000 people whilst Glasgow, Liverpool and Manchester changed out of all recognition, from small towns in 1700, with fewer than 10,000 people, to teeming cities of nearly 500,000 inhabitants by the 1870s.

Such phenomenal growth could hardly have left the rural landscape of 1700 unscarred and unpolluted. It caused major upheavals in the structure of society. Existing social and welfare provision was no longer sufficient. Improvements in both local and central government failed lamentably to keep pace with the growth of both the economy and the towns.

Becoming the 'Workshop of the World' raised many tough problems: in education; in the maintenance of law and order; in the provision of municipal services, such as mains water and drainage; in public health, such as the control of epidemic diseases; and in the scale, extent and type of welfare provision for the poor, the unemployed and the handicapped.

Not surprisingly, these major changes and the problems they created were met with mixed reactions from the people caught in the middle of this transformation of society. The working classes, without a vote in

1700 and unrepresented in Parliament, responded at times with violence but never with open rebellion, unlike many other European countries during this period. When they acted constitutionally, as at Peterloo in 1819, they were met by violence. Trade union growth was deliberately stifled; the legal position of the unions was still unclear in 1870, just three years after a substantial number of working-class men had been given the vote for the first time.

These many and varied activities and developments are described in this book. At times the relationship between these different strands of development may not always be clear or obvious. This is why you should find the Time Chart, on pages 321–4 useful. It has been designed to show at a glance, how these various elements were all part of the same social and economic revolution.

Some of the extracts and quotations used in this book have been simplified – in rare cases with the substitution of a modern word or phrase for one that is obscure or obsolete, more commonly by inserting the meaning in brackets adjacent to the word or phrase in the quotation (rather than as a footnote which might be overlooked). In a very few instances, link words have been added to smooth the juncture between separate extracts from the same source.

Lack of space has inevitably prevented the inclusion of many long quotations and the usual technique of eliminating unnecessary sentences or phrases has been adopted in order to cut these extracts down to comprehensible proportions. However, the convention of indicating such exclusions with rows of dots has not normally been followed, to avoid confusing the reader with broken dotted text.

Notes for Teachers

Questions and exercises have been numbered in the text. As a general, but not invariable, rule the simpler, easier questions come first, followed by the more complicated, interpretative questions.

As far as possible these questions and exercises have been designed to provide students at all levels of ability with an opportunity to demonstrate what 'they know, understand and can do' as preparation for the differentiated questions in the GCSE examination.

Chapter One

The Agrarian Revolution

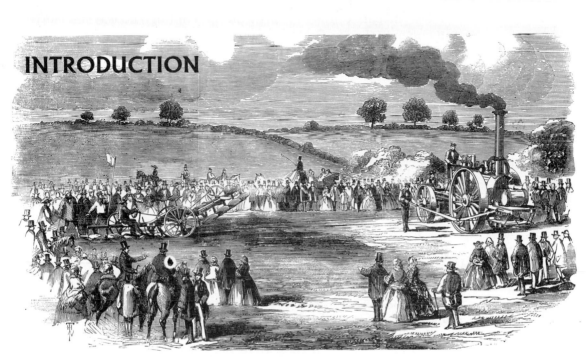

INTRODUCTION

Ploughing Meeting,
The Illustrated London
News, *17 October,*
1857

'The progress of our agriculture during recent years has been striking. The British farmer has awakened from his long trance, and with some few exceptions, is ever ready to seize upon the newest invention in farming implements: he seeks out the most fertilising manures, the best methods of drainage, and the best arrangements of farm buildings. He engages the most skilful servants and the most intelligent labourers; and, greatest and best of all improvements, he has chained the steam-horse to the plough and the thrashing machine. Wherever we find steam introduced, it is a significant mark of progress; and the more we can use it, the better. Steam-horses require no feeds of corn, and therefore leave all the more grain for the food of the people.'

Chambers's Journal 1856

1 *Name five improvements used by progressive farmers in 1856.*
2 *Which of these improvements did the writer think was the most important? Which improvement can you see in the picture?*

> **3** _What did the writer call a steam traction engine? Why? What did the writer say was one of its advantages? With what was the steam traction engine being compared?_
>
> **4** _What did the writer mean by the phrase 'The British farmer has awakened from his long trance'?_

Farming had come a long way over the previous hundred years. In the mid-eighteenth century much of the land in England was still cultivated in communal open fields instead of being divided into separate farms. In some areas farming had changed little since the Middle Ages. In other areas you could already see the beginnings of what was to become a revolution in agriculture.

There were very few sudden and dramatic changes. It was not like a real revolution at all. But by the middle years of the nineteenth century, almost all of the open fields had gone and new farming methods were talked about, even if they were not commonly used.

In this chapter you will see what progress was achieved, why it was so striking, and how and why these changes took place. You will also see that these changes brought poverty and distress to many of the people who lived, and worked, on the land.

REASONS FOR THE CHANGES IN AGRICULTURE

The reasons why the changes in agriculture took place can only be fully understood if looked at together with the other developments which were taking place in Britain at the same time.

(a) The growth of the population (see Chapter 5) created a constant demand for more food. The number of people in England and Wales probably grew by as much as 50 per cent between 1750 and 1800. It then doubled between 1800 and 1850. The old system of farming had only just been able to feed everyone in 1700. By 1850, the demand for food had trebled. Yet, despite the changes in agriculture, hunger was common among the poorest people in Britain.

(b) The rapid growth of the industrial towns (see Chapters 2 and 5). Before this most people (even the weavers and coal miners) had plots of land on which they grew some of the food they ate. However, with the growth of industry, the industrial workers who lived in the towns had to depend entirely on the farmers for their food. When corn prices rose, they had to pay more for their bread.

(c) The rapid improvement in transport and travel (see Chapter 3). Better roads, and later the railways, made it easier to take food from the countryside to the towns, and deliver coal and machinery to the farmer.

(d) The Revolutionary and Napoleonic Wars (1793 to 1815) prevented

European corn reaching Britain. Because grain was scarce, prices in Britain rose steeply, which gave big profits to farmers and provided them with an even greater incentive to produce more food from their land.

(e) People who had made money from trade bought land. They built mansions and applied their business skills to their estates. They wanted to make a profit from farming.

THE OPEN-FIELD SYSTEM

In 1700 the system of farming in many villages throughout England was little different from that of the Middle Ages. In many parts of southern and central England, farmland was still cultivated in huge open fields.

But, there were some signs of the changes to come. In many areas the open fields had already been wholly or partly enclosed. Land reclamation schemes in East Anglia had created large new areas of fertile soil. British travellers in Holland brought back new ideas, such as growing turnips as a fodder crop. But in 1700 these new methods were used by only a handful of farmers.

Open fields

Instead of being divided into hundreds of small fields, surrounded by hedges, land in the typical open field village was left as three huge fields, unfenced and divided into narrow strips of land. Each farmer held a number of these strips but they were scattered. Some were on good land, some on bad.

In practice, many strips had already been enclosed or combined into larger blocks of land by the beginning of the eighteenth century. Some farmers had become richer than others. The right to hold strips in the open fields was by no means equally shared by the villagers of 1700.

Many poor peasants had only one or two strips of land. The poorest – the cottagers – had no rights to any land. They scraped a meagre existence from the commons and woods, living in run-down cottages on the edge of the village or on the common.

Many farmers rented their land from the lord of the manor, as you can see in this extract from a letter by Henry Purefoy to Mr South, dated 'Wensday Nov ye 18th 1747'.

'Mr. Land the Attorney [lawyer] of Buckingham acquaints mee that you want a Bargain [small farm] of about three score pounds [£60] a year. I have a Bargain of seven yard lands [blocks of farmland] in the open ffeild with ye homestall to set [start] next Lady day [25 March]. The yearly rent is eight pounds the yard land and there is a close let with them which altogether make sixty three pounds a year. If this suitts you I shall be willing to accept you as a Tennant.'

From the *Purefoy Letters* edited by G. Eland

> 1 *Where were the yard lands situated?*
> 2 *What do you think the 'homestall' was?*
> 3 *Like farmland in many parts of Britain, a small part of the land had already been enclosed. How do we know this from Mr Purefoy's letter? What was the name for an enclosed field?*

Geography of the open fields

Area most affected by enclosure

The open-field system was not evenly spread across the British Isles. Many areas had never operated this system of farming, and as a result only the areas shown on the map were seriously affected by enclosure in the period between 1700 and 1850.

> 1 *Look at the map. Write one or two sentences to say in which parts of Britain most of the open fields were in 1700.*
> 2 *Do you think the farmers in the area where you live were affected when the open fields were enclosed?*

The three-course rotation

The open fields were cultivated in common. Farmers co-operated in order to do jobs which could be done more sensibly if they all worked together. They had to decide which crops would be grown in the fields, since it was nonsense for one farmer to grow root crops when all the others were growing wheat.

They used a simple system of crop rotation. In the first year they grew wheat. In the second year they grew barley or peas. In the third year they left the land fallow. This simply meant leaving it as stubble after the harvest, allowing weeds to grow, but letting the village cattle and sheep graze there. Their manure fertilised the soil. In the fourth year it was ready to start all over again with wheat.

The commons

Village cattle and sheep grazed on the common lands. Each of the villagers had the right to graze livestock there. The number of livestock they could graze depended upon the size of their holdings of land in the open fields and on past custom (whether their ancestors had also had these rights). The cows were looked after by an appointed cow keeper or hayward, the sheep by a shepherd and the pigs by a swineherd. The villagers had other rights as well, such as the right to take timber from the woods and turf from waste land for use as fuel.

We know a lot about these rights and the ways in which the open fields were run from old documents. In 1750, the rules at Shalstone (a village in Buckinghamshire) stated how many animals each farmer could keep on the common grazing lands, and when owners were to take their cattle away from the meadows (to let the grass grow). Some farmers had to supply a bull 'for the service of the Common herd'.

Farmers who let their pigs stray on to the open fields, or failed to keep the drainage ditches clear, were fined. Arrangements were made to hire a mole catcher, crow keeper (to shoot and keep crows and other vermin away), hayward (or cowkeeper) and two fieldsmen (to look after the open fields).

Ridge and furrow pattern in Northumberland. The ridges follow the line of the old medieval strips, when they were ploughed as part of the common fields. Why do they stand out in the snow?

Because farmers might have had strips scattered all over the village, farms and farm buildings were usually built in the village centre and not in the fields.

Advantages of the open-field system

(a) Most of the villagers had strips in the open fields, so a substantial number (but by no means all) of the people in the village were farming for themselves, rather than working as labourers for someone else.

(b) Because the strips were scattered, farmers could expect a fair share of the good and bad land.

(c) They shared rights to graze animals on the commons and had rights to timber and turf.

(d) The villagers were self-sufficient, growing their own food and rearing their own livestock.

(e) Because they were simple rather than sophisticated farmers, their requirements could easily be met by local tradespeople. Most villages had shops, an ale house or pub, a blacksmith, a carpenter and other craftsmen who could fashion the crude implements they needed to cultivate the land.

(f) Communal farming in the unfenced open fields meant that villagers had to co-operate to survive. So, they formed close-knit communities – helping each other but often bickering and even fighting among themselves.

Disadvantages of the open-field system

(a) Because the strips were scattered across the open fields, farmers wasted a lot of time travelling from one strip to another.

(b) Because the strips were small, there was little point in buying and using expensive new machinery like the newly-invented seed drill or the horse hoe in the early eighteenth century.

(c) Because the three-course rotation in the open fields left one year in every three fallow, crop yields were cut by a third.

(d) With no walls or hedges there was little to stop animals straying on to the open fields. Their owners were fined, but this was no compensation for the damage done to the harvest.

(e) Everyone had to grow the same crop. You could not grow turnips on your strip during the wheat year, since the sheep would feed on the stubble **and** your turnips, before they were ready for pulling.

(f) Paths and strips of waste land separated the strips, leaving a substantial part of the arable land uncultivated.

(g) Farmers were at the mercy of their neighbours. If the neighbours on both sides of a strip were lazy and did not weed their strips then the weeds spread to your land as well.

(h) Diseased and sick cows and sheep could infect the healthy animals on the common pastures. Selective breeding to improve the quality and quantity of meat, milk and wool was impossible.

(i) It was not usually sensible to try to drain the strips in the open fields, without the agreement of the other farmers.

(j) The common lands – grass, woodland, meadow land, waste land – occupied large areas of potential arable land. The richer farmers wanted to bring these common lands under the plough, so making more land available for cultivation.

(k) Few fodder crops were grown to feed the livestock in winter. As a result, many animals had to be killed at the end of the grass-growing season and before the onset of winter.

THE ENCLOSURE MOVEMENT

A farmer, called Thomas Tusser, wrote these lines in about 1570:

'More plenty of mutton and beef,
Corn, butter, and cheese of the best,
Where find ye (go search any coast)
Than there, where enclosure is most?'

> 1 *Which type of land did Tusser say produced the most food?*
> 2 *How can we tell from this that some parts of Britain were not farmed as open fields in the sixteenth century?*

Enclosure basically meant dividing the land into compact holdings, separated from other holdings by hedges, walls or fences. It meant getting rid of most of the common pastures and the common rights to woodland. These were allocated, instead, in parcels of land to those farmers who could prove they had a legal right to a share in the division of land.

Enclosing the open fields was not a new idea in the eighteenth century – it had been started hundreds of years earlier. In any case, many areas of Britain had not been farmed in open fields in the first place, such as Wales, Devon and Cornwall, parts of the north-west and the south-east. But, what was new in the eighteenth century was the speed with which enclosure began to take place, and the rapidity with which it altered the appearance of the country and changed methods of farming.

How the open fields were enclosed

The best method of enclosing the open fields was by agreement amongst those entitled to hold land. This was the method recommended by Arthur Young (see page 22). If there was no agreement, then enclosure could be forced through by law, provided the holders of 80 per cent of the land agreed to take joint action to enclose it.

Since a minority of the population – the richest farmers and land-owners – often held 80 per cent of the land anyway, it meant that they were usually able to enclose the open fields even if the majority of villagers opposed it.

The first thing they had to do was to tell the other villagers what they were planning. The law required that they did this by posting a notice of their intentions on the church door in the village on three Sundays in the summer.

Then, they could petition Parliament to pass a special law – an Enclosure Act – making it legal. In theory, Parliament tried to ensure that the enclosure of the open fields took into account the legal rights of all the landowners, not just those who were rich. Enclosure Commissioners were, therefore, sent to make a survey. They listened to the villagers, examined documents and drew maps.

On the basis of this survey, the Commissioners awarded blocks of land to the farmers. They usually tried to be fair, but since the richer landowners were often well known to them, it was inevitable that their awards were often unsatisfactory to the poorer villagers.

Getting the Enclosure Act through Parliament cost a lot of money and there were also legal fees to be paid as well. These costs all had to be met by the villagers. Later on, those farmers who got land had to pay for new roads, farm buildings and hedges, walls and fences. Enclosure was a costly business.

Some villagers, the cottagers, got no land at all. Others got parcels of land which were too small to be profitably farmed. As a result the poorest farmers had to sell the land they were awarded, either because they could not pay the costs of enclosure or because it was not profitable to farm it. Richer farmers bought their land and made their own estates even larger. The former farmers now became farm labourers, or left the countryside entirely, seeking work in the new industrial towns which were growing rapidly at this time.

You can see the effects of enclosure in the two maps of the village of Waltham in Lincolnshire – before and after enclosure in 1769–71.

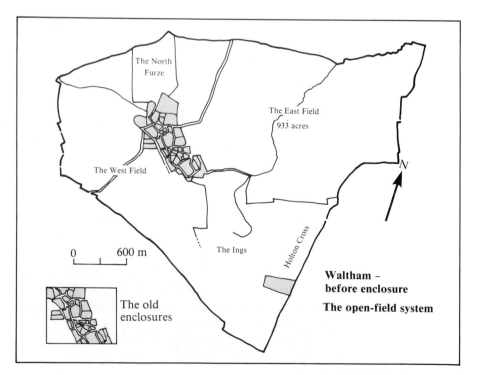

Open-field village before enclosure, based on the surveyor's map, c. 1769

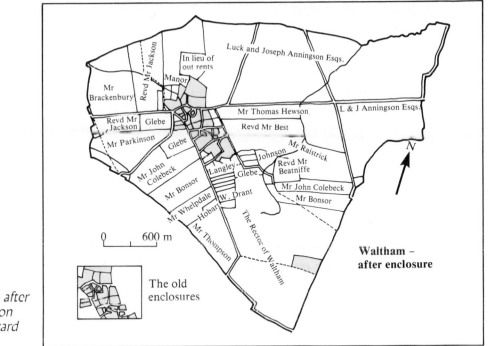

Open-field village after enclosure, based on the Enclosure Award map, c. 1771

---

1 *What were the names of the old open fields of this village?*
2 *Which part of the village was enclosed before 1769?*
3 *What happened to the East Field after enclosure?*
4 *Who took most of the area to the south of the parish?*

In 1771 Arthur Young wrote about:

> 'The amazing superiority of wool and profit in enclosed counties to open ones. The profit (per sheep) in enclosed grounds is 11s [55p] but in open ones only 2s 3d [11p] which is a prodigious difference. In the Vale of Evesham the average fleece is 9 lb [4 kg] in the enclosures; but only 3 lb [1.35 kg] in the open fields. Can there be a stronger argument for enclosing?'

---

5 *How much extra profit did he say there was per sheep in enclosed fields as opposed to open fields? By how many times were the sheep fleeces greater in weight on the enclosed lands? Was it a 'prodigious difference'?*
6 *Why would you have to treat these figures with a certain amount of caution? What would you want to know before accepting them as a decisive argument in favour of enclosure?*

The results of enclosure

Enclosure provided a solution to most of the problems caused by open-field farming (listed on page 6 under 'Disadvantages of the open-field system'). It also gave the landholders larger farms than they had held before enclosure. This was partly because some strip holders had been unable to prove they had a legal right to a share of the enclosures. It was also because much of the common lands, the woodlands and the waste lands were enclosed as well.

In the new, compact enclosed farms, farmers could breed and rear quality livestock. They saved time because their fields were close to one another. They suffered fewer problems from the spread of weeds and crop diseases from neighbouring land. Above all, they had freedom to use new methods of cultivation. They were no longer obliged to follow the old three-course rotation – wheat-barley-fallow. They could follow a new system, such as the four-course Norfolk Rotation (wheat-roots-barley-clover). The choice was theirs, not that of their fellow villagers.

Once land was enclosed it made more sense to buy expensive implements and machinery, such as the seed drill, horse hoe and Rotherham plough (see page 16). It also made sense to drain the land and improve its quality with manure and fertilisers.

But there were some practical problems as well. Each farmer had to plant hedges, erect stone walls or wooden fences to surround the new fields. At Cambo, in Northumberland, this even affected the type of farming adopted – as Arthur Young found when he visited farms in the area in 1769: 'About Cambo they keep no sheep, upon account of the white-thorn hedges in their new enclosures.'

---

1 *What reason was given for the absence of sheep at Cambo?*
2 *Can you think of a good reason why this deterred farmers from keeping sheep?*

One result of enclosure was that farmland prices and farm rents went up rapidly in value – to the advantage of those who owned land and to the disadvantage of those who did not. Food production increased, helping to support the growth in population and enabling the new industrial towns to thrive and expand.

But the pace of enclosure was not uniform. Nearly 1,500 Enclosure Acts were passed between 1790 and 1810 – half as many again as in the period between 1770 and 1790.

Effects of enclosure on the poor

Inside a farm labourer's cottage in Dorset, The Illustrated London News, *5 September 1846*

Enclosure brought poverty and hardship to many farm workers. In 1789, the Hon. John Byng went on a tour of the Midlands. Near Birmingham he talked to a lady in the village of Meriden:

> BYNG 'Has Meriden Common been long enclosed?'
> LADY 'Ah, lackaday, Sir, that was a sad job and ruined all us poor folk: and those who then gave into it, now repent it.'
> BYNG 'Why so?'
> LADY 'Because, we had our garden, our bees, our share of a flock of sheep, the feeding of our geese; and could cut turf for our fuel. Now all that is gone.'

From *The Torrington Diaries* edited by C.Bruyn Andrews and abridged by Fanny Andrews, published by Eyre and Spottiswode 1954

---

1 *What did the lady say enclosure had done for the poor people of Meriden?*
2 *What benefits had she enjoyed before enclosure?*
3 *Who did she say had had second thoughts about enclosure? To whom do you think she was referring?*

When he was in the Cotswolds in 1781, Byng had earlier said: 'As a sportsman I hate enclosures, and as a citizen, I look on them as the greedy tyrannies of the wealthy few'.

4 *What did he mean by that? How could enclosure affect him 'as a sportsman'?*

5 *In the light of this statement, can his dialogue with the lady in Meriden be taken seriously as reliable evidence that enclosure really did hurt the poor?*

6 *In what ways does the picture of a Dorset labourer's cottage, in 1846, support the view that there was considerable poverty and distress in the countryside after the period of the enclosures? Does this prove that the enclosures were the cause?*

Enclosure hit the poor farmers very hard indeed, giving them few advantages. The rewards went to the richer or more intelligent and adventurous farmers.

Poor farmers could not oppose the enclosure movement effectively, since they had to travel to London to present their case, or pay lawyers to do it for them. In any case, most were illiterate and ignorant of their rights.

Some poor farmers could not justify their claims to the land they held. Their only justification was that they had always farmed the land – it was a custom. This is why they were called customary tenants. The Commissioners, however, were only interested in legal documents entitling the owner to land or the right to lease or rent land and as a result many farmers lost their land.

The cost of paying for the survey put many farmers out of business. A small farmer with only 10 hectares could hardly afford to pay £30 in legal fees plus £100 or so for new roads and fences. Small farmers in one Northamptonshire parish calculated that it would cost each of them £250, just to hedge the small plots they were entitled to under the Enclosure Acts.

The people most affected were probably the poor cottagers who scraped a living from rough huts built near the commons. Here they kept a few hens and a pig and did odd jobs for a living. They had no right to any land, not even the sites of their huts. Many were evicted as a result of enclosure. In addition, they, and many other poor people, lost the right to graze animals in the meadows and on the common. They also suffered the loss of the woods, where they had earlier been able to snare rabbits and cut timber. In desperation, many turned to poaching to make ends meet – even if it meant the gallows, or transportation, if they were caught.

Enclosure greatly enlarged the labourer class of poor people who had been poor, but self-sufficient, farmers in the past. Rural poverty had always existed in England. But the extent of poverty in the countryside during the period of enclosures was probably greater and more widespread

Mill plaque in Snettisham in Norfolk. When was this flour mill built? Who paid for the mill? Why was it built?

than at any time since Tudor times and the Middle Ages. The new poor brought to a head the old arguments about poor relief (see Chapter 8).

To what extent this distress was caused by enclosure is a matter of debate. Enclosure was hastened by the Revolutionary and Napoleonic Wars which pushed up the price of bread and hit the poor people. Farmers made big profits during the Wars because the demand for wheat was always high. Farmers with land on the existing open fields soon saw that the only way to share this prosperity was by enclosure. This is why many more Enclosure Acts were passed during the Revolutionary and Napoleonic Wars than in the years preceeding 1793.

However, there was considerable opposition to enclosure. In 1765 *The Northampton Mercury* reported that a 'tumultuous mob' at West Haddon had destroyed fences intended for the enclosure of the common field after first assembling there to play football!

Social effects of enclosures

Prominent among the social effects of enclosure was the change in village life. Many farmers no longer took a prominent part in village life, since they built their new houses and farm buildings away from the village and on the site of the land awarded to them by the Enclosure Commissioners. One consequence of this was an increased feeling of isolation.

In 1832, William Cobbett, then in Northumberland,

'saw in one place more than a hundred corn-stacks in one yard, each having from six to seven Surrey wagon-loads of sheaves in a stack; and not another house to be seen within a mile or two of the farm-house.'

The village tended to tear apart. There were empty, run-down buildings along the village street. In a poem called 'Our Village', written in 1839, Thomas Hood said there were fifty-five private houses in the village and 'six empty'.

The life of the affluent farmer and family contrasted sharply with that of the poor labourer. The villagers no longer farmed in common, so many of the old village occupations disappeared, such as those of the fieldsmen, cowherd, swineherd and hayward. Ploughs and other field implements were manufactured in towns rather than by village smiths and carpenters.

At the same time, many country people in the North and Midlands, left the land, of their own free will, to work in town factories – even though they were no worse off after enclosure than they had been before. The rapidly growing industrial towns offered better paid jobs, better living standards (despite the slums) and excitement. They were more interesting places in which to live than sleepy country villages. So on the one hand there was pressure to leave the land, and on the other, a real incentive to go and work in the towns.

AGRICULTURAL IMPROVEMENTS

Enclosure was often prompted by the desire of farmers to take advantage of the new improvements in agriculture which were being talked about in the eighteenth century.

A number of farmers tried out new crops, new methods of cultivation and selective breeding after enclosure. They used fertilisers, new implements and machines. The people responsible for these new ideas and innovations are sometimes called the agricultural improvers.

Ploughing, The Illustrated London News, *17 October 1846*

New implements

Foremost among the agricultural improvers at the start of the eighteenth century was the Berkshire farmer, Jethro Tull (see below) who invented the seed drill.

Jethro Tull (1674 1741)

Jethro Tull was born in 1674. His main interest was in the use of the horse hoe to kill weeds in growing corn crops. He said you did not need manure to grow corn, provided you hoed between the rows instead! His book, *Horse Hoeing Husbandry*, was published in 1731.

Since you can only use a hoe if the corn seed is sown in rows, he invented a seed drill. It was this seed drill (1701) which really made his name famous as an agricultural improver, although it did not come into general use until the middle of the nineteenth century.

Corn seed had always been sown 'broadcast'. The farmer carried a bag of corn seed and scattered it by hand across newly-cultivated soil. In Jethro Tull's drill the corn seed was held in boxes. An ingenious device controlled the flow of seeds out of these boxes into shallow rows in the soil, which were made by the machine as it went up and down the length of a cultivated field. A harrow at the back of the machine covered the seeds with soil to prevent birds pecking at them.

Until the later years of the eighteenth century, farm implements were usually made by local craftsmen. In 1736, Elizabeth Purefoy wrote to 'Goodman Zachary a ploughmaker at Helmdon' in a nearby village, saying that the people in her village had recommended him:

'I desire you will make mee a very good plough and bring it over as soon as possible you can. Pray bring it in two or three days for wee shall want it'.

1 *How do you think a modern farmer would buy a plough? What does this letter tell you about country life in the middle of the eighteenth century?*
Look at the pictures on pages 14 and 16.
2 *How many labourers and how many horses were needed to pull a plough?*

Drilling corn seed and harrowing, The Illustrated London News, *7 November 1846*

3 *Draw a sketch of the seed drill and label it to show how it worked.*

4 *How many furrows were turned by the plough at a time? How many furrows were turned by the plough pulled by a steam engine, shown in the picture at the start of this chapter?*

The Rotherham plough

By the time of Elizabeth Purefoy's letter, however, a new implement, the Rotherham plough, had already been invented in Firbeck, a small village about 15 km from Rotherham in Yorkshire. But it was not until 1760, that it came into general use.

The Rotherham plough was easier to use than existing ploughs, even in very dry weather when the ground was hard. It could plough deep or shallow furrows, as the farmer required, and it was stronger than the usual plough. The inventors claimed it had 'Less wood and fewer joints, requiring fewer repairs than the common sorts of ploughs'.

The first Rotherham ploughs were made of wood (with iron plough-shares) but by the early nineteenth century, they were much stronger, being made completely of iron.

The threshing machine

Another important invention was that of the threshing machine – invented by Andrew Meikle, a Scottish millwright, in 1786. It did not become widely used until after 1840. In his machine, ears of corn were separated from the stalks when the corn was fed into a revolving drum, causing it to rub against the sides. Power was needed to turn the drum and this was provided by the 'gin'.

The 'gin' was a relatively simple engine which employed cogs and wheels to make use of the power provided by a team, or 'gang' of horses, going round and round in a tight circle. Special buildings, called 'gin-gang houses', were built on farms to make use of this machine.

The Norfolk Rotation

One of the most significant innovations was that of the Norfolk crop rotation. In the first year a field was sown with wheat, then came a root crop, such as turnips, in the second year. In the third year another grain crop was grown, usually barley, and in the fourth year a grass was grown, such as clover or lucerne.

The Norfolk Rotation had several main advantages. Chief of these was the fact that it increased the amount of cropland since land did not lie fallow. Under the old three-field system an area of say 600 hectares of arable land was often divided into three fields – growing 200 hectares of wheat, 200 hectares of barley and a third field with 200 hectares of land lying idle as fallow.

Under the Norfolk Rotation, the same 600 hectares of land could be sown with 150 hectares of wheat, 150 hectares of turnips, 150 hectares of barley and 150 hectares of clover.

---

1 *What was the total area of land sown with crops under the three field system?*
2 *What was the total area of land sown with crops under the Norfolk Rotation?*
3 *What percentage increase in cropland could be achieved by changing from the three field system to the Norfolk Rotation?*
4 *Did this mean that farmers could expect a similar percentage increase in the value of their crops?*

The Norfolk Rotation also helped to increase the yield of crops at harvest time. The different crops put fertility back into the soil. For example, clover puts nitrogen back. When roots were grown the land was cleansed of weeds, since the young turnips were well-hoed between the rows of plants in the early summer. When sheep were folded (allowed to graze) on the stubble in the wheat and barley years, their feet trod down their own manure well into the soil. Different crops took nutrients from different levels in the soil, because some had long roots and some had short.

Farmers experimented with other rotations as well, seeking the system best suited to their own land and their type of farming. One such rotation followed a five-course – 1 clover or peas, 2 wheat, 3 oats, 4 turnips, 5 wheat or barley. Arthur Young described a seven-course rotation – 1 potatoes, 2 carrots, 3 cabbages, 4 barley, 5 clover, 6 clover, 7 wheat.

New crops

Roots and sown grasses (such as lucerne and clover) increased the quantity of fodder crops which could be stored and fed to the livestock in winter. Some of the root crops (such as turnips), seed grasses and rape had been grown in Britain in the seventeenth century, but it was not until the eighteenth century that they became widespread. One of the pioneers of the new crops was 'Turnip' Townshend.

Viscount Townshend (1674–1738)

Viscount Townshend was born in the same year as Jethro Tull. He was called 'Turnip' Townshend because he persuaded other farmers to use turnips as part of a four-course rotation, to provide fodder crops for livestock in winter. He also promoted the use of marl (a type of clay) to improve sandy soil.

These ideas had already been introduced into England in the seventeenth century but Townshend did a lot to make their advantages well known.

Townshend was already well known in Britain as a former ambassador and government minister. In fact, it was not until 1730, when he was 56, that he retired to his estates at Raynham in Norfolk.

Arthur Young thought it odd that he should be remembered for his farming activities, rather than for his work as a statesman and politician. But it is doubtful whether he would have had quite so much influence with farmers, had he not been a man of some importance. Later writers wrongly gave him the credit for inventing the Norfolk Rotation and introducing turnips.

Fertilisers

Look at the picture opposite showing a new dung-pit in 1756.

1 Why did farmers keep dung?
2 At which time of the year was dung collected in the farmyard?
3 Why do you think the dung-pit was lined with bricks? What was wrong with a hole in the ground?
4 What were the reasons for putting the dung-pit below the level of the farmyard?

Contemporary print of a dung-pit in 1756

Most farmers (apart from Jethro Tull) recognised the need to add manure to the soil to help it produce bigger and better crops. Animal manure was the easiest type of fertiliser to use, since it was produced in large quantities on the farm already, as a by-product of keeping livestock.

As early as the 1750s farmers were building special underground tanks and pits to hold this manure in order to prevent it being weathered away by exposure to sun and rain.

Farmers also used other fertilisers, such as human manure from the towns (called night soil – because it was carted away at night), soot from chimneys, and marl (a clay with a high lime content). Marl was added to light soils to make them heavier and better able to retain moisture.

In north-west Norfolk the rental value of farmland with sandy soils was only 5s 0d [25p] an acre in 1780. After treatment with marl it became so productive it was worth £1 5s 0d [£1.25] an acre in 1855.

Drainage

Farmers with enclosed fields found it profitable to drain their fields, to stop them getting waterlogged in wet weather. Draining a field in the eighteenth century involved digging trenches at regular intervals across the land and filling them with stones and rubble. The soil was then replaced on top. When it rained, water drained through the soil into these stone-filled trenches and out into ditches at the sides of the field. Much later, in the 1840s, cylindrical clay pipes were used instead of stone-filled trenches.

New methods of breeding livestock

New and exciting methods were also being used to improve the quality of livestock, particularly cattle, sheep and horses. One of the leading pioneer breeders at this time was Robert Bakewell of Dishley, in Leicestershire, with his Leicester and New Leicester sheep and improved Longhorn cattle. However, Bakewell (see below) was by no means the first or the only farmer to use selective breeding in the eighteenth century. There were many others.

Selective breeding simply means picking the finest animals and breeding from them. Only the best of each new generation of lambs or calves is used to breed the next generation, and so on. In this way farmers can develop breeds of cow which give higher yields of milk and lambs which fatten quickly or produce finer wool. To do this a breeder must keep a careful record of each animal's family tree or pedigree. Selective breeding can only be done if the animals are kept apart from inferior breeds and their progress carefully monitored.

Other important breeders, at this time, included Thomas Coke of Holkham in Norfolk, who favoured the Southdown breed of sheep. These breeders were so successful that by 1800 their top pedigree bulls, cows, rams and ewes were fetching high prices at auction – as much as £1,000 each – an enormous sum of money in those days.

How news of the Agricultural Revolution spread

The improvements in agriculture would have been of no great consequence had they only been used by the innovators themselves. At that time there were no cheap newspapers or magazines to spread the news of innovations to the poor farmer. Information travelled slowly.

However, two great agricultural improvers – Thomas Coke of Norfolk (later Earl of Leicester) and Francis, Duke of Bedford – did a lot to promote the new methods of farming at their Holkham (Norfolk) and Woburn (Bedfordshire) sheep-shearings respectively. You can read about Coke on page 23. It was these events which a writer in *The Illustrated London News* 1857 wrote:

> 'fixed the type of our modern agricultural shows and festivals; entertaining hundreds of agricultural-minded guests, conducting them every morning over the best farms of their vast domains, examining crops and stock, testing newly-devised implements, and winding up each day with a dinner, at which agricultural questions – such as the results of drilling roots, the comparitive value of the new Leicester and the Southdown, the Longhorn and the Devon – were fully and freely discussed amid the cheering influences of numbers and generous wine.'

Robert Bakewell (1725–95)

Robert Bakewell followed the work done by other breeders in the early years of the eighteenth century. His main claim to fame was that he was the best known and, at first, the most successful.

Bakewell bred sheep which fattened quickly and to a much greater size than ordinary animals. Unfortunately, the meat was fatty and of relatively poor quality. Eventually, the Southdown took over from his Leicester and New Leicester breeds as the preferred breed of sheep of many farmers in the nineteenth century.

Bakewell was no more successful with his improved Longhorn cattle. These quickly grew to a good size but what they gained in weight they lost in milk and, like the sheep, their meat was fatty. The Longhorn was destined, too, to decline in popularity and, eventually, to die out completely as a significant British cattle breed. Instead, farmers preferred the Durham Shorthorn which was bred by the Colling brothers at their farm at Ketton, near Darlington, in County Durham. One of their bulls sold for £1,050 in 1810 – more than the combined annual earnings of fifty farm labourers at that time.

Nonetheless, despite the long-term failure of his own breeds Bakewell was highly regarded in his day. Visitors were very impressed with his farms and his methods. Arthur Young noted 'the amazing gentleness' with which he reared his bulls, so that they were easily managed, instead of being troublesome.

He was undoubtedly one of the greatest agricultural innovators of the eighteenth century. He established the principles for breeding farm animals and provided other breeders with the know-how to continue this work.

Robert Bakewell on horseback, portrait painted by John Boultbee in about 1780

The Duke of Bedford's sheep-shearing party in 1811, contemporary engraving

Royalty often attended as well as large crowds – some on foot, some on horseback. There were competitions, exhibitions, demonstrations, banquets, speeches, presentations of cups. In 1800 at the Woburn sheep shearing the *Farmer's Magazine* reported that:

> 'Several improved implements in husbandry were exhibited, particularly a chaff cutter, ploughs, harrows, etc. At three o'clock, the Duke entertained about two hundred of the company in the great hall in the Abbey with an elegant dinner.'

1 *Who attended these sheep-shearings? What did the visitors see at these demonstrations?*

2 *In what ways does the picture support the evidence given in the two extracts?*

3 *How did the sheep-shearings help to promote the new improvements in agriculture?*

4 *What were the mid-nineteenth-century equivalents of these sheep-shearings? What are their modern counterparts? How do modern farmers learn about new improvements and developments in farming?*

Writers also helped to spread the news about these farming improvements to other farmers. One of the most famous of these writers was Arthur Young, but there were others as well, such as William Marshall. Even the Royal Family played its part. King George III was known as 'Farmer' George because of his keen interest in the royal farms at Windsor.

Arthur Young was born in 1741 and died in 1820. He began his career as a farmer, near Bury St.Edmunds, in Suffolk. But when he failed to make it pay he turned to writing instead. He travelled throughout the

British Isles, taking careful note of what he saw, and used this information to spread the ideas and methods of the agricultural improvers. In 1771, he said that:

'The great improvements [in farming in Norfolk] have been made by means of the following circumstances.
First. By inclosing without the assistance of parliament.
Second. By a spirited use of marl and clay.
Third. By the introduction of an excellent course of crops.
Fourth. By the culture of turnips well hand-hoed.
Fifth. By the culture of clover and rye-grass.
Sixth. By landlords granting long leases.
Seventh. By the country being divided chiefly into large farms.'

Arthur Young's influence in spreading new ideas achieved even greater prominence when he was made the first Secretary of the new Board of Agriculture when it was founded in 1793.

Thomas Coke (1754–1842)

Thomas Coke was highly respected, in his own lifetime, as an outstanding pioneer of the new improvements in farming. He was made Earl of Leicester in 1837, although he farmed at Holkham Hall in north-west Norfolk. It was here that he showed his fellow landowners the value of granting long leases to tenants and insisting they use crop rotations to conserve the soil.

Long leases of 21 years had been agreed by some Georgian landowners fifty years earlier. But it was Coke who showed how they could be profitable both for the landlord and the tenant. The security of being able to rent a farm for a long period made it worthwhile for a farmer to spend money on improvements, such as drainage schemes. When one of his tenants reclaimed meadowland from a marsh, Coke renewed the tenant's lease for a further 21 years as a reward for his 'very great exertion'.

Coke was also famous throughout Britain for the agricultural meetings he held on his estates, his selective breeding of cattle and sheep, and his new plantations of pine trees which made good use of land unsuited for crops or grazing livestock, by producing timber.

He was so successful in promoting these improvements that later writers incorrectly gave him most of the credit for introducing them in the first place. They measured his success in financial terms, applauding the fact that the value of his estates rose from £300,000 when he took over, in 1776, to £1,200,000 at the time of his death, in 1842.

Thomas Coke at Holkham Hall, painting by Thomas Weaver

Look at Sources A, B, C, D, E, at the quotation from Arthur Young (page 23) and at the information on Townshend and Coke (pages 18, 23).

Source A

'Mr Coke had for some years directed his mind and his fortune to bringing a poor soil into cultivation by a system then new to agriculturists.'

R. N. Bacon 1844

Source B

'The present pre-eminence of the county in improved husbandry is due alone to the celebrated Coke of Norfolk.'

James Caird 1850

Source C

'Both Townshend and Coke introduced into Norfolk new crops and new methods – above all, root crops and the marling of light land. Their example put their backward county at the head of English agriculture.'

G. M. Trevelyan 1944

Source D

'This county [Norfolk], before the great works done by enclosing and marling was all a wild sheepwalk; but through the uncommon spirit of many great farmers, has been advanced in value to an amazing degree.'

Arthur Young 1771

Source E

'Suffolk is also remarkable for being the first where the feeding and fattening of sheep as well as black cattle with turnips, was first practised in England.'

Daniel Defoe 1722

---

1 When did Thomas Coke take over the estate at Holkham in Norfolk? How old was he in 1771? When did Viscount Townshend retire to his estates at Raynham in Norfolk?

2 To whom were the vast improvements in Norfolk agriculture attributed by James Caird in Source B? Which of the other sources can be used to prove that he was wrong?

3 *Which of the improvements listed by Arthur Young and Daniel Defoe were credited by G. M. Trevelyan in Source C to Viscount Townshend and Thomas Coke? How can you prove that he was completely wrong about Coke and probably wrong about Townshend?*

4 *Take each of the sources A,B,C in turn and write a sentence to say whether you think the writer was justified or not in making that statement. Give reasons for your answers.*

EFFECTS OF THE REVOLUTIONARY AND NAPOLEONIC WARS OF 1793–1815

The wars against France had a crucial effect on British agriculture. This was because Napoleon Bonaparte was able to stop large quantities of European corn reaching Britain. As a result prices for British corn rose steeply. This was good news for farmers and landowners but bad news for the landless poor and the workers in the towns. Much distress was caused by rising bread prices, as you can see in the photograph (page 13) and in the chapter on the Poor Law (page 266).

When the Wars ended, British merchants expected they would be able, once again, to import grain from countries like France and Prussia. People thought that bread prices would fall, making it easier for the poorest people to buy enough food to live on. However, farmers were worried that corn prices would fall and they would be forced out of business. Many Members of Parliament were themselves farmers or landowners, and not surprisingly, they gave their support when the Government introduced the Corn Laws at the end of the war in 1815.

The passing of the Corn Laws

The Corn Laws were passed in 1815. They enacted (made law):

- 'that such foreign corn, meal or flour, may be imported into the United Kingdom, for home consumption, without payment of any duty whatever, whenever the average prices of the several sorts of British corn, shall be at or above the prices hereafter mentioned;
- that is to say, whenever wheat shall be at or above the price of eighty shillings [£4] per quarter;
- whenever rye, pease and beans shall be at or above the price of fifty-three shillings [£2.65] per quarter;
- whenever barley shall be at or above the price of forty shillings [£2] per quarter;
- and whenever oats shall be at or above the price of twenty-seven shillings [£1.35] per quarter.

● And be it further enacted, that whenever the average prices of British corn be below the prices stated, no foreign corn, or meal, or flour, shall be allowed to be imported into the United Kingdom for the purpose of home consumption.'

N.B. Corn was measured by volume and a quarter of wheat was roughly 200 kg in weight.

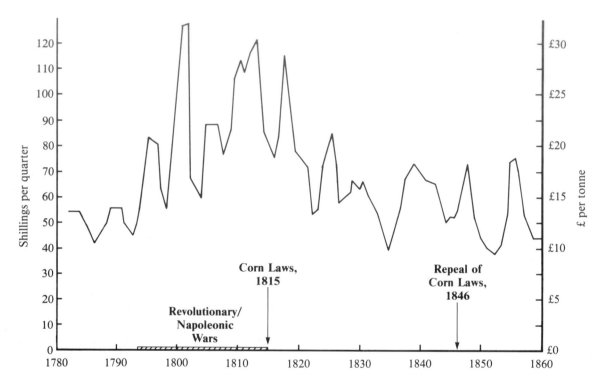

The rise and fall in the price of wheat.

1 *Which corn crop do you think usually fetched the highest price on the market? Which usually fetched the lowest?*

2 *The Corn Laws of 1815 only permitted foreign wheat to be imported into Britain if the average price of wheat per quarter reached a certain level. Was it more than:*
   (a)   40 shillings,
   (b)   27 shillings,
   (c)   80 shillings,
   (d)   53 shillings?
   What was the permitted price level for barley?

3 *What did the Act say was to happen if the average prices for British corn fell below those listed in the Corn Laws?*

4 *Look at the graph showing average wheat prices in Britain between 1782 and 1860. In how many of these 78 years did the average price of wheat fall below 80 shillings per quarter? In which years, between 1820 and 1845, would it have been possible to import foreign wheat into Britain (under the 1815 regulations)?*

5 *What happened to wheat prices in the years 1816, 1817, 1818 and 1819?*

The immediate result of the Corn Laws in 1815 was a rise in bread prices, since foreign wheat was no longer cheaper than British wheat. This was also a time when there was great distress and poverty amongst the working classes (as shown in Chapter 7). The introduction of new machines in factories created unemployment in some industries. Thousands of soldiers and sailors had returned from the wars and joined the growing numbers of former farm labourers who were seeking employment in the towns. Factories which had made uniforms, bullets and munitions for the army and navy now found their order books empty and so they sacked many workers.

Opposition to the Corn Laws was part of the general unrest in the country which led to the Peterloo Massacre and the Six Acts of 1819 (see Chapter 7), limiting the freedom of working people to protest against the decisions of the Government.

In the 1820s there was a move, led by William Huskisson, President of the Board of Trade, to modify the effects of the Corn Laws by bringing in a sliding scale of duties on imports of foreign grain. An Act of this type came into force in 1828 and Sir Robert Peel made further modifications to the Corn Laws in 1842.

AGRICULTURAL UNREST IN THE NINETEENTH CENTURY

1 *Look at the text, pictures and captions on the following pages. Write an essay to describe the buildings, surroundings and general living and working conditions of farm workers in the the nineteenth century. Do you think they were justified in their complaints (see the section on Captain Swing page 30), in wanting to leave the land for the towns, and in criticising their employers, the farmers?*

The hard life of the farm worker

Farm workers worked as long in the fields as workers in factories and coal mines – usually for less pay. In Dorset, a writer in 1846, said: 'The wages here in very few instances exceed seven shillings [35p] per week.'

Haymaking and harvesting seemed never-ending, even though crowds of people were employed. The shepherd, on the other hand, lived a lonely life with his flock. Driving them to market was an escape from boredom.

'Shepherds who attended with their flocks from long distances started from home two or three days, or even a week, before the fair, driving their charges a few miles each day – not more than ten or twelve – and resting them at night in hired fields by the wayside.'

Thomas Hardy, *Far From the Madding Crowd*

2 *Why did the shepherds not use some form of transport for driving their sheep to market?*

Hiring fairs

Hiring fair in Warwickshire, The Illustrated London News, *October 1871*

'It was the chief hiring fair of the year. The long bonnets of the women, cotton gowns and checked shawls mixed with the carters' smock frocks; for they, too, entered into the hiring. An old shepherd had planted the stem of his crook in the gutter and was resting upon the bow.'

Thomas Hardy, *The Mayor of Casterbridge*

Farm labourers and servants could be sacked at a moment's notice. If they had to find a new employer they could go to the nearest hiring fair and stand in line there, offering their services as maid, cook, shepherd, carter, ploughman.

3 *Do you think the artist thought the hiring fair was picturesque or degrading? Which do you think it was?*

Village life

Dorset village, The Illustrated London News, *5 September 1846*

'The first feature which attracts the attention of a stranger on entering the village is the total want of cleanliness which pervades it. A stream, composed of the matter which constantly escapes from pigsties and other receptacles of filth, meanders down each street, being here and there collected into standing pools, which lie festering and rotting in the sun so as to create wonder that the place is not the continual abode of pestilence.'

Description in *The Illustrated London News*, 5 September 1846, of the village shown in the engraving

Houses

This is how a writer described farm labourers' cottages in Dorset, in 1846, like the one shown on page 11.

'The atmosphere to an unpractised nose is almost insupportable. Dishes, plates, and other articles of crockery, seem almost unknown.

Bread forms the principal kind of food which falls to the labourer's lot. In no single instance did I observe meat of any kind.

A labourer and his family – in all eight persons – are the occupiers of a hovel, in which there is but one bedroom. There is a small opening about a foot square which is unglazed [i.e. no glass in it] and serves the purpose of a window. The furniture – a rickety table and two or three foundered chairs. Want, famine and misery are the features of the village.'

The Illustrated London News, 5 September 1846

---

4 *In what ways do the pictures of the village, and of the labourer's cottage, support or contradict the written descriptions which accompanied them, in the same issue of* The Illustrated London News, *5 September, 1846?*

5 *What do your comparisons between artist's illustrations and written descriptions tell you about their use as historical evidence? In what ways are they misleading? Would a photograph be more reliable than an artist's drawing? In what ways can a photograph lie or show bias?*

Captain Swing

In 1830 trouble erupted all over southern England – in the south coast counties, the Midlands and in East Anglia. Hay ricks and corn stacks were set on fire and threshing machines destroyed. Many of these incidents in different parts of the country were said to have been the work of 'Captain Swing'.

THE HOME OF THE RICK-BURNER.　　*A cartoon from* Punch

We can read about the troubles in the local newspapers of the time. For instance, in December 1830, a local newspaper carried an item about a Warwickshire woman whose new threshing machines had been set on fire. In another item, farm buildings and 32 stacks of hay or corn had been burnt down in Cambridgeshire.

The authorities acted harshly. Some of the rick burners were executed, such as James Passfield, aged 23, convicted at Essex Assizes (law courts) of setting fire to a farmer's stackyard. In 1831, a curate wrote to *The Sussex Advertiser* describing the fate of seven villagers. They had joined a Captain Swing demonstration and been charged by cavalry. One had a fractured skull, another an amputated arm (from a sword wound), one had fled the village, three had been arrested and were likely to be hanged, whilst the seventh had been trampled on by horses and was thought unlikely to survive.

These farmworkers were protesting for a variety of reasons. Distress and poverty were common throughout the rural counties of southern England. This was partly because there were no factories there, offering alternative employment to those out of work.

Farmers had cut the wages of their workers because they were facing problems of their own. Prices for farm produce had dropped, despite the Corn Laws. But many farmers had agreed to pay high rents for their farms during the Napoleonic Wars, when farm prices were high. After 1815, rents still stayed high but the prices farmers got for their produce dropped.

---

1 *What was the easiest way for farmers to cut the cost of growing crops and rearing livestock on their farms? How did the use of a threshing machine help farmers to cut their costs? Why did farm workers destroy threshing machines? What other grievances did they have?*

2 *How were these problems aggravated by the enclosure of the open fields and high bread prices?*

3 *Look at the graph of wheat prices on page 26. Work out, roughly, what the average price of wheat was in the years between 1810 and 1820. What was the average price of wheat between 1820 and 1830? By what percentage had it fallen?*

4 *Look at* The home of the rick burner *opposite. Write two or three sentences to describe this farm cottage and its inhabitants. Why do you think the cartoonist drew a ghostly figure of a man with a blazing torch? What was the point of the cartoon?*

THE PREMIER'S FIX.
FREE TRADE AND AGRICULTURE.

Robert Peel sitting on a fence separating Cobden and Bright on one side of the gate and the Protectionist bull (marked with P) on the other
Punch *(1845)*

PEEL'S CHEAP BREAD SHOP,
OPENED JANUARY 22, 1846.

Punch *(1846)*

The repeal of the Corn Laws

By the late 1830s there was much opposition to the Corn Laws throughout the country. Workmen and farm labourers bitterly complained that the Corn Laws kept bread prices higher than they need be, since cheaper foreign grain could not be imported into Britain, to compete with British wheat.

Manufacturers and industrialists thought they were being unfairly treated by the Government. The Corn Laws prevented foreigners selling corn to Britain and as a result they could not pay for British manufactures. So, the landowners appeared to get all the benefits whilst the factory owners got all the hardship.

In 1839 the Anti-Corn Law League was founded by John Bright and Richard Cobden. They wanted Free Trade (see Chapter 4) which would allow foreigners to buy and sell goods in Britain without paying customs duties. Bright and Cobden argued that by charging tariffs (customs duties) on foreign imports of corn, the Government was depriving British manufacturers of markets for their goods.

Exports of British cloth, for instance, depended partly on the ability of other countries to pay for the goods they imported. By restricting corn imports from abroad, the British Government was helping to prevent the expansion of cotton exports. This cut jobs in the industry. Greater exports of manufactured goods would mean more jobs in factories and less unemployment.

The Corn Laws kept bread prices high, which aggravated the problems of the poor and created unnecessary distress and unrest. Lower bread prices would mean less poverty. This in turn would mean fewer people turning to the workhouse to take advantage of the Poor Law (see Chapter 8).

Cobden and Bright entered Parliament to fight the case for the industrialists. They had to convince the landowners of the Tory Party, led by Sir Robert Peel the Prime Minister. Peel was himself the son of a cotton manufacturer and was torn between the two sides. He could see the merits of the case for Free Trade but he had to get support from his own party to carry such a measure through the Houses of Parliament.

The Anti-Corn Law League was supported by most of the major industrialists. As a result it was rich and powerful and could afford to sponsor protest meetings all over the country and to print pamphlets and posters publicising opposition to the Corn Laws and getting popular support for the campaign.

Supporters of the Corn Laws even formed their own pressure group – the Anti-League – to oppose them. They argued that the only reason why the manufacturers wanted to repeal the Corn Laws was to bring down the price of bread and so lessen demand for higher wages among the working classes. The Anti-League members were supported in Parliament by politicians like Benjamin Disraeli, who later became Prime Minister.

However, Sir Robert Peel was by this time convinced of the advantages of Free Trade and in 1842 he reduced Customs duties on many goods (see Chapter 4) and in succeeding years abolished many other duties completely.

Events in the mid-1840s helped him to take the decisive action needed to convince Parliament that the Corn Laws should be abolished. These were:

(a)   the poor harvest of 1845 which pushed corn prices even higher, and,
(b)   the complete failure of the Irish potato crop.

The people of Ireland were faced with a dreadful and terrible famine, which eventually led to the deaths of hundreds of thousands of people, and the emigration of huge numbers of people to America. Sheer necessity added its weight to the convincing arguments of the Free Traders.

> **1** *Who founded the Anti-Corn Law League? How did they take effective action to try to persuade the Government to repeal the Corn Laws?*
> **2** *Look at the cartoons from* Punch *on page 32. In which year did Peel repeal the Corn Laws? How did* Punch *portray this in a cartoon?*
> **3** *Write a sentence to say what is meant by 'Free Trade'.*
> **4** *Why do you think farmers and landowners were afraid? How were they portrayed in the* Punch *cartoon published before the repeal of the Corn Laws? How did* Punch *depict Peel?*

THE GOLDEN AGE OF AGRICULTURE

In 1849 the Californian Gold Rush began, followed shortly afterwards by the discovery of gold in Australia. People dreamed of making a fortune. Why, then, do you think Punch *captioned this cartoon –* AN ENGLISH GOLD FIELD, *in July 1852?*

The repeal of the Corn Laws did not have the disastrous effect on farming which the landowners and farmers had feared – at least not in the twenty years or so after 1846. Instead, the price of wheat remained steady but the farmers' costs went down because of increased efficiency. As a result many farmers became prosperous and the time was known as the 'Golden Age of Agriculture' or the 'Golden Age of High Farming'.

Wheat prices remained relatively steady for two main reasons. In the first place the demand for wheat in Britain kept pace with the growing quantities of foreign corn imported into the country. Secondly, there was only a limited amount of corn available for import. The prairies of North America could not yet be cultivated on a grand scale, since there were no trans-continental railways to take corn to the Atlantic ports for shipment to Britain and Europe.

So most British farmers became prosperous and able to take advantage of the latest improvements in machinery and farming methods. This made them even more prosperous. Many of these improvements are highlighted in the pictures and in the extracts which follow.

The impact of the Transport Revolution on the farmer

The new railways (see Chapter 3) made it possible for farmers to sell their produce in markets at a considerable distance from their farms. A writer, in 1850, told how Mr Hodson, a farmer who lived 100 miles away from London, reckoned that before the coming of the railway he had to drive his livestock to London to be sold – the sheep lost 3 kg and the bullocks 13 kg on the journey – a loss equivalent to over £600 per annum. Once the railway arrived he only had to pay the cost of transporting the animals by train. They did not lose weight on that journey.

Meeting of the Royal Agricultural Society at Chelmsford, in Essex, The Illustrated London News, *19 July 1856*

The coming of the railway meant that farmers could also travel to agricultural shows and demonstrations. The first Royal Agricultural Show was held at Oxford in 1839. Six years later the Royal Agricultural College was opened at Cirencester.

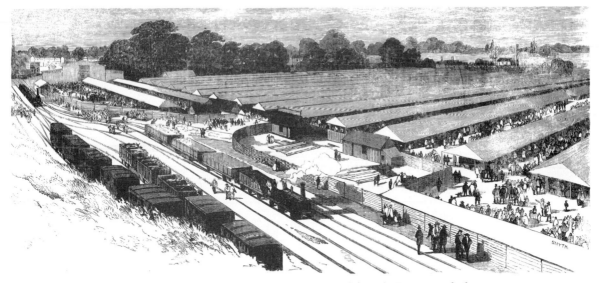

A writer in a journal, published in 1857, argued that

'The railroad compresses, by its easy cheap conveyance, what was formerly the work of a week into a day. The farmer is no longer isolated. Within seventeen years the great railroad net has been spread out and completed. Wherever there is a railroad there comes a reporter with his notebook and pencil. In one week in one newspaper we learn more agricultural facts than the genius of Arthur Young was able to collect in a year.'

The Illustrated London News, 17 October 1857

According to a newspaper item in 1866, the daily supply of milk brought into London by the North Western Railway had risen sharply from 1,300 litres to 9,400 litres, whilst the Great Western Railway, which had previously brought little milk to London, now delivered nearly 8,000 litres a day. The Great Eastern Railway brought in 12,000 litres and the South Western Railway 14,000 litres. In total the railways brought in about one third of London's daily requirement for milk.

---

1 *How did the railways benefit the livestock farmer and those farmers keen to find out about the latest developments in agriculture? How were railways used at the Royal Agricultural Show in 1856?*
2 *Why did the newspaper claim that the farmer was no longer 'isolated'? What had farmers been isolated from in the past and how had developments in the middle of the nineteenth century helped to lessen that isolation?*

New agricultural machinery

The Industrial Revolution (see Chapter 2) made a big impact on farming in the nineteenth century. Without it, there could have been no steam engines, new implements or precision-made machines. It also stimulated the investigations which led to the use of new fertilisers.

Even simple farm tools changed in the nineteenth century. Hand sickles had always been used for cutting corn at harvest time, until it was shown that it was cheaper to use scythes. Tests showed that it cost about 13s 0d [65p] to cut 10 hectares with scythes, compared to £1 2s 0d [£1.10] with sickles.

---

1 *Why was the scythe more efficient than the sickle?*
2 *What is the difference between these two implements?*

As new machines came into use the number of people employed on Britain's farms began to fall. In 1851, about 2 million people were employed in agriculture, according to the Official Census. By 1871, the number had dropped to 1.8 million – even though the population of Great Britain, as a whole, had risen from 21 million to 26 million in the same period.

The speed with which the new machines were introduced can be seen from this account of new farming methods, published in *The Illustrated London News* in 1857.

'Fifty years ago thrashing-machines were recommended by Arthur Young, and used by a few great English landlords; but it is only within seventeen years that their use has become universal.

Fifteen years ago the use of a steam-engine for agricultural purposes was considered a wild and dangerous innovation.

Six years ago the reaping machine was unknown in England, except as a mechanical curiosity. It has now been established as a standard implement.'

Agricultural implements at the Smithfield Cattle Show, The Illustrated London News, *12 December 1846*

Bell's Improved Reaping Machine, from a Victorian encyclopaedia, c. 1850. Why did the horses not pull the machine?

The first reaping machine was invented in 1827 by Dr Patrick Bell, a Scottish clergyman. Before that time corn was cut by hand, using either the sickle or the scythe. The machine was later perfected by manufacturers, such as Crosskill of Beverley in Yorkshire, and became an important labour-saving device on the farm.

In 1808 Robert Ransome made the first all-iron plough at his implement works in Ipswich (opened in 1785). Soon manufacturers were producing a wide range of implements, tools, engines and farm machinery.

The steam traction engine

To the Victorian farmer, the most exciting invention was the steam traction engine. Already, many farmers had altered the 'gin-gang house', so that the threshing machine could be powered by a stationary steam engine. This explains why some old farms appear to have factory chimneys. One writer described its advantages in 1845:

'Compare the simple flail of our ancestors with the improved steam thrashing-mill of the present day - moved by steam, and not only thrashing out the grain, but winnowing it, dressing it, and sacking it quite ready for the market. The farmer need never unyoke his horses from their ordinary field-work, so far as thrashing is concerned; he has only to light his furnace in the morning, by breakfast the steam is up, and before dinner as much grain is thrashed, cleaned, and ready for sale, as a dozen flail-men could have prepared in a month.'

Chambers's Journal 1845

Progress was also being made in developing steam traction engines which could move, literally, 'under their own steam'. These were the fore-runners of the tractor. Their main disadvantage was that they were far too heavy and often sank into soft ground. In 1843 there was only one steam engine in the whole of Norfolk, the richest of the arable counties. Fourteen years later one firm in Lincoln, alone, was making 500 steam engines a year.

---

1 *Which modern machine has replaced the reaping machine?*
2 *Name four machines in use on farms in the 1850s, which would have been new to Arthur Young in 1800.*
3 *How does a scythe differ from a sickle? What were the advantages of reaping machines for the farmer?*
4 *Why do you think some farmers continued to use the old methods (such as cutting corn with scythes) long after the invention of the new machinery?*
5 *Why was it only possible to use these new machines on farms in areas like East Anglia **after** the coming of the railways?*
6 *At the start of the nineteenth century over one worker in every three had been employed in agriculture. By 1871, the proportion had dropped to less than one in every six. Why was this?*

Improving the land

Farmers improved much of their land by digging drains to stop fields becoming waterlogged. Competitions were sometimes held to see who could dig a drainage trench in the shortest possible time. New methods of drainage were introduced.

Scientists also turned their attention to manures and fertilisers – with very profitable results. One landowner, Sir Tatton Sykes, noticed that grass grew more luxuriantly near his dog's kennels. He attributed this to powdered bones – one of the most sought-after fertilisers in the 1840s.

'The subject of manure, the last and least thought of by our fore-fathers, who allowed their dung-heaps to run to waste, exposed to the sun and rain. Now every scrap of farm manure, and every drop of animal liquid, is collected and preserved with as great care as is the grain that is reaped and thrashed. Nay, farther, the droppings of sea-birds, under the name of guano, are imported from South America at many pounds per ton.

Crushed bones are regarded as one of the finest manures for light turnip soils. How our forefathers would have laughed at the prediction of bone-mills, and British soil fertilised with ship-borne bones from Germany and Prussia. The same may be said of soot, night-soil, urine, and the waste substances which used to flow from gas-works, and from the factories of the soap-boiler, sugar-refiner, and others.'

Chambers's Journal 1845–6

Sir John Bennet Lawes (1814–1900) and Sir Joseph Henry Gilbert (1817–1901) were two of the greatest innovators in this field. They were partners in the Rothamsted Agricultural Laboratory which was founded in 1843 and which performed pioneer work in investigating the properties of various types of fertiliser.

They made a careful scientific analysis of the soil, studied plant nutrition and proved that land could retain its fertility with artificial fertilisers rather than with manure. By field experiments Lawes was able to show that it was perfectly possible to grow the same crop year after year in the same plot of land, provided the appropriate nutrients were put back into the ground after harvesting each year.

In 1842 Lawes opened a phosphate factory at Deptford Creek in London, the first factory in Britain to manufacture artificial fertilisers. In 1858 it was said that wheat yields had improved by 25 per cent, in the previous 15 years after using these artificial fertilisers and manures.

1 *Name five different fertilisers used in the 1850s. Name two fertilisers which were brought by ship to Britain in the 1840s.*
2 *Describe the tanker shown below. How did it work? Do you think this was an effective way to spread manure?*
3 *How did Lawes and Gilbert prove that crop rotations were not essential?*
4 *Refer back to an earlier illustration in this chapter. Was it correct to say that earlier farmers had allowed 'their dung-heaps to run to waste, exposed to the sun and rain'?*
5 *How did artificial fertilisers make it possible for farmers to specialise in arable farming – growing nothing but crops?*

Tanker holding about 1,000 litres of liquid manure, The Illustrated London News, *1844*

Effects of agricultural changes on society

One of the most important results of the improvements in agriculture was its effect on food supplies. There was less chance of people starving, when food from one part of the country could be taken by railway to another. Meat, milk, butter, cream, fruit and vegetables could be produced at a distance from the urban areas and sent by rail for sale in the towns. Farmers on the outskirts of towns began to specialise, producing milk, vegetables and fruit for the market. In general, people began to eat better food and more of it. And better food meant better health. The food industry had really begun. By 1852 there were sugar beet factories in Britain and a growing food canning industry.

FURTHER QUESTIONS AND EXERCISES

1 *Name four people who made important contributions to the Agrarian Revolution in the eighteenth century. Write a sentence to say what each of them did.*

2 *What were the main advantages and disadvantages of the open-field system?*

3 *Imagine you are a small farmer in 1810. The open fields in your village were enclosed five years ago and you were allocated a smallholding. Describe the events leading up to the enclosure of the fields. Explain why you have had to give up your farm.*

4 *Which of the people named in the list on the left is associated with the developments listed on the right?*

Jethro Tull	the New Leicester sheep
Andrew Meikle	long leases
Robert Bakewell	books about new farming methods
Thomas Coke	the repeal of the Corn Laws
Patrick Bell	the horse hoe
Viscount Townshend	the turnip
Arthur Young	the threshing machine
Robert Peel	the reaping machine

5 *Look at Sources A and B below.*

Source A

'Sir

Your name is down amongst the Black Hearts in the Black Book and this is to advise you and the likes of you, to make your wills. Ye have been the Blackguard Enemies of the people on all occasions, ye have not done as ye ought

Swing'

Letter received by a farmer in 1830

Source B

'At the Huntingdon Assizes, GIFFORD WHITE, aged 18, was sentenced to transportation for life for sending a letter to a farmer, threatening to burn his farm and the farms of others.'

News item 1844

(a) Who was 'Swing'?

(b) How do you account for Gifford White's conduct?

(c) Explain the circumstances which led up to these troubles.

6 Name five significant improvements in farming methods which took place in the working lifetime of a farmer who farmed between 1800 and 1860.

7 Study the sources below.

Source C

'bones are sought in every quarter, gathered at home, and shipped from abroad'

Source D

'fourteen acres have been devoted to the continuous growth of Wheat since 1843, eight acres to the continuous growth of Turnips from the same date'

(a) To which developments in farming do you think Sources C and D refer?

(b) Who is most likely to have made the statement in Source D?

(c) Explain how and why Source D contradicts the thinking of 'Turnip' Townshend and Arthur Young.

8 Write two or three sentences to say why farmers prospered between 1850 and 1870.

9 What do you think were the three most powerful arguments in favour, and the three most powerful arguments against, the enclosure of the open fields?

10 Write a short essay about the Corn Laws. In your essay explain what they were, and say when, and why they were passed. Describe the effects of the Corn Laws on poor people and say what opposition there was to this legislation. Show how, and why, the Anti-Corn Law League was formed and what its members hoped to achieve. What did they do to promote their cause? When, and why, were they successful? Who was the Government minister responsible for the repeal of the Corn Laws? What did he hope to achieve? What opposition did he meet? Was he successful?

11 *How, when and why were British farmers able to make use of, and benefit from, the following:*
 (a) the coming of the railway
 (b) steam power
 (c) the development of new machinery
 (d) scientific analysis of the soil
 (e) the effects of the Napoleonic Wars?

12 *Explain why British farming changed in the period between 1750 and 1850.*

13 *Describe the extent to which the agricultural changes between 1750 and 1850 can be said to have created more problems than they solved. Who gained and who lost as a result of these changes? How did it affect the everyday life and social structure of the British countryside?*

14 *Look at these cartoons which appeared in* Punch *in 1863 (left) and 1854 (right).*

THE PIG AND THE PEASANT.

PEASANT.—"AH! I'D LIKE TO BE CARED FOR HALF AS WELL AS THEE BE!"

AGRICULTURAL DISTRESS.

BRITISH FARMER.—"WELL! HERE'S A PRETTY BUSINESS! I'VE GOT SO MUCH CORN, THAT I DON'T KNOW WHERE TO PUT IT!"

 (a) Why does the farm worker in THE PIG AND THE PEASANT *say: 'Ah! I'd like to be cared for half as well as thee be!'?*
 (b) Why does the farmer in AGRICULTURAL DISTRESS *grumble: 'Well! Here's a pretty business'. I've got so much corn, that I don't know where to put it.'?*

(c) Explain the full significance of these cartoons. What do you think
the Punch cartoonist thought about farmworkers and farmers in the
middle years of the nineteenth century? How far does this confirm
what you have learned about the development of agriculture in the
nineteenth century?

15 Study Sources E, F, G.

Source E

THE NEW STEAM-FARMER – Boydell's Traction Steam-engine
'The engine walked from Camden-town to Acton, taking in tow its
four-wheeled wagon, with coals, and four heavy iron ploughs, and
water enough for four hours' work. It can ascend a slope of one in
three. It can back, advance or stop instantaneously; and the power
may be used for driving thrashing-machines, mill-stones or other
purposes.
    Instead of a farmer sending for and sending back a six horse
power engine and thrashing machine, requiring in each trip four
horses, this machine will move itself anywhere – draw the corn to
market, bring home manure, and do the cultivation and work of the
farm.'

                                                    Chambers's Journal 1856

Source F

'The steam traction engine with three double ploughs, ploughed
about 8 acres in one day of ten hours, at a cost for labour and coals
of £1 12s 0d [£1.60], whilst the work performed by six single
ploughs with eighteen horses in the same time would only be 4 acres,
and this at a cost of about £2 11s 0d [£2.55]. The cost of the
engine with the ploughs would be about the same as the eighteen
horses; while the wear and tear would be the greater on the latter.'

                                        The Illustrated London News, August 1857

N.B. 1 acre = 0.4 hectare

Look carefully at the picture on the next page and at the ploughing
scene with horses shown on page 14.
(a) How many labourers were needed to operate the steam traction
engine and its ploughs?
(b) How many horses and single ploughs would have been needed to
plough 8 acres in one day. How much would it have cost?
(c) How many labourers were usually needed to work with a plough
team of three horses and a single plough? How many would have
been needed to plough 4 acres with eighteen horses and six single
ploughs? How many would have been needed to plough 8 acres?

Source G

Steam ploughing with Boydell's Engine, near Louth in Lincolnshire, The Illustrated London News, *15 August 1857*

(d) *What advantages did horses still have over steam traction engines? Were they more reliable? What happened if the steam traction engine broke down? Were they as easy to use as horses on sloping ground or in small fields?*

(e) *Compare this method of steam ploughing with the method shown at the start of this chapter on page 1. What is the main difference? How do you think the steam traction engine pulled the plough in each of these examples? Which method was closest to the method used by the modern tractor and plough? What advantages did Boydell's steam traction engine have over other steam engines? Quote your evidence.*

(f) *What do you think were the disadvantages of using steam traction engines in wet weather? What were the disadvantages of using steam traction engines a long distance away from the farm buildings?*

(g) *Write the report you think a farm manager might have written to his rich employer, had he attended the trials at Louth in 1857.*

(h) *What would you have found worrying about these figures had you been a farm worker at this time? Imagine you have been chosen by the workers on a farm to try to persuade a farmer not to buy a steam traction engine in 1857. Write down the arguments you think you might have used.*

Chapter Two

The Industrial Revolution

INTRODUCTION

Contemporary illustration of a cotton mill in about 1830

Look at this report of a speech made by the Mayor of Bradford in October 1853. He was reminding an audience of textile workers, of the changes which had occurred 'within the memory of persons present in the building' in the textile industry.

> 'Instead of the manufacture being confined to the cottages, they had built palaces of industry equal to the palaces of the Caesars (Applause); instead of hand labour, they had, to the utmost, availed themselves of the almost miraculous resources of mechanical science; instead of a master manufacturer carrying a week's production upon his own back, he harnessed the iron horse to the railway train, and daily conveyed away their goods by the ton.'
>
> *The Illustrated London News,* October 1853

1 What do you think the Mayor meant by 'the iron horse'?
2 What were
  (a) 'the almost miraculous resources of mechanical science',
  (b) 'palaces of industry'?
Does the picture of a cotton mill justify either, or both, of these descriptions?

> **3** Which of his statements do you think he exaggerated? Give reasons for your answer.
> **4** What were the three basic changes he said had taken place in the textile industry within living memory? Write down one word to summarise each of these three striking changes.

In this chapter you will see how, and why, these changes took place in the organisation of industry and in the methods of production. You have already seen something of the extent of the changes in agriculture (Chapter 1) and in Chapter 3 you will see how the changes in methods of transport were both a result, and a cause, of industrial progress.

In later chapters you will see how the working class reacted to these changes (Chapter 7) and how far they brought advantages, and misery, to the working family (Chapters 6 and 8).

These changes are all part of what we call the Industrial Revolution. But, like the Agrarian Revolution, it was not something which happened overnight. In some industries there were indeed dramatic changes in the space of ten years or so. But startling changes occurred at different times in different industries. We cannot say exactly when the Industrial Revolution began or when it ended.

Signs of the changes to come had already been apparent in the seventeenth century, when the first effective steam engine was invented. The process of industrial change does not stop but continues towards the twenty-first century. The computer and the silicon chip of today have caused changes in recent years, every bit as striking as those which stemmed from the use of the steam engine. Industry has not, and does not, stand still.

INDUSTRY IN THE EARLY EIGHTEENTH CENTURY

In about 1720, Daniel Defoe (author of *Robinson Crusoe*) journeyed to Halifax in the West Riding of Yorkshire. This is what he saw.

> 'The sides of the hills, which were very steep every way, were spread with houses. We found the country one continued village, though mountainous; hardly a house out of speaking distance from another.
>
> We could see at every house there was a tenter, and on almost every tenter, a piece of cloth. We found at every one of them a gutter of running water; tinged with the drugs from the dyeing fat, and with the oil, the soap, the tallow, and other ingredients used by the clothiers in dressing and scouring the cloth.
>
> Every clothier must keep a horse to fetch and carry for the use of his manufacture, to fetch home his wool, to carry his yarn to the spinner, his cloth to the fulling mill, and, when finished, to the market to be sold. Every one generally keeps a cow or two for his

family, and this employs the two, or three, or four pieces of enclosed land about his house, for they scarce sow corn enough for their cocks and hens.

There is scarce a hill but you find a spring of water, and a Coal Pit. Having thus fire and water at every dwelling, there is no need to enquire why they dwell upon the highest hills.

Within we saw the houses full of lusty fellows, some at the dye-vat; some at the loom, others dressing the cloths; the women and children carding, or spinning; all employed from the youngest to the oldest; scarce anything above four years old, but its hands were sufficient for its own support.'

Two apprentice weavers in a silk-weaving workshop, a Hogarth engraving of 1747. How does this scene differ from the one in 1830 shown at the beginning of this chapter? What changes had happened in the textile industry over those eighty years?

1 (a) *Why did the clothiers keep horses?*
  (b) *How do we know their houses were close to one another – but not too close?*
  (c) *What was a 'tenter'?*
2 True *or false?*
  (a) *The villages were farmed in open fields*
  (b) *Many of the people of the area were part-time farmers as well as being cloth manufacturers*
  (c) *The cloth was spun and woven in factories*
  (d) *Children were employed in the industry at an early age*
  (e) *Cloth was dyed in a vat and washed in fresh water with soap, oil or candle wax.*

Woman spinning in cottage, contemporary print

3 *In what ways does this picture confirm what Daniel Defoe said about the domestic textile industry in 1720?*

4 *What did Daniel Defoe mean by:*
  (a) *'one continued village';*
  (b) *'tinged with the drugs from the dyeing fat';*
  (c) *'anything above four years old, but its hands were sufficient for its own support'?*

5 *Why did 'they dwell upon the highest hills'? What advantage was this when there were no steam-powered machines in the woollen industry?*

The domestic system

Almost all the industries of Britain at the start of the eighteenth century were organised on a small-scale basis as described above. But some workers were employed in small workshops rather than in their own cottages. They included the apprentices you can see in the picture, on page 47, of a silk-weaving workshop in Spitalfields, London. This was drawn by Hogarth in 1747.

Even the coal mines were small, employing only a handful of miners; so too were the iron furnaces and forges scattered across the country. In 1785, Thomas Newte noted that near Birmingham, 'are many nailers, who work in their own cottages, and employ every hand in the family, whether male or female'.

This type of organisation of work is called the domestic system, because much of the work was done at home ('domestic' means belonging to the home). But this did not mean that the workers made everything from start to finish in their homes. Many industries were organised so that different workers did different jobs. In 1724, Daniel Defoe said that, 'The vast manufactures carried on chiefly by the Norwich weavers, employ all the country round in spinning yarn for them.'

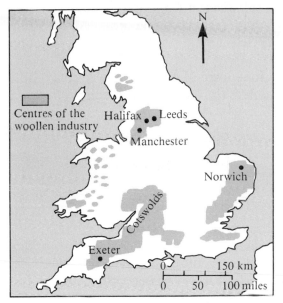

Map of the woollen industry in the early eighteenth century

1 *Look at the map of the woollen industry. Which regions of Britain were important centres of this industry at the start of the eighteenth century?*
2 *Which region was your nearest woollen industry in 1700?*

In the woollen industry some workers cleaned and scoured the raw wool, before it was carded (brushed) with prongs to separate out the fibres or combed by the handcombers to get the fibres parallel. It was then spun on a spinning wheel, usually by a woman (hence the term spinster). The lengthwise warp thread was sometimes dyed in a vat by a dyer and the cloth woven on a handloom by the handloom weaver before being sold by the clothier as a 'piece' of cloth.

The clothier was the merchant who organised the work – giving the wool to the spinner to spin and the spinner's yarn to the weaver to turn into cloth.

Advantages of the domestic system

The advantages that the domestic system had over the factory system were thought to be:
(a)   In theory, the worker and family were free to work for themselves, at their own rate, and in their own time. They could work on their small farms during the day and at their looms and spinning wheels when the farm work was done.
(b)   In theory, child workers were treated with greater kindness at home (by their parents) than in factories (by foremen and overseers), as you will see in Chapter 8. Women worked at home, and could look

after the children. When women later went to work in factories, it was claimed that many young children died from neglect.

(c) Working conditions at home, with a spinning wheel or handloom, were far better than in the factories where people spent long hours minding power looms or spinning machines in a crowded, noisy, suffocating atmosphere.

(d) Skilled workers got more satisfaction from their cottage spinning wheels and handlooms, than factory textile workers, watching over, but not controlling, 'self-acting' power looms and spinning machines.

(e) Strikes and other disruptions were almost unknown, since most workers worked for themselves or in small workplaces with only a few employees.

Disadvantages of the domestic system

The domestic system also had many disadvantages:

(a) Time and money were lost taking raw materials to different workers – the raw wool to be cleaned and scoured, the yarn to the weaver, the cloth to the fulling mill where it was beaten with hammers and shrunk to make it heavier and firmer. It was more sensible to have these jobs performed under one roof.

(b) It was difficult, if not impossible, to ensure that goods made in different workplaces were all of the same quality. Machine-made products were usually identical in quality – though frequently produced to a lower standard of workmanship than the best handmade goods.

(c) Most workplaces were far too small to make effective use of water power (see page 52).

(d) Skilled workers in the domestic industry were often underpaid for the amount of work they did. Clothiers and iron masters were no more inclined to treat them with generosity than were the later factory owners.

(e) As Daniel Defoe's account of Halifax showed, children as young as 4 years old were sometimes employed in cottages, crowded with workers.

(f) Country cottages, such as the one shown in the picture on page 11, were usually no better than town slums. They were cold, damp and far from comfortable.

(g) These cottage workplaces were often polluted with waste-products and dirt - such as the dregs of fat, soap and tallow described by Daniel Defoe.

> Study the advantages and disadvantages of the domestic system closely.
>
> **1** Which do you think were the most significant advantages and disadvantages of the domestic system of industry?
>
> **2** Which would you have preferred – to work in a factory or in a cottage?

The first factory

By 1700, a substantial number of people worked in town workshops – apprenticed to a master (like the apprentices in the picture on page 47), or employed as journeymen craftsmen (skilled day workers).

The advantages of the factory system were already apparent in 1720. Read this description by Daniel Defoe of a factory making silk thread in Derby.

> 'Here is a curiosity in trade worth observing, as being the only one of its kind in England, namely a throwing mill, which performs by a wheel turned by the water; and though it cannot perform the doubling part of a throwster's work, which can only be done by a handwheel, yet it turns the other work, and performs the labour of many hands. Whether it answers the expense or not, that is not my business.'

> **1** What was the name used to describe the job of a mill hand in this silk-throwing factory?
>
> **2** What did Defoe think was the principal advantage of the water wheel? Which part of the silk thread manufacturing process could not yet be powered by the water wheel? How was that work done?
>
> **3** Which part of the evidence tells you that Defoe had not seen a factory like this before? Do you think it was the factory he found unusual, or, the fact that it used a water wheel to power the silk-throwing machines?
>
> **4** Was the experiment successful or not? What evidence would have convinced Defoe that it was?

The silk-throwing factory had been built by John Lombe on an island in the middle of the river Derwent between 1717 and 1721. It was an enormous building for that time – 150 metres in length, 16 metres in width, several storeys high and fitted with 468 windows. It employed about 300 workers.

John Lombe was said to have acquired the secret manufacturing process by bribing workers in an Italian silk-throwing mill. He died shortly afterwards, in mysterious circumstances, and his half-brother, Thomas Lombe, took over the mill.

> **5** *What modern phrase best describes John Lombe's activities in Italy? How can the inventors of a process protect their invention?*

Not everyone was impressed with the silk-throwing mill at Derby. William Hutton (1723-1815) wrote in 1791, 'To this curious, but wretched place, I was bound apprentice for seven years and put to labour before Nature had made me able'.

> **6** *Between which dates do you think it most likely that William Hutton worked at this factory? Which evil of the factory system is illustrated by his experience?*

Water power

Water wheel at Kilhope

Water power had long been used in some industries. Water mills ground corn in the Middle Ages. Fulling mills, powered by water wheels, scoured woollen cloth during the Crusades. Grindstones, turned by water wheels, sharpened Sheffield knives at the time of the Armada. Bellows and hammers were worked by water power in the seventeenth century.

It was not unusual, therefore, to find the new inventions of the eighteenth century powered by water in the early stages of the Industrial

Revolution. This is why the earliest sites for factories were in valleys, by the banks of rivers and streams.

There were three main types of water wheel. In slow-moving streams, water wheels were undershot – water pushed the wheel at the bottom rather than at the top. With fast streams water could be taken through a channel and made to overshoot the wheel at the top. This was the most efficient form of wheel. Halfway between the two was the breast shot wheel.

The period when water power played a significant part in the location of new industries, was short-lived. The first cotton spinning mill to use water power was opened in 1771, and was followed nine years later by the first to use steam power. However, many works continued to use water power until well into the nineteenth century. In some places, steam engines were even used to pump water to the reservoirs which controlled the flow of water to the water wheels.

New water wheels were still being installed as late as 1860, like the one you can see in the photograph, which provided power to crush lead ore at the Kilhope lead mine in the Pennine hills, in County Durham.

---

1 Describe the water wheel in the photograph.
2 Why do you think they used water power there in the 1860s instead of steam power?
3 What type of water wheel is it?

THE AGE OF STEAM

The development of the steam engine

Appropriately enough, the reason the first steam engines were developed, was because the mining of coal (used to heat the boilers which produced steam), and the mining of tin in Cornwall, were often impeded by flooded mine-workings. An effective mechanical pump was needed to drain the mines, instead of the inefficient horse-driven water pumps in use at the time.

In 1698, Captain Thomas Savery invented a pump, which used steam and atmospheric (air) pressure to draw water up a pipe in the mine shaft. It was not an engine.

Savery's machine was followed by Thomas Newcomen's steam engine in 1712. This, too, was mainly used to pump water out of underground mine workings. In the picture on the next page, which was drawn in 1717, you can see Newcomen's 'ENGINE for Raising Water (with a power made) by FIRE'.

Newcomen's engine was atmospheric. It used atmospheric pressure to

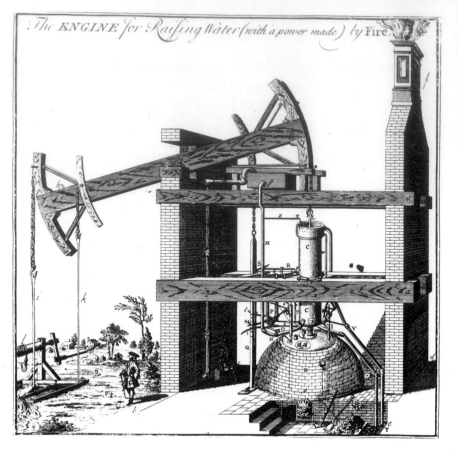

Engraving by H. Beighton of Newcomen Engine (1717)

move the piston down the cylinder, not steam. Steam from the boiler entered the cylinder, causing (but not forcing) the piston to rise. When it reached the top, cold water was fed into the chamber, making the hot steam condense, thus creating a partial vacuum inside the cylinder. This allowed atmospheric pressure (the weight of the air in the atmosphere) to push the piston back down the cylinder again. When steam was readmitted, the vacuum disappeared and the piston rose up the cylinder once more, assisted by a heavy counterweight attached to the beam at the top. This is why it was sometimes called a beam engine.

There were several drawbacks to the Newcomen engine. For one thing it could only produce an up and down motion, not the rotary action of a water wheel or a windmill. It was large and cumbersome for the power it produced and used a lot of fuel. But it did the required job and there was plenty of fuel at the coal pits anyway.

It was only when James Watt (see below) developed his improved version of the Newcomen engine in the second half of the eighteenth century that steam engines rapidly began to replace the water wheel. A hundred years later, there were more than 110,000 steam engines in use throughout Britain.

James Watt (1736–1819)

Engraving of James Watt

James Watt was an extraordinary genius, who made an immense contribution to the Industrial Revolution.

In 1763, when employed by Glasgow University as a scientific instruments maker, he was asked to repair a model of Newcomen's steam engine. Watt decided to improve it and built a new engine with a separate chamber in which to condense the steam. In this way, the main cylinder stayed hot, and so saved fuel.

Watt, like many great inventors, lacked his own capital (the money needed to build machines and factories). He joined forces with John Roebuck of the Carron Ironworks to build steam engines, but their first full-scale steam engine failed, largely because the quality of the workmanship could not match the strains put on the machine.

In 1774, Watt went into partnership with Matthew Boulton and a new version of the steam engine was built at Boulton's Soho engineering works in Birmingham. It used an accurately-machined cylinder made by John Wilkinson, at his ironworks at Broseley (see below).

In 1776, the first genuine Boulton-Watt **steam** engine began to work. It was still a reciprocating engine (i.e. an engine which produces an up-and-down motion). But it produced as much power from one tonne of coal as the Newcomen engine did from three tonnes.

In 1781, Watt, and his foreman William Murdock, developed a new system of gear wheels, known as the 'sun and planet' system, which converted the up-and-down motion of the beam engine to one of rotary motion. It was now possible to use a steam engine to power machinery instead of using a water wheel. Soon, vehicles would be developed which would move 'under their own steam'.

In 1782, Watt made his steam engine even more efficient by making steam drive the piston up the cylinder, as well as down. This is why it was called the double-acting steam engine.

By 1800 there were at least 500 Boulton and Watt steam engines in use in Britain, many of them in mines and ironworks. About 40 per cent were in cotton mills, but only 4 per cent were in woollen mills.

The steam engine was a remarkable development and it created a huge new demand for coal, iron and precision machinery. Progress in transport (see Chapter 3) also played an important part. The manufacture of steam engines benefitted from the growth of canals and railways. In turn the steam engine made steamships and steam railways possible.

THE COAL-MINING INDUSTRY

In 1700, British coal production was about 4 million tonnes a year. Demand was growing all the time, largely to supply the domestic market with fuel for home fires. But, in the following 50 years, coal began to be used as fuel for steam engines and blast furnaces, as well. Annual production rose by 50 per cent to 6 million tonnes in 1750, and then by a further 66 per cent to 10 million tonnes in 1800.

In the early nineteenth century, the needs of a rapidly expanding population, the phenomenal speed with which factories began to use steam power, the coming of the steamship and the creation of a railway network, stimulated demand for coal to even greater heights. By 1850 coal production had risen by a staggering 500 per cent in 50 years, to 50 million tonnes. In 1900, coal output was 230 million tonnes a year.

The location of the coalfields in 1700 was very much the same as today, with the exception of the Kent coalfield, which was not discovered until the nineteenth century. The most important was the Northumberland and Durham coalfield. Coal was mined close to Newcastle-upon-Tyne and shipped from the estuary of the Tyne to London and to ports along the coasts of Britain.

Many of the pits were owned by the aristocracy, since the coal was found on their estates. At first only the coal which was on, or near, the surface was mined. Deeper coal was being mined from tunnels in the sides of valleys, called adit mines, and from pit shafts in what were known as bell pits.

By 1700 some pits were already as much as 50 metres in depth. The pit owners knew there was coal deeper in the ground, but there were difficult problems to overcome to be able to mine it. As demand

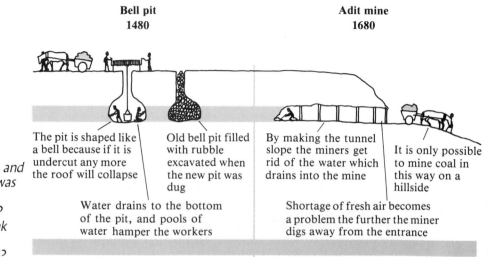

**Bell pit
1480**

**Adit mine
1680**

The pit is shaped like a bell because if it is undercut any more the roof will collapse

Old bell pit filled with rubble excavated when the new pit was dug

By making the tunnel slope the miners get rid of the water which drains into the mine

It is only possible to mine coal in this way on a hillside

Water drains to the bottom of the pit, and pools of water hamper the workers

Shortage of fresh air becomes a problem the further the miner digs away from the entrance

Diagram of bell pit and adit mine. Which was the more wasteful method of mining? Which do you think was the more dangerous method?

increased in the eighteenth century, and then rocketed in the nineteenth century, there was great pressure on pit owners to solve these problems, in order to get the maximum amount of coal possible from each pit – sometimes at great risk to the miners.

Problems in the coalmines and attempted solutions

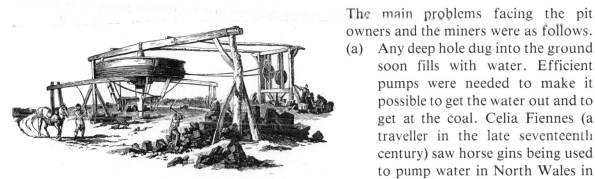

Horse gin at a colliery, from Pyne's Microcosm, c. *1805. How many horses were needed to work the 'gin'?*

The main problems facing the pit owners and the miners were as follows.

(a) Any deep hole dug into the ground soon fills with water. Efficient pumps were needed to make it possible to get the water out and to get at the coal. Celia Fiennes (a traveller in the late seventeenth century) saw horse gins being used to pump water in North Wales in 1698. 'They have great wheels that are turned with horses that draw up the water and so draine the Mines which would else be overflowed so as they could not dig the coale.'

However, these simple pumps could not cope with deep mines. The invention of the Newcomen engine and later, the development of the Boulton-Watt steam engine, were therefore of vital importance to the coal-mining industry to pump water out.

(b) There was always a danger from fire-damp (a mixture of air and methane gas found in coal deposits). When it escaped it would easily explode if exposed to a naked flame. Miners often worked in the dark, as candles were far too dangerous to use. Some method of providing safe lighting underground was essential.

In 1815 Sir Humphry Davy invented a safety lamp in which a cylindrical gauze sheet surrounded an oil lamp. Light could shine through but the gauze prevented the heat of the flame igniting methane gas in the mine workings.

(c) Choke-damp (carbon dioxide) was another fairly dangerous gas found in mines. It snuffed out the candle light and could suffocate miners if they could not get to fresh air in time.

An efficient system of ventilation was needed. For a long time the only method used was to sink two shafts and to light a fire in one of them. Warm air rose up the ventilation shaft and fresh air was drawn down the other shaft. This caused air to circulate through the workings. Children, called trappers, squatted in the dark tunnels underground, and opened and shut gates, called traps, to control the flow of air and to allow miners and wagons through.

In the 1790s an exhaust pump was invented by John Buddle. His pump sucked foul air out of one shaft, and fresh air was drawn in down another shaft. Thirty years later some pits had even installed steam-powered mechanical fans. But this still did not cure the problem, as the frequency of accidents and mine explosions showed only too clearly in the nineteenth century.

(d) As mine shafts became deeper the strains imposed on the ropes which lowered miners down the shafts and raised tubs of coal to the surface increased. In the early 1800s wire cables were successfully introduced but not before many miners had lost their lives in accidents, when ropes frayed or snapped in two.

(e) The great difficulty of transporting a dirty, heavy and bulky product like coal cheaply, both above and below ground, presented a very real problem. It could only be transported over a distance when cheap and efficient forms of transport were available.

At first women and children dragged heavy wagons of coal underground, and sometimes carried it on their backs (see also Chapter 8). Later on, pit ponies were used to pull the wagons.

On the surface, one of the first uses of the new canals, was to get coal to the customer. As Chapter 3 shows, the Duke of Bridgewater's spectacular canal (completed by James Brindley in 1761) reduced the cost of sending coal from the Duke's Worsley Colliery to his customers in Manchester by 50 per cent.

In Northumberland and Durham, in the late eighteenth century, coal was loaded into wagons, which ran on primitive railways running down the valley sides of the River Tyne. They were drawn by horses and the coal was loaded from wharves, on the river bank, on to boats for shipment to London. The horses pulled the empty wagons back up the railway lines to the coal mine.

In the nineteenth century, the development of the steam railway locomotive (see Chapter 3), completely transformed the way in which coal was distributed, since it provided the cheapest and most efficient form of transport overground. In time, underground railways solved the problem of transporting coal along the mine workings.

(f) Working underground was dangerous. Problems were caused by falling rock and the collapse of underground tunnels. Miners inhaled dust. Long hours working underground made them tired and as a result their lives were often put at risk through carelessness.

Miners still hewed coal with picks and shovels for much of the nineteenth century, as they had done in the eighteenth century. Originally they left pillars of coal to support the roofs of the workings. But this method of supporting the roof was unreliable and there were many rock falls. Pit props of timber or metal were later used instead.

Women and very young children ceased to be employed underground after the Coal Mines Act of 1842. In Chapter 8 you can see how this law affected the collieries and how it put an end to the appalling conditions in which many young children and women had worked. In the 1830s, it was a common sight to see women bent double, straining to carry heavy baskets of coal, and young children with ropes or chains around their waists and through their legs, hauling tubs of coal along the underground railway lines.

Look at Sources A, B, C, D, E.

Source A

Painting of a colliery in about 1790

Source B

'We found a prodigious large fire engine at work, draining the water from the pit; and adjoining to it a circular aperture of a tolerable diameter, filled with smoke. We were gently lowered by the operation of six horses employed for that purpose, till we found ourselves at the end of about five minutes safely landed on solid ground, and with a huge fire burning on one side, to keep the air in proper temperature.

'What surprised me the most, were the horses I found living there. The miners do not continue in the pits above twelve hours at a time. The coal is wound up in baskets, and these baskets again are emptied into carts, which are placed upon cylindrical wheels.'

From a contemporary account of a visit to a Northumberland coal mine, 1778

Source C

'I had to wait a few minutes, till a huge deep iron tub, containing about two tubs of coal, discharged its load. We were then swung off and let down, sinking the eighteen hundred feet [550 m] in what seemed to me little more than two minutes. The tub was brought to a level with a kind of gallery, along which was a tramway for wagons. A few candles and lamps gave light to the scene.

'Every hundred yards or so [about 90 m] a horse and laden wagons go tearing and clanking past one's very breast. At intervals along the passage, I found it closed up with coarse wooden doors, each attended by a boy, who opened it for the passing of the wagons, and then shut it again. These form a part of the arrangements for ventilating the mine. Every two yards [1.8 m] a wooden beam, prevented falls of the sandstone ceiling.

'At length we came to two human figures, naked all except the smallest possible kilt; the one wielding a mattock [pick] against the solid wall of coal, the other shovelling the resulting loose materials into a wagon. Having taken a hasty peep at the vast furnace used for the ventilation of the pit, I stepped once more into the metal tub and was quickly hoisted to the upper world.'

From a contemporary account of a visit to a Durham coal mine, 1844

Source D

THIS MONUMENT was erected to perpetuate the remembrance of an awful visitation of the Almighty which took place in this Parish on the 4th day of July 1858. On that eventful day the Lord sent forth His Thunder, Lightning, Hail and Rain, carrying devastation before them, and by a sudden irruption of Water into the Coalpits of R. C. Clarke Esq.ʳ twenty six human beings whose names are recorded here were suddenly Summon'd to appear before their Maker.

Monument at Silkstone Church, near Barnsley, to a pit disaster in 1838

1 Which mining problem caused the accident at Silkstone? Which problem probably caused the accident shown in the picture opposite of Page Bank Colliery, in 1858?

2 How did the miners underground move coal from the coal face to the bottom of the pit shaft at the colliery in Northumberland in 1778, and at the colliery in Durham in 1844?

3 Write down two of the ways in which the extracts show how these collieries differed from one another. Which was the more important of the two mines?

4 Is there anything in the picture of a colliery, drawn in about 1790, which confirms any of the facts about the colliery visited in 1778?

5 Which passages in the two extracts describe (a) pit props, (b) the work of a 'trapper', (c) a horse gin, (d) a Newcomen engine?

6 Both extracts describe vast or huge furnaces underground. But only one correctly explains why a furnace was situated there. Which

source is correct? Write a sentence to the other author explaining why he is wrong.

7 What changes took place between the end of the seventeenth and the end of the eighteenth centuries in the methods used to drain the pits?

8 The pictures enable you to compare two collieries from 1790 and 1858. How was the 1790 colliery drained? Where was the engine house at the 1858 colliery? Write two or three sentences comparing these collieries under the headings (a) buildings, (b) transport, (c) machinery.

Source E   *Accident at Page Bank Colliery, County Durham,* The Illustrated London News, *16 October 1858*

9 At a meeting in 1816, to congratulate Sir Humphry Davy, the committee concerned recognised 'the great merit of its inventor' in making it possible to use 'coal mines where inflammable air prevails'. They saw the safety lamp as making it possible for mineowners to open new seams at even deeper levels. Accordingly, some critics have said that he only made matters worse for the miner. What do you think?

10 What evidence is there to show that the Davy Safety Lamp was not in universal use after 1815?

THE IRON AND STEEL INDUSTRY

Basic processes The basic processes in the iron and steel industry, at the time of the Industrial Revolution, were:

(a) **Smelting** – heating iron ore in a furnace, together with limestone (to get rid of impurities in the ore) and a fuel. In 1700 this fuel was charcoal. Bellows were used to pump a blast of air through the furnace to raise the temperature high enough to melt the iron. Molten iron was run off into moulds, called pigs. Pig iron is hard but brittle. It can be melted again and poured into moulds of different shapes to make cast iron goods.

(b) **Forging** Many iron products are made from a slightly softer, less brittle iron. In 1700 this was done by reheating the pig iron in a furnace, with the aid of bellows, and repeatedly hammering (forging) the molten iron into shape to remove the impurities which weakened it. This was wrought iron.

(c) Steel is stronger and tougher than iron but greater care has to be taken to remove the impurities. In 1700 there was no effective way of doing this.

In the eighteenth century, Abraham Darby began producing cheaper pig iron by using coke in a blast furnace. Henry Cort made it possible to use coke in a forge to produce cheaper wrought iron, whilst Benjamin Huntsman developed the crucible method of making high quality steel.

Iron-making in 1700

At a number of sites in Britain, it is possible to visit reconstructed forges which date back to the eighteenth century and the days when water was used to provide power. In cutlery forges in Sheffield, water wheels turned grindstones for sharpening blades. In many ironworks, water wheels operated bellows, which blasted air through the furnaces. They also powered the heavy hammers which shaped wrought iron.

The main problem was one of ensuring a regular supply of water to the 'goit' or channel which carried water to the wheel. Often, a dam was built behind the forge to hold a reservoir of water, called a hammer pond.

Water wheel and heavy helve hammer at Wortley Forge, near Sheffield. How do you think a water wheel, turning round and round, could make a hammer go up and down?

Charcoal was used to heat the furnaces. This had to be made by slowly baking a pile of wood, covered with turf (to stop the heat getting out). It took five days to burn and three days to cool down. When coke was later made from coal, a similar process was used – until coking ovens were invented.

By 1720, the days of the hammer pond and the charcoal furnace were already numbered. Daniel Defoe discovered why, when he visited ironworks in Kent and Sussex.

'I had the curiosity to see the great foundries, or iron works, which are carried on at such a prodigious expense of wood, that even in a country almost all over-run with timber, they begin to complain of the consuming for those furnaces, and leaving the next age to want timber for building their navies.'

> 1 What was the problem Daniel Defoe discovered?
> 2 How was it aggravated by the need to build, heat and furnish houses and by the increasing demand for iron?

Two solutions were possible. One was to try to find new sources of timber supply. This was why some iron makers built furnaces in areas of woodland some distance away from the areas where deposits of iron ore were found. They even built furnaces in the remote highlands of Scotland.

The other solution was to use coal as the fuel. Since it was already used as a fuel in other industries, it seemed sensible to see if it could be used to smelt iron ore. But a coal-fired furnace on its own could not reach the high temperatures needed to smelt iron – at least, not until Abraham Darby used coal in the form of coke.

The Abraham Darby family

Abraham Darby I (1677–1717) owned an ironworks at Coalbrookdale in Shropshire. He discovered that a strong blast of air could raise the temperature in a coke-fired furnace high enough to melt large quantities of iron ore.

The local 'clod coal' in Shropshire made excellent coke, unlike coal in other districts. It was this new smelting process which he successfully launched in 1709. Coke as a fuel was ideal in several respects. At that time, seams of coal were often found close to deposits of iron ore – which saved ironworks the cost of transporting heavy raw materials. Coke was stronger than charcoal, so heavier loads of iron ore could be smelted at one go, in bigger and taller furnaces.

Abraham Darby I was shrewd. He did not readily pass on his discovery to other ironmasters, preferring to reap the benefits himself. As late as 1750, most of the new coke-burning blast furnaces were still in Shropshire. But in the next fifty years, the industry was transformed. By 1788, nearly five tonnes of pig iron were being smelted with coke, for every tonne smelted with charcoal. A traveller in Scotland, noted in 1760, that at the Carron Ironworks, 'instead of burning wood, they use coal, which they have the art of cleaning in such a manner as frees it from the sulphur, that would otherwise render the metal too brittle for working.'

Abraham Darby II (1711–63) was also an innovator. He continued to develop Coalbrookdale as an ironworks and in 1743 made a major change in the industry, when he used a Newcomen steam engine to power the bellows in a blast furnace.

An engraving from a 1782 painting of the Iron Bridge near Coalbrookdale. Are bridges like this built today? Which types of bridge still require large quantities of iron or steel?

During the lifetime of Abraham Darby III (1750–91), the family tradition continued. The Coalbrookdale Works made the first iron railways in 1767 and from 1777–81, built the celebrated Iron Bridge across the Severn. This proved that iron could be used as a building material, as well as for making machinery and steam engines. Since thousands of visitors from all over the world came to see the bridge, Darby got excellent publicity for his ironworks and established the reputation of the rapidly expanding British iron and steel industry.

Steel

Sheffield was one of the earliest centres of the iron industry. It was here, in 1740, that Benjamin Huntsman (1704–76) developed the first effective method of making steel.

Iron was too brittle and snapped too easily for some manufacturing purposes, even when toughened in a charcoal furnace over a period of several hours (the so-called 'blister' method). Huntsman's solution was to melt this 'blister steel', in a clay crucible, in a coke-burning furnace which burned off the impurities, turning it into high quality steel.

Crucible steel was used whenever manufacturers wanted a metal that was hard and tough but also flexible (as in a spring, for instance). Its main disadvantage was that it was a costly method, producing only small quantities of steel at a time. By 1770, there were still only 5 steel manufacturers in Sheffield. In 1856 there were 135.

Increasing iron production

The growth of industry in the eighteenth century meant an increased demand for iron.

1 In what ways did the following developments create a demand for high quality iron. (a) the Agrarian Revolution; (b) the use of steam-powered machinery; (c) wars in the eighteenth century?
2 Why was the iron produced in Darby's coke-fired blast furnaces not sufficient in itself to satisfy the rising demand for more iron to make machines and weapons?

The demand for wrought iron was only met when some way of speeding up the forging process was devised. As late as the 1780s, red hot pig iron was still repeatedly hammered in a forge to get rid of impurities and make it suitable for rolling into bars and plates.

A number of ironworkers were trying to solve the problem. Although Thomas and George Cranage of Coalbrookdale and Peter Onions of Merthyr Tydfil were working on similar processes, it was Henry Cort (1740–1800), who in 1784, developed and got the credit for the 'puddling' process.

Cort owned ironworks in Hampshire. He heated the pig iron in a special white-hot, coke-burning furnace. This reverberatory furnace was shaped like a long oven rather than a tall funnel. The metal rested on sand and did not come into contact with the coke. Flames were deflected on to the surface of the iron from the roof of the furnace.

Workmen stirred ('puddled') the molten iron with iron rods to dislodge the impurities which made the metal brittle and unreliable. These were burned off in the intense heat. When the stirring rods got too hot they were cooled in water. At the end of the process, the 'puddler' stirred the iron into lumps, called 'blooms'. These were about 40 kg in weight and were hammered roughly into shape before being rolled between iron rollers to get rid of any remaining impurities. The iron bars could then be shaped on a forge or rolled into any desired form – bars, plates, ingots, etc.

The two most important results of this 'puddling' process were (a) economy, and (b) speed. Cort used coke instead of charcoal and he could produce 15 tonnes of bar iron in the same time it took other iron masters to produce a tonne of wrought iron in a forge.

A contemporary print of Lymington ironworks, Northumberland, in 1835

---

3 *Can you locate: (a)   a puddling furnace, (b)   a blast furnace, in this picture?*

4 *What jobs are being performed by the three men in the foreground of this picture?*

5 *How were heavy raw materials moved from one part of this works to another? What different types of power were used?*

6 *Write an extended caption for this picture, explaining clearly everything you can see there.*

The puddling process enabled the ironmasters to meet the rapidly increasing demand for metal and caused the output of iron to shoot up. In 1786, Britain still made less than 70,000 tonnes of pig iron a year. In the next ten years the output of iron nearly doubled to about 130,000 tonnes. It doubled yet again in the next ten years after that, until total iron production stood at 250,000 tonnes (in 1806). By 1850, it had increased by nearly ten times, to a massive 2,250,000 tonnes – all within the lifetime of an ironworker.

The ironmasters also began to use steam engines to power a number of important processes. In 1786, steam was first used to power grindstones in the Sheffield cutlery industry. It was so effective that within ten years, more grindstones were being turned by steam engines than by water wheels.

The ironmasters

Forges, like Kirkstall Forge, in Leeds, owed much of their prosperity to the skills of the ironmasters who owned them. One of the most famous of these ironmasters was John 'Iron-mad' Wilkinson (1728–1808). He was called 'Iron-mad' Wilkinson because of his obsession with iron and its products. (He even stipulated that he was to be buried in an iron coffin, he built a Methodist chapel made of iron, and it was said of him that he always mentioned the magic word 'iron' in every letter he wrote!)

Wilkinson owned several iron works in the Midlands. His skilled workforce could bore cylinders with a high degree of accuracy. It was their precision and accurate machining, which made it possible for James Watt to make a successful steam engine.

Wilkinson began to use the Boulton-Watt steam engine to power the bellows which blasted air through his iron furnaces. In 1787 he built the first iron ships. These were designed to carry his iron manufactures on the River Severn.

Changes in location and importance of the iron and steel industry

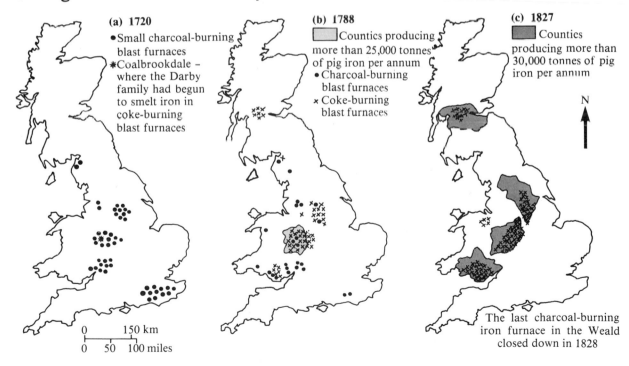

(a) 1720
• Small charcoal-burning blast furnaces
✳Coalbrookdale – where the Darby family had begun to smelt iron in coke-burning blast furnaces

0   150 km
0   50 100 miles

(b) 1788
▢ Counties producing more than 25,000 tonnes of pig iron per annum
• Charcoal-burning blast furnaces
× Coke-burning blast furnaces

(c) 1827
▢ Counties producing more than 30,000 tonnes of pig iron per annum

N

The last charcoal-burning iron furnace in the Weald closed down in 1828

Location of the iron and steel industry: (a) 1720; (b) 1788; (c) 1827

The location of the iron and steel industry changed between 1720 and 1827, as you can see from the three maps on the previous page. So too, did its importance, as you can see from this article from a newspaper of the early nineteenth century – the *Dumfries Courier*.

'Witness some of the wonders of the present century : such as 300 furnaces in full operation, iron bridges, boats built of the same material, locomotives rivalling the eagle's flight. In the absence of iron, the steam-engine and spinning-jenny would have been things in abeyance to the end of time.

In 1740, the quantity of pig iron manufactured in England and Wales, the united product of 50 furnaces, merely amounted to 17,000 tons [17,272 tonnes], or less than a fortieth part of the returns given for the year 1827, when the furnaces in Staffordshire, Shropshire, Wales, Yorkshire, Derbyshire and Scotland, had increased to 284 and their product as near as may be to 700,000 tons [711,200 tonnes] of pig iron.

A very great increase has taken place in the iron trade during the nine years that have elapsed since that period. The demand for railroads has given a fillip to the manufacture.'

1 *In which year was the article written?*
2 *Which developments did the* Dumfries Courier *think had helped to boost the iron industry in the early years of the nineteenth century? What did the writer think would have been the fate of the steam engine and the spinning jenny without iron?*
3 *Name two areas which produced iron in 1720 but were no longer important iron-producers in 1827. What reasons help to explain this change?*
4 *Write a paragraph to describe and explain the location of the iron and steel industry in 1827.*
5 *By how many times had the output of pig iron risen between 1740 and 1827? What was the average output of iron in each furnace (a) in 1740, (b) in 1827? What conclusion can you draw from these figures?*

By 1800 some of the ironworks had grown to a great size. The different processes – smelting pig iron in a blast furnace, removing impurities in a puddling furnace, shaping the iron in a rolling mill – necessitated the spending of large sums of money and the erection of huge new buildings.

Iron and steel works, such as the Carron Iron Works in Scotland and Richard Crawshay's Cyfarthfa Works in Merthyr Tydfil, were a far cry from the small forges and furnaces which had produced iron in 1720.

THE POTTERY INDUSTRY

Restored 'beehive' pottery kiln at Stoke-on-Trent. Pottery was baked by coal-burning furnaces in these kilns until fairly recently. Why do you think they are now disused?

The pottery industry of Staffordshire thrived in the late eighteenth century, largely as the result of one man's enterprise and skill. That man was Josiah Wedgwood (see below). Other fine pottery works were also established by men like Josiah Spode, but it was Wedgwood who made the six towns of the Potteries (Stoke-on-Trent, Tunstall, Fenton, Longton, Burslem and Hanley) famous throughout the world for their fine china and earthenware.

In 1697, Celia Fiennes 'went to Staffordshire to see them making the fine teapots, cups and saucers of the fine red earth, in imitation and as curious as that which comes from China'.

In 1771, Arthur Young said:

'It dates its great demand from Mr. Wedgwood introducing, about four years ago, his cream coloured ware, and since that time the increase has been very rapid. Large quantities are exported to Germany, Ireland, Holland, Russia, Spain, the East Indies, America, France. Common clay of the county is used for the ordinary sorts; the finer kinds are made of clay from Devonshire and Dorsetshire but the flints from the Thames are all brought rough by sea, either to Liverpool or Hull.'

1 *Why are cups, saucers and plates called china?*
2 *Was the pottery industry of Staffordshire started by Josiah Wedgwood? Quote your evidence.*
3 *How can you tell it was an industry of world-wide importance by 1771? What reason was given for this rapid growth?*
4 *Name one of the advantages of the area for pottery-making and one of the disadvantages.*

Josiah Wedgwood (1730–95)

Josiah Wedgwood

Josiah Wedgwood was born into a family of potters. He began work as a child of nine and soon showed an aptitude for the business. He was primarily interested in making beautiful pottery and in 1763 designed a cream-coloured pottery, called Queen's ware. He also introduced the blue Jasper ware in which exquisite designs were left in white and slightly raised above the surface of the pottery.

In 1769, he opened his new Etruria Works. His pottery was soon sold all over the world and graced the tables of kings and nobles. The Empress Catherine of Russia bought two magnificent 950-piece dinner services, which can still be seen in Leningrad today. Wedgwood also made pots and plates for ordinary homes.

Pottery, as an industry, was not easily mechanised, but Wedgwood made the best possible use of steam power and other new developments. Coal from the Staffordshire coalfield fired the kilns and steam engines processed raw materials, grinding flints and mixing colours and clays.

But pottery was still mainly made by hand, employing skilled craft workers. Wedgwood got the best out of his workforce, dividing the jobs, so that each worker became skilled in a particular technique.

Wedgwood soon saw the benefits that would come from linking his pottery works by canal to the port of Liverpool. He was the main power behind the canal company which began the Grand Trunk (or Trent and Mersey Canal) at Burslem, in 1766. In 1769 he built his new Etruria Works on the banks of the canal. The section linking Burslem to the Mersey was opened in 1770.

Nineteenth-century engraving of the Wedgwood Works at Etruria, showing the canal

> **5** *Draw a simple diagram of the Etruria Works from the picture opposite.*
> **6** *Mark on your diagram:*
> (a) *the canal,*
> (b) *a pottery kiln,*
> (c) *the wharves where the clay was unloaded,*
> (d) *a barge,*
> (e) *a sailing ship,*
> (f) *the main works.*

Reasons for Wedgwood's success

(a) Staffordshire was already famous for its pottery in the seventeenth century, as the quotation from Celia Fiennes's travels showed. Local raw materials, marl clay ('the fine red earth') and coal (used to fire the pottery kilns) helped a thriving pottery industry to develop, long before Wedgwood was born. However, it was still only a domestic cottage industry.

(b) Wedgwood used the natural resources and the existing craft skills of the potters of Staffordshire well. He fulfilled, and created, an increasing demand throughout Britain, for good quality china. More people were drinking tea, coffee and chocolate. Affluent people wanted better pottery than that produced by the local potters, who were to be found in most towns. As Arthur Young's account showed, in 1771, there was also a large demand from Europe and America for Wedgwood's chinaware and earthenware products.

(c) Wedgwood was a first-class businessman. He sent travellers, armed with catalogues (in French and German, as well as in English) to sell his pottery. He advertised his wares in the newspapers and put them on display in his splendid London showrooms. He understood that it was not enough to make a good product; you had to be able to sell it as well.

(d) He made his pottery works at Etruria as efficient as it was possible to do at the time. He quickly saw the advantage of using kaolin from Cornwall and china stone to produce fine quality china. The kaolin was taken by sea from Cornwall to Liverpool and from there to Etruria by land. Wedgwood was active in promoting the construction of the Grand Trunk Canal, which linked his works with the Mersey in 1770. He also made good use of the turnpikes.

(e) Good communications, at that time, meant that he assembled raw materials and distributed finished goods as cheaply as possible in the pre-railway age. Canals provided a safe method of transporting a breakable item such as china. He used steam-powered machinery to grind materials. He employed fine artists to create new designs and introduced new glazes to improve the appearance of his pottery.

THE LANCASHIRE COTTON INDUSTRY

Reasons for the original location of the industry

Cotton mills in Manchester, Victorian engraving, c. 1890. In what way is the situation of this cotton mill similar to that of Wedgwood's Etruria pottery works in Burslem?

The first textile industry to become industrialised along modern lines was the Lancashire cotton industry. The industry thrived in Lancashire for a number of reasons:

(a) The existing woollen industry in the county meant that there was already a workforce skilled in spinning and weaving.

(b) The port of Liverpool imported raw cotton from Turkey and the Middle East at that time. As the cotton industry grew, Liverpool reaped the benefits of being ideally placed, on the west, Atlantic-facing coast, to import cotton from the plantations of the southern states of North America.

(c) Coal from the Lancashire coalfield could be used as a fuel for some processes, such as dyeing and washing cotton.

(d) Fast streams flowing off the Pennine hills could be used to power water wheels. Their soft water was ideal for washing purposes.

(e) The dampish climate was suitable for the industry, since it kept the cotton thread moist enough to stop it snapping when under strain. A dry atmosphere would have been a serious disadvantage.

(f) Cotton manufacture was a relatively young industry and the manufacturers were less conservative than those in the woollen industry. They were usually more prepared to take risks than the woollen manufacturers, who had made money from traditional methods and could see little point in changing to something new and risky.

(g) The cotton industry had few of the restrictions from which the traditional woollen industry suffered, such as guild and craft regulations. These often stood in the way of industrial expansion, since they had originally been designed, in the Middle Ages, to protect weavers and cloth merchants from unfair competition. They were not designed to meet the requirements of the factory age.

Kay's flying shuttle

The most important initial requirement in the cotton industry was to find a method of speeding up the spinning process. In 1715, it took the work of ten spinners to supply the yarn used by each weaver in the woollen industry. The invention of Kay's flying shuttle in 1733 only made the problem worse since it speeded up the weaving process. However it was thirty years before it came into widespread use.

John Kay came from Bury in Lancashire but invented his flying shuttle when employed in Colchester, in Essex, in 1733. Until then the maximum width of cloth a weaver could make was limited by his reach, since he had to pass the weft thread across the width of the warp threads which ran lengthwise along the loom. If a wider cloth, called broadloom, was woven then two weavers were needed, one on either side of the loom.

Kay's flying shuttle, was designed for use on this broadloom and was operated by only one weaver. He (most weavers were men) pulled a cord and this caused the shuttle to 'fly' through the warp threads.

---

1 *How many weavers were needed on a broadloom (a) before, (b) after, the invention of Kay's flying shuttle?*
2 *Why do you think Kay became very unpopular in Colchester in 1733?*
3 *Why was his invention unnecessary at that time?*
4 *Why do you think it was 30 years before its use became widespread in the textile industries?*

The pressure to speed up the production of yarn led to the development of three outstanding new spinning machines in the 1760s and 1770s. The first of these, the spinning jenny, was designed for use in the spinner's cottage, although it was often used in a mill; the second, the water frame, could only be used in a mill or factory, since it required water power (later steam power); the third, the mule, later became the main type of spinning machine in textile mills.

The spinning jenny

The spinning jenny. Write two or three sentences comparing this spinning jenny with the hand-operated spinning wheel shown in the picture on page 48.

James Hargreaves was a carpenter and weaver who lived and worked near the cotton textile town of Blackburn in Lancashire. It is said that he got the idea for his spinning jenny, in 1764, when he saw the wheel and spindle of his wife's overturned spinning wheel turning round and round, even though it was upside down on the floor. It occurred to him that a machine could be produced, like this, which could spin several threads at the same time.

In 1767, he perfected this spinning jenny, as it was called. Tradition has it, that it was called a 'jenny' after his wife, but the term may have come from 'gin', since this was a popular abbreviation for 'engine'.

The original spinning jenny had eight spindles, used the spinner's hands and feet to operate the machine, and had the capacity to spin eight times as much yarn as an ordinary hand spinning wheel. Its main disadvantage was that the yarn it produced was very fine and not very strong and tended to snap easily. As a result, it could only be used for the weft threads which were woven through the lengthwise warp threads.

Hargreaves kept the machine secret, and used the yarn produced by his own family as weft yarn for his own loom. However, he sold a few machines to make some extra money, and a mob of spinners then broke into his house and destroyed his jenny and his loom. Hargreaves left the district in disgust and went to work in Nottingham, where he opened a small cotton mill in partnership with a man called James.

By the time of his death, in 1778, many of his spinning jennies had been fitted with 80 spindles instead of eight. It was later estimated that, in 1784, there were 20,000 jennies at work in the cotton industry.

1 *Why was Hargreaves well qualified to invent and make a spinning machine?*

2 *Why do you think the mob destroyed his spinning jenny? Did they achieve anything by this action? How do people react today, to the invention of machines which speed up industrial processes?*

3 *Did Hargreaves completely solve the problem of how to cope with the increased demand for yarn, which had been caused by the invention of the flying shuttle?*

4 *How many spinners were needed to operate the estimated number of jennies at work in the cotton industry, in 1784? How many spinners would have been needed to produce the same amount of yarn with the old spinning wheel?*

The first factories

Thomas Lombe's silk-throwing mill had shown how a textile factory could make use of water power. James Hargreaves's spinning jenny had shown how a machine could increase output of cotton yarn. Richard Arkwright (see over), who was born in Preston in Lancashire, put both ideas together. He opened a cotton spinning mill in Derbyshire, in 1771, equipped with a machine, the water frame, which was powered by a water wheel.

Arkwright's mill at Cromford in Derbyshire

Richard Arkwright (1732–92)

Some people believe that Richard Arkwright's water frame was based on an earlier design for a spinning machine, invented by Lewis Paul and John Wyatt, in 1738. Arkwright installed it in the world's first cotton mill.

Instead of installing his water frame in a cotton mill in Preston, he kept the idea secret and moved to the Midlands. There, in partnership with Jedediah Strutt, a stocking manufacturer, he installed his spinning machines in a mill on the river Derwent, at Cromford, in Derbyshire, in 1771. Each frame could spin four spindles at a time.

His water frame had one great advantage over the spinning jenny which was that it made a tough, stronger yarn. This could be used in the stocking and knitting industries of Nottingham, Derby and Leicester. It was also suitable as a yarn for the stronger lengthwise warp threads fastened to the loom, through which the finer weft threads (from the spinning jenny) could be woven. Up until then these warp threads had been made from linen yarn rather than from cotton.

The Cromford mill was an outstanding success. Arkwright became rich, famous and was knighted. He built other cotton mills, and after the development of the Boulton-Watt steam engine adapted them for use with steam power. His cotton mill at Wirksworth was the first to use steam power, in 1780.

Arkwright was a highly efficient and ruthless businessman. He organised his factories efficiently, putting his workers on 12-hour shifts, in order to operate the machinery 24 hours a day.

By 1782, he was employing over 5,000 cotton workers in his mills. He, more than any other person in the textile industry, made the factory age possible.

Arkwright's water frame

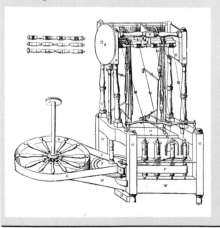

Sir Richard Arkwright

1 *Why do you think Arkwright built his mill in Cromford, in Derbyshire, and not in Preston, in Lancashire?*

2 *Was it an advantage, or a disadvantage, that the water frame could only be used in a factory rather than in the spinner's own cottage?*

3 *Imagine you are a cotton spinner visiting a friend in Derbyshire, in 1772. Write a short letter to a relative in Lancashire, commenting on the new mill at Cromford.*

4 *What is there in the photograph on page 75 to suggest that this cotton mill at Cromford is not the original 1771 building? (It was actually built by Arkwright in 1783.)*

5 *Why do you think the water frame and the spinning jenny both did well in the 1770s and 1780s, even though they produced the same product – cotton yarn?*

6 *The water frame and the jenny were soon challenged by a machine which produced yarn, combining the strength associated with the water frame, with the finer quality produced by the jenny. Because it was a cross between the two it was called a mule. Why?*

The spinning mule

The spinning mule was invented by Samuel Crompton, a spinner from Bolton, who had been very dissatisfied with his spinning jenny, as the thread it produced kept breaking. Between 1774 and 1779 he developed an improved spinning machine, combining techniques used in Arkwright's water frame (the rollers) with those used in the spinning jenny.

The machine he completed in 1779, combined the virtues of both – producing strong, reliable yarn which was also fine enough to satisfy the demand for high quality cloth.

Crompton designed his mule as a hand-operated spinning machine, which could turn 48 cotton spindles at a time. It was subsequently improved in many ways. Steam-engines powered bigger and better mules and one machine was eventually made, in which a single operator controlled 1,200 spindles at the same time.

Despite these improvements, it was not until 1830 that a completely 'self-acting' (automatic) spinning mule was perfected. After that time, the services of skilled spinners were no longer needed in cotton mills.

The power loom

The new spinning machines could produce so much yarn that the weavers were always kept extremely busy. As a result weavers were constantly in demand and were paid high wages – until Edmund Cartwright invented the power loom (see next page).

Edmund Cartwright (1743–1823)

Edmund Cartwright

Unlike most of the other people who invented machines for the textile industry Cartwright was not originally employed in the industry himself. He was a clergyman and also a poet.

In 1784 he visited Arkwright's mill at Cromford and was reported to have told Arkwright, that because he had greatly increased the output of yarn, he ought to invent a power loom. Cartwright thought this should not be too difficult and set about inventing a rather clumsy power loom himself. This was not very successful but he went on to develop the idea further and built a prototype power loom which was installed, in 1787, in a small factory in Doncaster.

At first the power for his loom came from the weaver's feet but by 1789 a steam engine was used to provide the power. In 1791, a cotton firm in Manchester agreed to buy 400 of his power looms. Looms powered by steam engines reduced the cost of weaving cloth by half the amount it cost to employ hand-loom weavers to do the same work.

The mill was burned down soon after installing the looms – possibly by dissatisfied and worried handloom weavers. They stood to lose most from the introduction of the power loom – both their jobs and their relatively high rates of pay as skilled workers. However, sooner or later the power loom was bound to succeed. In the early years of the nineteenth century it was modified and successfully introduced into most cotton and woollen weaving mills in the country.

As it transformed the textile industry, it created widespread unemployment and distress amongst the skilled handloom weavers.

Number of weavers and spinners in the cotton industry between 1820 and 1890

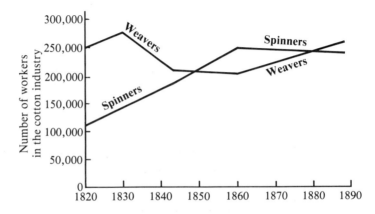

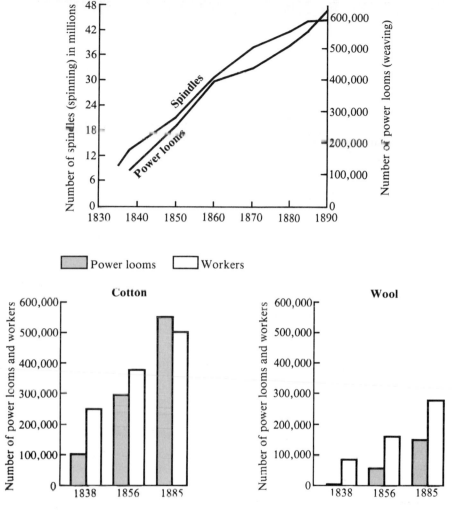

Number of spindles and power looms in the cotton industry between 1830 and 1890 (note the different vertical scales on this graph)

Number of power looms and workers in the woollen and cotton industries in 1838, 1856 and 1885

Look at the graphs.
1 Why did the number of weavers in the cotton industry suddenly drop between 1830 and 1840?
2 Approximately how many spindles were needed for every power loom in the cotton industry in the nineteenth century? Did the proportion change significantly during that time?
3 Approximately how many weavers were needed for each spinner (a) in 1820, (b) in 1850? Why did the proportions change? How were these ratios vastly different from those in 1715, when it was said that ten spinners were needed for every one weaver?
4 Write two or three sentences commenting on the graph, comparing progress in the cotton and woollen industries in 1838, 1856 and 1885.

THE WEST RIDING WOOLLEN INDUSTRY

The West Riding woollen industry was much slower than the Lancashire cotton industry to make use of the new machines. The first worsted spinning mill in Yorkshire, using a water wheel and spinning frames, was not opened until 1787 (at Addingham, on the river Wharfe) sixteen years after Arkwright opened his cotton mill at Cromford. Benjamin Gott, one of the pioneers of the factory system in Yorkshire, built a large woollen mill in Leeds in 1792, but even this used spinning jennies and handlooms at first. In 1800, the first steam-powered spinning mill in Yorkshire was opened in Bradford.

By this time, however, the advantages of the new manufacturing processes were already becoming obvious to most people in the woollen and worsted industries. Where in the eighteenth century, 160 workers had been needed to make a given quantity of cloth, by 1800 the same work could be done in the same time by only 77 workers – thanks to the invention of shearing frames and other machines. However the same number of weavers (24) was still required.

As in Lancashire, the introduction of power looms was greeted with bitter opposition. A power loom installed in a mill near Bradford in 1822 was smashed to pieces by angry workers. In 1836 there were still only 2,800 power looms in Bradford, even though it was the most progressive town in the worsted industry. Five years later there were 11,500 power looms, 19,000 by 1845 and 30,000 by 1850. The use of power looms in all of Britain's textile industries rose sharply from 14,000 in 1820 to 250,000 in 1850 and 400,000 in 1861.

Similar progress was also made in other parts of the industry. In 1845 there were 10,000 handcombers in Bradford. But after Samuel Cunliffe Lister introduced a new combing machine, the number of handcombers was cut by half, by 1851. Six years later, handcombing as a craft was almost extinct.

The number of spindles turned by Bradford's spinning machines doubled between 1839 and 1856. They were also much improved and rotated faster, increasing productivity by 30 per cent. Better steam engines made more efficient use of fuel, doing the same amount of work using less than half the amount of coal. New safety valves made it possible to use higher steam pressures and better lubricants made the machines more reliable.

The West Riding was ideally placed to take advantage of the development of steam power. At Linfits Mill, near Huddersfield, coal was taken straight from the pit head and put into the furnaces feeding the boilers in the mill. By 1834, Edward Parsons could write of the area around Leeds, 'The majority of the population is employed in manufacture, and the smoke of countless mills ascends to the skies'.

The Cotswold, West Country and Norwich woollen and worsted industries could not compete with the West Riding industry. The high cost of shipping coal, even by canal, to provide power, put them at a serious disadvantage. By the 1850s, the industry had severely declined in these regions with the result that the worsted industry in Britain was then almost entirely concentrated in the West Riding of Yorkshire. Of the 32,000 power looms in the industry in 1850, 30,000 were in Yorkshire, as were 71,000 of the 79,000 workers. Over half of these were in one parish alone – that of Bradford.

A contemporary print of steam-operated power looms in 1844. Write two or three sentences comparing this picture with the Hogarth engraving of hand looms in 1747 (on page 47).

By 1870 the textile industries were almost completely mechanised. The handloom weavers and the handcombers had finally disappeared. So, too, had the factories and mills which were still using water power in the early years of the nineteenth century. They were unable to compete when the opening of the railways brought cheap coal to all parts of Britain.

A model textile mill

As Chapter 8 will show, factory conditions had improved by 1870. Some manufacturers had even made an effort to build model factories and better quality housing for their employees.

In September 1853, Titus Salt opened his 'stupendous Model Mill' (shown in the picture on the next page) at Saltaire, near Bradford, in Yorkshire. He entertained over 3,000 guests to a huge banquet at the opening. They included 2,420 workers 'brought by railway from his works at Bradford.'

Titus Salt said he had determined some time before 'to leave Bradford' and had looked around for a suitable site for his new factory. He promised:

'He would do all he could to avoid evils so great as those resulting from polluted air and water; and he hoped to draw around him a population that would enjoy the beauties of the neighbourhood, and who would be a well-fed, contented, and happy body of operatives (Applause).'

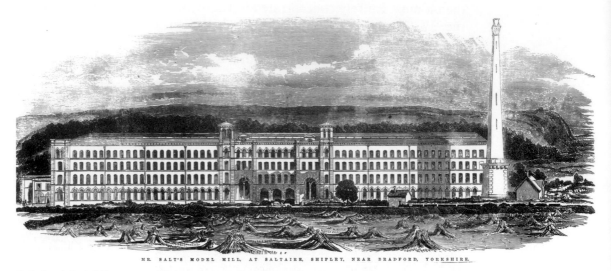

MR. SALT'S MODEL MILL, AT SALTAIRE, SHIPLEY, NEAR BRADFORD, YORKSHIRE.

Saltaire Model Factory at Saltaire, near Bradford, The Illustrated London News, *1 October 1853*

'Mr. Salt is one of the most eminent of the Bradford worsted manufacturers, employing a vast number of hand-loom moreen [a heavy cloth] weavers.

Saltaire is situated about four miles from Bradford in the beautiful valley of the Aire. Offices are now being built, facing the new road made by Mr. Salt which commences close by the Bingley turnpike-road, crosses the railway, the river, and canal [the Leeds and Liverpool] by two iron bridges.

The engines are supplied with water from the river by tunnels passing under the whole buildings, and when used, is again, carried back to the river. A branch from the Midland Railway, at the south front, will pass under the central arches, where there will be hoists for loading and unloading.

When the works are finished, 4500 hands will be required to keep them going. The weaving shed will contain 1200 looms; the length of the shafting will be 9870 feet [3,000 m]; the steam-engines to work these shafts are equal to 1250-horse power.'

The Illustrated London News, 1 October 1853

1 *Why was the new town called Saltaire?*
2 *Why did Titus Salt choose the site at Saltaire? What were its attractions as the site for a huge new textile mill? What did he, and his architects, do to make the best of these advantages?*

3 *What type of looms did his Bradford workers use? What type of looms were his Saltaire workers going to use? Did Titus Salt's plans involve a cut, or an increase, in jobs in the textile industry?*

4 *Examine critically the evidence given here. What were Titus Salt's real chances of avoiding 'polluted air and water'? How did the artist of the picture try to emphasise the fact that the new mill at Saltaire was situated in the countryside? Did his mill add to, or detract from, 'the beauties of the neighbourhood'? Do you think his attitude to his employees was likely to produce a 'contented and happy body of operatives'?*

'WORKSHOP OF THE WORLD'

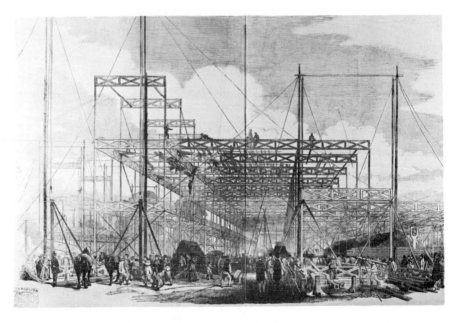

Building the Crystal Palace, The Illustrated London News, *1851. Why was the construction of a building like this only possible after the Industrial Revolution?*

The Great Exhibition of 1851

On 1 May 1851, Queen Victoria opened the Great Exhibition in a spacious new building in Hyde Park, which had been designed by Joseph Paxton, an architect well known at that time for his greenhouses. It was popularly known as the Crystal Palace but one critic said it was neither crystal nor a palace!

In fact, it was really a showcase for British industry. The light and airy building was itself a splendid advertisement, since it was made of iron and plate glass. Inside it was a remarkable display of machinery, including James Nasmyth's massive steam hammer (see page 86) and a hydraulic turbine.

The Great Exhibition confirmed the view that Britain was at that time the 'Workshop of the World'. If foreigners wanted to buy a railway, power loom, or a pin, they came to Britain for it.

Rapid growth in output

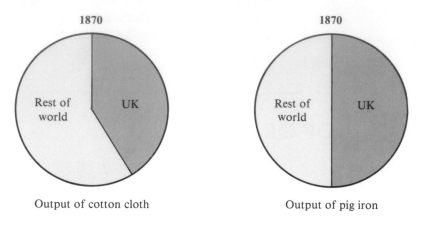

Pie diagrams showing output of cotton cloth and pig iron

1 *Write a sentence to say how these graphs support the view that Britain was the 'Workshop of the World' in the middle of the nineteenth century.*

2 *In 1867, nearly 10 million tonnes of coal was exported from Britain to different parts of the world. What is surprising about the fact that Russia imported 0.5 million tonnes of this coal, and Germany and Prussia imported 1.2 million tonnes? What does this tell you about the Industrial Revolution in Europe and about the position of Britain as 'Workshop of the World'?*

3 *Draw a graph to show the following statistics, comparing the performance of four British industries in 1800 and 1880.*

	1800	**1880**
coal	10,000,000 tonnes	147,000,000 tonnes
iron	200,000 tonnes	7,700,000 tonnes
cotton imported	22,000 tonnes	650,000 tonnes
shipping launched	50,000 tonnes	660,000 tonnes

4 *Which of these industries made most progress in the space of 80 years?*

The growth and development of the engineering industry

The engineering industry was another major contributor to Britain's reputation as 'Workshop of the World'. By 1855, Kirkstall Forge, in Leeds, was supplying steam hammers to India, Australia and Italy, steam engines to Egypt and machine tools to Russia.

The engineering industry had developed out of the small workshops, where skilled smiths and other craftsmen had shaped tools, weapons and implements in the past. By the start of the nineteenth century the industry was growing fast. In 1811, Louis Simond, an American visitor to Birmingham, saw:

> 'In one place five hundred persons were employed in making plated ware of all sorts, toys and trinkets. In another place, three hundred men produced ten thousand gun-barrels in a month.
>
> Bars of iron, presented to the sharp jaws of gigantic scissors, moved by the steam-engine, are clipped like paper. Iron-wire, from an inch to the tenth of an inch [25 mm to 2.5 mm], is spun out with as little effort, and less noise, than cotton thread on the jennies.'

Although the mass production lines of today did not exist at that time, many workers were doing one job only, rather than having to learn a number of different skills. A visitor to a large Birmingham button factory in 1844, noted that, 'Each species of button had its own department, and, there was a minute division of labour.'

---

1 Which new inventions were mentioned by Louis Simond on his visit to a Birmingham factory?

2 What is meant by the phrase 'division of labour'?

By 1851, many new engineering works had been started all over Britain, making engines and parts for ironclad steamships, steam locomotives, threshing machines, steam traction engines and many other machines. Few businesses were untouched by the growth of the engineering industry.

The engineering industry, and the other industries which depended on it, owed a lot in the nineteenth century to the work of a remarkable group of engineers. Joseph Bramah (1748-1814), for example, was an inventor who helped to found the machine tools industry. He invented patent locks and built machine tools to make them.

His leading pupil, Henry Maudslay, made two important contributions to the engineering industry. He built a machine which would cut screws, and developed methods of measurement which allowed engineers to work to much finer limits of tolerance than had previously been the case.

Whitworth's drilling machine on display at the International Exhibition in 1862, The Illustrated London News, *12 July 1862. Are exhibitions like this still held today?*

One of Maudslay's pupils, Joseph Whitworth, went on to develop a standardised system for classifying screws and screw threads. Engineers could now rely on being supplied with accurate spare parts for a machine.

Another of Maudslay's pupils, James Nasmyth, was the inventor of a steam hammer in 1839. Its great merit was that it enabled industry to produce the huge girders and metal bars required by other expanding engineering industries, such as shipbuilding.

Monster Steam-Hammer

'On Saturday the largest and most powerful steam-hammer which Mr. J. Nasmyth has yet constructed, was by him set to work at Sir John Guest's extensive iron-works at Dowlais. The hammer or block of cast iron which gives the blow to the iron on the anvil is upwards of six tons in weight, with a clear fall of seven feet [over 2 m] perpendicular. The force of the blow which this gives out is tremendous indeed, but is under such control as to be made to drive a nail into soft wood, with a succession of the most delicate taps.'

The Northampton Herald, Saturday 18 April 1846

3 *How did the journalist, who wrote this article, show the great power of the new hammer?*

4 *How did he describe the fine control an operator had over the machine?*

The growth and development of the shipbuilding industry

The shipbuilding industry was dominated by the wooden sailing ship until well into the nineteenth century (as shown in the section on sea transport in Chapter 3).

At the start of the nineteenth century, shipyards employed carpenters and joiners rather than metal workers. Even when iron was used, it was usually to cover a timber structure with iron plating. This is why the first iron ships were called ironclads.

The shipbuilding industry was originally concentrated in two main estuaries – those of the Thames and Tyne. The latter area was renowned for its colliers – the sturdy wooden sailing boats which took coal from the Tyne to the ports along the coast, notably London.

In the days of the wooden sailing ship the Thames was at an advantage as a shipbuilding centre as London was a great port, with by far the largest population in Britain. But it was at a very considerable disadvantage when iron steamships started to dominate the seas.

London was a long way from the coalfields, which provided most of industry's power requirements in the nineteenth century. It was also a long way from the main iron and steel producing areas, whose ironworks provided the pig iron for the iron plating, girders, tools and engines needed to build an iron steamship.

Great Eastern *steamship under construction,* The Illustrated London News, *13 June 1857*

Yet ironworks and marine engineering factories were built by the Thames shipbuilders in an attempt to keep the Thames industry competitive. In the 1850s, the shipbuilding yards at Millwall built the world's largest ship (for that time) – the *Great Eastern*.

It took a long time for the shipbuilding industry to change. Early steamships were built with sails, as well as with steam engines. The *Great Eastern* even had two – a gigantic screw propeller and a huge pair of paddle wheels – in addition to its massive sails (see also page 144).

By the middle of the nineteenth century, shipyards near coalfields and ironworks were beginning to dominate the industry, for example, Birkenhead on the Mersey, Barrow-in-Furness, Tyneside and above all the shipbuilding yards situated on the river Clyde in Scotland.

---

1 *What building materials were used to build the* Great Eastern*?*
2 *What debt did the shipbuilding industry owe to the work of James Watt, Henry Cort and the great engineers of the early nineteenth century? Why was it impossible to build ships such as the* Great Eastern *in the eighteenth century?*
3 *Why is London no longer an important shipbuilding centre?*

The growth and development of the iron and steel industry

Some of the most significant industrial changes of the nineteenth century affected the iron and steel industry. Ironically, their use in Germany and in the United States, led eventually to the decline of Britain as 'Workshop of the World'.

In 1828, John Neilson began to use pre-heated air – a 'hot blast' – to raise the temperature in a blast furnace. This made much more economical use of coal as a fuel and so reduced the cost of pig iron.

The most important innovation, however, was undoubtedly the discovery of cheap and effective ways to make steel. The first process introduced was pioneered by Henry Bessemer (see opposite) in 1856.

'This new process of Mr. Bessemer's consists merely in forcing air through the molten pig-iron. The molten iron is received red-hot into a sort of basin with holes at its bottom, communicating with a very powerful pair of blast-bellows, worked by steam. The air blast is turned on before the red-hot liquid metal is received into the basin.

The fierce air-blast forces the carbon combined with the iron into a furious combustion. A bright flame and an eruption of sparks burst from the mass.

There is to be one roasting and one melting, in the place of half-a-dozen tedious and costly fusings; air is to be blown through the molten liquid, and presto! in a few short minutes, huge masses of the finest iron are to be ready for the hammer and the anvil. If this promise be fulfilled, the best steel, which is now worth from £20 to £30 the ton, will be furnished in any required quantity at the cost of £6 the ton.'

Chambers's Journal, 15 November 1856

Henry Bessemer (1813-98)

Henry Bessemer was the son of an inventor and began his career inventing (among other things) a printing machine, a method of producing embossed velvet, a sugar refining machine and a process for making bronze powder and gold paint!

During the Crimean War he worked on the problem of how to improve the quality of the guns used by the army in Russia. Some of them shattered into pieces when fired. Bessemer wanted to find out why. His experiments, and a chance observation, led him to invent the converter method of changing iron into steel.

Its main advantage was that it could convert a substantial amount of iron to steel in a relatively short time. Its disadvantage was that it could not be used with iron made from ores containing phosphorus. As a result only the ironworks of Cumbria, such as those at Barrow and Workington, were able to use the Bessemer Converter with iron made from local ores. Other plants had to use iron ores imported from Sweden and Spain.

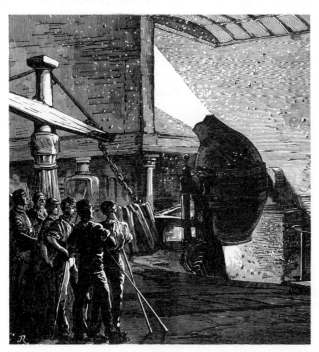

Bessemer Converter, The Illustrated London News, *5 July 1873*

Bessemer's steel-making process was so efficient, it could produce twenty times as much steel as by Huntsman's crucible steel method but in less than a quarter of the time. For the first time, good quality steel was cheap and plentiful.

1 *What effect did the writer (see page 89) think the new process would have on the price of steel?*
2 *Which stage in the process is illustrated in the picture on the previous page?*
3 *Why was this machine called the 'Bessemer Converter'? What did it convert?*

The haematite iron and steel works, Hindpool, Barrow-in-Furness, The Illustrated London News, *19 October 1867 (see extract below)*

'As a result of the high iron content of the Furness haematite ore, its easy fusibility, intense heating power, and great strength, as well as of the fine Durham coke which is used for fuel, the eleven large furnaces at Hindpool are capable of making iron at the rate of 500 tons a week each, at a price of £4 per ton. The steelworks when in full operation would convert weekly about 1000 tons of pig iron into Bessemer steel, selling for £12 to £14 per ton.'

The Illustrated London News, 19 October 1867

4 *How many tons of pig iron could the Barrow iron works make in a week? How much was it worth?*
5 *What proportion of that pig iron was made into steel? How much was that steel said to be worth? Was this an estimated or an actual value?*
6 *Where did the iron ore come from? What were the special advantages of this 'haematite' iron ore? Where did the coke come from? What single reason best explains why this iron and steel works was built at Barrow-in-Furness? Why was it built by the sea?*
7 *Does this news item confirm or contradict the expectations about the cheapness of Bessemer steel, raised by the extract on page 89, from an article in* Chambers's Journal, *in 1856? Why would you have to exercise caution in comparing the two estimates?*

The Bessemer Converter was followed soon afterwards by the open-hearth process, invented by a German scientist called William Siemens, who was working in Britain at the time. The open-hearth process was easier to control than the Bessemer Converter, and eventually took over from it. But, like Bessemer's process, the open-hearth furnace could not use iron produced from ores containing phosphorus.

WHY BRITISH INDUSTRY DOMINATED THE WORLD BY 1870

The reasons why Britain became the first industrialised nation in the eighteenth century, and the 'Workshop of the World' in the nineteenth century, are many and complex. They can only be summarised here.

1. Power and mineral resources

Water power was freely available. The wet climate of the British Isles and the hills of the north and west provided industry with many fast-flowing streams and rivers when water-wheels powered machinery.

Britain was rich in excellent coal. In 1700, much of it still lay close to the earth's surface. First-class iron ore was also available, often in close proximity to the coalmines. In the early stages of the Industrial Revolution coal and iron ore were sometimes brought up the same shaft.

2. Transport (see Chapter 3)

Canals and navigable rivers provided industries with a network of waterways to enable them to assemble raw materials.

The early development of a complete network of railways provided an enormous boost to British industry in the nineteenth century, since it made it much cheaper and easier to assemble raw materials and send finished products away to be sold. At the same time it provided the coal-mining and iron and steel industries with a huge new market for their products – both at home and overseas.

Similar advantages arose from the development in Britain of the steam-powered iron ship, with its great need for iron and coal. Britain's merchant shipping fleet began to dominate the world.

3. Inventors

Britain was fortunate in having many resourceful and ingenious inventors, who were able to solve many of the technical problems which arose when manufacturers wanted to increase output.

People like Cort, Watt, Hargreaves, Kay, Cartwright, Arkwright, Bessemer, Nasmyth and Wedgwood led the world in pioneering new processes and new inventions.

4. Population

The rapid development of industry in Britain was assisted by the growth in population which took place between 1750 and 1870 (see Chapter 5). This provided industry with a market for its goods and a steady and increasing supply of factory workers. Farmworkers forced from the land also helped to enlarge the industrial workforce.

5. Lack of foreign competition

Unlike most of the other major countries in Europe, Britain escaped invasion and revolution between 1700 and 1870. Germany and the United States, Britain's two great rivals of the late nineteenth century, were both involved in wars in the 1860s. It was not until after German unification in 1871 and the end of the Civil War in the United States in 1865, that these two great industrial powers were able to challenge Britain's industrial supremacy. Unlike Germany and the United States, Britain was governed by one central government, and was not split into different states each with conflicting interests.

6. Finance

Industry could only expand if money was available to purchase land, machinery and equipment. In the eighteenth century, Britain was lucky in having many private individuals with capital (money) available for investment, who were prepared to take a risk with new projects (in the hope of making a big profit). Much of the money available had been made by merchants trading abroad. In the nineteenth century, investors used the Stock Exchange to buy shares in the big companies. The development of the Bank of England and the growth of hundreds of banks helped to make it possible for companies to borrow money.

Many factory owners, ironmasters and industrialists ploughed their profits back into their businesses and financed the building of new works and the purchase of new machinery from their own resources.

7. Empire

The growth of the British Empire provided British industry with raw materials, such as wool from Australia. At the same time, the people of the Empire provided British factories with a huge new market for exports. Some of the profits from British industry were invested in overseas enterprises, in Europe and America, at first, but later in the Empire, such as on railways and plantations in India.

FURTHER QUESTIONS AND EXERCISES

1   Look at the above engraving from 1783.
    (a)   What product is being made in this cottage?
    (b)   What phrase is used to describe this system of industry?
    (c)   What were its main advantages and disadvantages?
    (d)   How had this method of manufacturing changed by 1870?

2   How was the industrial development of Britain helped by the work of
    any three of the following?
    (a)   Henry Bessemer   (f)   Josiah Wedgwood
    (b)   James Watt   (g)   Richard Arkwright
    (c)   the Abraham Darby family   (h)   Samuel Crompton
    (d)   Sir Humphry Davy   (i)   John and Thomas Lombe
    (e)   Sir Titus Salt   (j)   John 'Iron-mad' Wilkinson?

3   In an article on Accidents in Mines in Chambers's Journal, in 1844, a
    writer said:

    'It appears from a list of published cases, that explosions of fire-
    damp, choke-damp, falls of the roof, breaking of the rope or other
    apparatus in descent, fall of stones down the shaft, and bursting in
    of water, are the main causes of accident. Now, all of these
    casualties are clearly capable of being either altogether prevented, or
    diminished in frequency.'

    How were these problems tackled in the period 1700-1870 and with
    what success?

KNOCKER-UP. | REELER. | HOT-WATER WOMAN. | HAND-MULE SPINNER. | WINDER. | OVERLOOKER TO SELF-ACTING MULES. | POWER-LOOM WEAVER. | SELF-ACTING MINDER. | WEAVER. | THROSTLE-DOFFER.
HALF-TIMER. | SCAVENGER. | THROSTLE-SPINNER. | CARDER. | POWER-LOOM WEAVER. | JACK-FENTER.

Cotton workers outside a cotton mill in Manchester, The Illustrated London News, *22 November 1862*

4　Look at this picture from The Illustrated London News. *The captions indicate the jobs performed in the mill by each of these different types of worker.*

(a)　One of these jobs was the 1862 equivalent of an alarm clock and performed in the streets near the cotton mill early in the morning. Which job was that? How did the worker do the job?

(b)　Had child labour been stopped in the cotton mills by that time? What do you think a 'half-timer' was?

(c)　What jobs do you think the following workers did: (i) a carder, (ii) a scavenger, (iii) an overlooker?

(d)　At the time of Kay's invention of the flying shuttle in 1733, most weavers were men. What changes had taken place in the weaving industry by 1862?

(e)　Imagine you are one of the textile workers in this picture. Write about your place of work and about your fellow workers. Compare your working life with that of the workers shown in the picture on the previous page.

5　What was meant by the following lines from the old coal miner's ballad, The Pitman's Pay?

> 'Of all the toils and tears it gives
> To warm the shins of London city.'

Write two or three sentences explaining, with examples, what you think the writer meant by this poem. What was 'it'? What were the 'toils'? What caused the 'tears'?

6 Read this extract from an article published in Chambers's Journal *on 10 October 1846.*

WHAT IS MACHINERY DOING FOR US?

'At the beginning of the current century, the mechanical apparatus of Britain was of a simple and scanty description: agriculture could boast of nothing like machinery; spinning and weaving were done by hand; our ships were wafted by the breeze. Now all this is changed, and there is scarcely a single manual operation, which is not less or more facilitated by mechanical aids.

There can be little doubt that, without the aid of the steam-engine, many of them would have never been thought of, or at all events never brought to their present perfection. It is to this that the modern world owes its astonishing advances. It is in our mines and beside our furnaces; in our factories and workshops; in our mills, bakehouses, and breweries.'

(a) What did the writer mean by ships 'wafted by the breeze'?

(b) From which date did the writer think these striking changes in the use of machinery had taken place? Was it (i) after 1700, (ii) after 1750, (iii) after 1800?

(c) Is this piece of evidence about the progress made in industry by 1846, (i) fact, (ii) a statement of opinion? In what ways is the extract biased or inaccurate?

(d) Imagine you are either, (i) the owner of a stage-coach or, (ii) a Yorkshire handloom weaver. What do you think about the uses to which the steam engine had been put in the years before 1846? In what ways might your statement be biased?

(e) Write a short essay assessing the significance of the steam-engine to the Industrial Revolution and comparing it with other inventions and other developments.

7 What were the main improvements made by James Watt to the steam engine? How did his machines differ from those of Thomas Newcomen? What were their main advantages? What were their main disadvantages? How were they used:
(a) in coal mining   (c) the pottery industry
(b) textile manufacture   (d) ironworks?

8 Describe and account for the changes in the location of the following British industries in the eighteenth and nineteenth centuries:
(a) iron and steel
(b) shipbuilding
(c) worsted and woollen textiles.

9   *Study the following sources carefully. Note that they were both written in the same year – 1825.*

Source A

'Sixty years ago there was not a cotton mill. At present there are no fewer than sixty-five, of which all, except two, have been built during the present century. These mills, which are wholly employed in spinning cotton, are all worked by steam, and there are, within the same limits, one-hundred and forty steam engines, used in the various processes of manufacturing and mining.

   The vicinity of Oldham to Manchester, the great market for cotton goods, the advantages of water, but above all the abundant supply of coal, from the mines in the surrounding townships, have constituted this one of the most extensive and improving seats of manufacture in the county.'

Description of Oldham, Lancashire by Edward Baines 1825

Source B

PAINSWICK, GLOUCESTERSHIRE
───
EXTENSIVE MILL PREMISES
TO BE LET, ON LEASE
With about Eighteen Acres of excellent Pasture and
Orcharding Land, comprising

A LARGE well-built FULLING MILL, constructed to be driven by steam or water, and 3 floors, 42ft by 24ft [12.8m by 7.3m] for machinery, with a steam engine of 30 horse power, and a water-wheel 40 feet [12.2m] diameter, having a reservoir of water 2½ Acres. The whole of the premises are situated within a quarter of a mile of the turnpike road leading from Stroud to Gloucester, and are well worth the attention of any manufacturer requiring an extensive power.

Advertisement, *Cheltenham Journal*, 11 July 1825

(a)   *What advantages did Painswick have as the site for a textile mill? How was its machinery powered?*

(b)   *What advantages did Oldham have as a cotton spinning town?*

(c)   *In what ways had the Oldham textile mills made the Painswick mill obsolete by 1825?*

(d)   *Why was there a reservoir at the Painswick mill?*

10   *How important was the role of the individual – inventor or industrialist – in the growth and development of industry in Britain in the eighteenth and nineteenth centuries? Select two or three key figures and assess their importance to the Industrial Revolution.*

11   *What industrial changes do you think would have most impressed Daniel Defoe, had he been able to see the textile industries of Lancashire and Yorkshire in 1870?*

Chapter Three

The Transport Revolution

INTRODUCTION

'Perhaps the most wonderful forms in which its power now manifests itself are the railway locomotive, shooting along at the rate of sixty or eighty miles an hour [about 100 to 125 kph]; and in the giant iron steamer, crossing the waters of the Atlantic in as brief a space as, a century ago, our forefathers would have required to pass from Edinburgh to London.'

Chambers's Journal, 10 October 1846

1 *What was the writer describing? What was 'its power'?*
2 *With what type of transport was the steamer being compared?*
3 *From what you have already learned, write two or three sentences to say how the Transport Revolution affected farmers, manufacturers and ordinary people.*
4 *The picture above was drawn in 1843. Which two types of transport does it illustrate? Write a paragraph explaining why you think the artist drew this picture and what he or she was getting at. Write a short but appropriate caption for the picture.*

As shown in Chapters 1 and 2, the improvements in agriculture owed a lot to the advances made by engineers in developing steam engines, in making cheaper and better quality iron and in developing artificial fertilisers. Yet, without the extra food produced by the farmers, there would have been insufficient bread to meet the needs of the thousands of people living in the expanding towns and working in the factories. Agriculture and industry both needed each other.

They also needed transport. Without the dramatic and exciting changes, which improved and speeded up communications between 1700 and 1870, the pace and nature of industrial change would have been different. In 1700, it was extremely difficult to take heavy goods from one part of Britain to another, except by sea and, in some cases, by river. Many roads were impassable in bad weather, even to heavy carts pulled by large teams of horses.

Private travellers also had problems. Coaches were slow and uncomfortable vehicles in which to travel any distance. There were many accidents, and the poor state of the roads meant that travellers were often black and blue by the end of their journey. Most travellers preferred to go on horseback, despite the danger of meeting highwaymen.

IMPROVING ROAD TRANSPORT
The state of the roads in 1700

A contemporary engraving of a country road in the middle of the eighteenth century

In 1697, Celia Fiennes described a road near Bath, as:

'a narrow Causeway that a Coach can scarce pass, all pitched with slatts and stones, our Coach was once wedged in the wheels in the stones that several men were forced to lift us out; its made only for Packhorses which is the way of Carriage in those parts.'

From *The Journeys of Celia Fiennes* edited by Christopher Morris

In 1702, a royal party travelled 64 km from Windsor (in Berkshire) to Petworth (in Sussex).

'We set out at six in the morning and did not get out of the carriages (save only when we were overturned or stuck fast in the mire) till we arrived at our journey's end. 'Twas a hard service for the Prince to sit fourteen hours in the coach that day without eating anything, and passing through the worst ways I ever saw in my life.'

Annals of Queen Anne 1704

1 *Describe the country road shown in the picture. What types of transport can be seen? Is the road clearly marked? What is the road surface made of? What do you think it would have been like in:*
   (a)   wet weather
   (b)   hot, dry weather?
2 *What were the main complaints about the state of the roads in the eighteenth century?*
3 *What type of transport did Celia Fiennes think the road near Bath had been made for?*
4 *What was the average speed of the Prince's coach on the journey from Windsor to Petworth? Would it have been quicker to walk?*

Packhorses were used by merchants to carry heavy goods, such as packs of wool, or cloth, to be processed by workers in their cottages (see page 46), or to be sold at markets and fairs. Long trains of thirty or forty packhorses were led along narrow pathways, crossing streams by special narrow bridges. The leading packhorse carried a bell to warn other travellers. Many of these packhorse bridges can still be seen today, particularly in northern England. They are easily recognised, since they are usually quite small, humpbacked in shape, and built of stone with a road surface paved with cobbles.

Packhorse bridge near Penistone in Yorkshire

5 *How can you tell from the photograph, that Celia Fiennes was perfectly correct in suggesting that a causeway intended for use by packhorses, was unsuitable for coach traffic?*

In muddy or dusty conditions, it was almost impossible to tell where the road began and the fields ended. One landowner even erected a beacon to guide travellers across Lincoln Heath. The condition of the surface of the roads was not helped by farmers driving cattle, sheep and geese to market along them.

Turnpikes and turnpike trusts

The appalling state of most of the roads in Britain had arisen chiefly because no one had overall responsibility for constructing a comprehensive network of good roads. In 1555, the roads had been made the responsibility of the Justices of the Peace. Local people had to provide road building materials and their labour free, to repair the sections of public road which passed through their districts. But they complained that most of the damage to the roads was done by strangers passing through the parish. Why should they work, to benefit 'foreigners' from other districts? The most they did was to fill the ruts with stones.

The first significant change was made in 1663, when the first Turnpike Act was passed. This gave the local justices, in what is now Cambridgeshire and Hertfordshire, the right to levy tolls from travellers, in order to pay for the upkeep and repair of their section of the Great North Road (from London to York).

It was some time before this idea of charging tolls to maintain roads became widespread. But in the early eighteenth century, the first Turnpike Trusts were formed. These were formed by groups of gentlemen and local business people, who were given power, by a local Act of Parliament, to take responsibility for maintaining a small section of road.

The Turnpike Trust either repaired the road, or built a completely new road in its place. The money to build new roads was raised from business people and from banks. In return for their investment these people took a share of the profits derived from the tolls charged on the new turnpike road. The money to pay for maintenance also came from this toll. Turnpike gates were erected across the road to bar the way and prevent travellers going through without paying. Tollkeepers were appointed and small tollhouses built for them, since the gate was manned 24 hours a day.

Hunter's Bar, Sheffield

'Turnpikes or toll-bars have been set up on the several great roads of England, beginning at London; at which turn-pikes, all carriages, droves of cattle, and travellers on horseback, are oblig'd to pay an easy toll; that is to say, a horse a penny, a coach three pence, a cart four pence, a waggon six pence; but in no place is it thought a burden that ever I met with, the benefit of a good road abundantly making amends for that little charge the travellers are put to at the turn-pikes.'

Daniel Defoe 1724

1 *How much did it cost a horseman to travel on a turnpike road? What was the charge for a coach?*
2 *Where were most of the turnpike roads situated in 1724?*
3 *The photograph was taken in the suburbs of Sheffield. What do you think it shows? How did the 'turnpike gate' and the 'toll bar' get their names?*
4 *What did Defoe mean when he said 'in no place is it thought a burden'?*
5 *What evidence did Defoe have for saying that travellers did not object to paying the toll? Can we rely on this as fact or do we have to treat it as an opinion?*

On payment of the toll, the traveller was given a ticket with the name of the Gate or Bar, the date, the amount of toll paid, and the names of any other toll bars along the road, through which the traveller was now entitled to pass, free of any further charge.

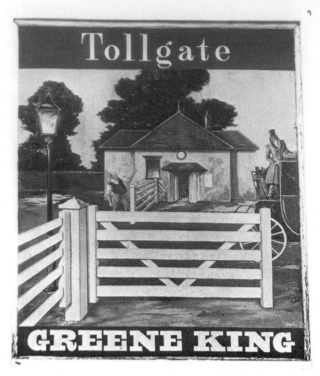

Tollgate Inn, Bury St.Edmunds, Suffolk

6 *Make a tracing of the inn sign shown in the picture. Find and label:*
(a) *the toll-house*
(b) *turnpike gate*
(c) *mail coach*
(d) *turnpike keeper*
(e) *guard on the coach*
(f) *lamp used to light up the gate at night*
(g) *toll board listing different tolls.*

Despite being welcomed by traders and travellers, there was often considerable opposition to the erection of turnpike gates and the charging of tolls. It may not have been a burden to Defoe, but it was a burden for local people. They had used the roads without charge in the past. Why should they suddenly have to pay?

Gates and tollhouses were destroyed and there were serious riots. In 1749, the *Gentleman's Magazine* reported that 'almost all the turnpikes and turnpike-houses' in the neighbourhood of Bristol had been demolished. Similar riots broke out in Leeds and at Selby in Yorkshire, in 1753.

Advantages of the turnpikes

The advantages of turnpike roads, according to Daniel Defoe, were:

(a) That the carriage of heavy goods was much easier, since wagons could take heavier loads and fewer horses were needed. Journey times were cut. People could expect to pay less to have goods carried by road.

(b) Travellers could travel to London in comfort and in greater safety. There were fewer hazards.

(c) Fat cattle and sheep could be driven to market with greater ease and speed. They lost less weight on the journey.

(d) Turnpikes made it possible for postboys to ride faster and so speeded up the delivery of mail.

As you can see, some of these advantages cancelled each other out! Flocks of sheep on a turnpike road were hardly likely to speed travellers on their way!

---

1 *Why did the fat cattle and sheep lose more weight when driven over bad, rather than good, roads? What was the advantage of the turnpike road to the farmer?*

2 *Which of Defoe's reasons do you think would have most impressed:*
(a) a lady or gentleman living in London
(b) a poorly paid worker in Birmingham?

Disadvantages of the turnpikes

(a) It was not a uniform system. There were over a thousand Turnpike Trusts and their attitude to the roads entrusted to their care was not the same everywhere. Some had over a hundred members, but were responsible for only a short 20 km of turnpike! Some made a profit, some made a loss.

(b) Travellers on many main roads wasted time and money passing through a large number of tollgates and travelling on a succession of different road surfaces, good, bad or indifferent. There were over one hundred turnpike gates and toll bars within 6 km of London's Charing Cross and ten on one stretch of road only 5 km long.

The turnpikes were usually better than the old parish roads, but in the eighteenth century there was still plenty of room for improvement – as you can see from Arthur Young's experiences in about 1770.

Wigan. 'I measured ruts four feet [1.2 m] deep, floating with mud from a wet summer; what must it be like after a winter? The only mending it receives is the tumbling in of some stones.'

Kendal to Windermere. 'Turnpike; now making. What is finished, is as good, firm, level a road as any in the world.'

Driffield. 'Most excellent. Firmly made of good gravel; free from ruts and loose stones, and of a proper breadth'.

Sudbury. 'Ponds of liquid dirt and a scattering of loose flints, sufficient to lame every horse that moves near them.'

Rotherham to Sheffield. 'The road is execrably bad, very stony and excessively full of holes.'

Brentford to London. 'Turnpike. Excellent. But much too narrow for such vast traffic.'

---

1 *What were Arthur Young's complaints about the turnpikes?*

2 *What qualities did he most admire?*

3 *Write the comment you think Arthur Young would have made about the road shown in the picture on page 98.*

4 *Arthur Young admired one road because it was 'free from ruts'. From this we can deduce that many bad turnpikes had ruts in the road surface. What other defects can be deduced in this way from the praise lavished on the good turnpikes?*

5 *Do you think he over-praised the good roads and condemned the poor roads too harshly? Modern historians have calculated that he described two-thirds of the turnpike roads he travelled on as 'good' and the remainder as 'bad' or 'middling'. How far can we use his evidence to draw conclusions about the state of the roads in 1770? What does he tell us about the effect of the Turnpike Trusts on Britain's roads?*

The great road engineers

Road engineers were needed to plan, organise and supervise the building of the new turnpike roads and to undertake the repairs needed to maintain existing roads. New roads had usually been made by laying down large stones and covering them with a layer of smaller stones, mixed with earth, which was then given a pronounced curve to let rain-water drain away. In practice, coaches and wagons tended to stick to the centre of the road, to avoid the steep camber at the sides. This caused the central part of the road to be flattened, leaving ruts. These filled with rainwater, which softened up the rest of the road.

Three outstanding civil engineers were responsible for most of the great improvements between 1770 and 1830. They were John Metcalf, Thomas Telford and John McAdam (see below and overleaf).

John Metcalf (1717–1810)

'Blind Jack of Knaresborough', as John Metcalf was called, was the first of the great road builders. He was a remarkable man, who had been blind since the age of six, but went on to build about 300 km of turnpike road, mainly in Lancashire, Derbyshire, Cheshire and Yorkshire, in the period 1765–92.

Metcalf believed that a good road should have good foundations, be well drained and have a smooth convex (rounded) surface to allow rainwater to drain quickly into ditches at the side of the road. He established his reputation as a road builder, particularly, by building a good, dry road across marshland. Other engineers thought it could not be done, but Metcalf accomplished the task by first making a foundation of brushwood. He showed the importance of good drainage, since it was rain which caused most of the problems on the roads.

Thomas Telford (1757–1834)

Thomas Telford came from Scotland and started work as a stonemason but eventually became one of the greatest of all civil engineers, building canals (such as the Caledonian), docks in London, over 1,200 bridges (including the Menai Suspension Bridge) and well over 1,500 km of excellent new road.

In 1819, he told Parliament what was wrong with the roads:

'There has been no attention paid to constructing good and solid foundations. The materials, whether consisting of gravel or stones, have seldom been sufficiently selected and arranged. The shape of the roads is frequently hollow in the middle; the sides blocked by great banks of road dirt, which prevent the water from flowing into the side drains.'

Thomas Telford

Telford built many turnpike roads in Scotland but his greatest achievement was the construction of the 500 km long, London to Holyhead road. It was 10 m wide and so soundly built, that parts of the road are still in use today on the A5. He took care to avoid steep gradients and sharp bends on his roads. He made the camber across the road gently convex, instead of resembling the side of an orange, as in the older roads!

John Loudon McAdam (1756–1836)

John Loudon McAdam

McAdam, like Telford, also came from southern Scotland. He had long been interested in the principles of road-making but it was not until he was nearly 60, that he began to make his name as a road engineer. In 1815 he was appointed surveyor-general of the roads in the Bristol area.

McAdam had a rather different method of constructing a road to that of Telford and Metcalf. He believed that solid stone foundations were unnecessary. He claimed that a shallow layer (20–25 cm deep) of small stone chips, not larger than 40 mm in diameter, was the best material for ordinary roads, not the large setts (rectangular blocks of stone) or cobbles (rounded stones), which were usually used, particularly in towns.

This layer of broken stones (usually granite) knitted together (because of the different edges and angles of the chips) especially when compacted down by the weight of traffic. This caused the road surface to become smooth and hard, making coach journeys more comfortable and letting rainwater run off quickly into drains at the sides of the roads.

This 'macadamised' surface, as it was called, was cheaper to use than the solid, more permanent methods favoured by Telford. It had a particular appeal, therefore, to the Turnpike Trusts and to the Government. McAdam told Members of Parliament:

> 'I consider that the expenses would be materially reduced; the convenience of passing over the surface would be generally facilitated; and the same weight of stone, now put upon streets as pavement, would be obtained at infinitely less expense, for the purpose of road-making.'

Tar was later used to produce the smooth, hard-wearing road surfaces we use today – called tarmacadam.

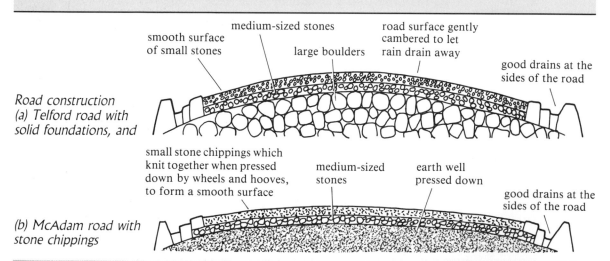

Road construction (a) Telford road with solid foundations, and

medium-sized stones
smooth surface of small stones
large boulders
road surface gently cambered to let rain drain away
good drains at the sides of the road

(b) McAdam road with stone chippings

small stone chippings which knit together when pressed down by wheels and hooves, to form a smooth surface
medium-sized stones
earth well pressed down
good drains at the sides of the road

> Look at the diagrams of different types of road construction.
> 1 Which was the cheaper road to build? Why?
> 2 What were the chief advantages of the McAdam roads? What were the chief advantages of the Telford and Metcalf roads?
> 3 What features did both types of road have in common?
> 4 Write a short comparison of the roads shown in the diagrams.

The coaching age

Regular coach services began in the seventeenth century and by the early eighteenth century they were common, as you can see from the advertisement and the scene at an inn in 1740 on the next page.

YORK Four Days Stage-Coach.

Begins on Friday the 12th of April 1706.

ALL that are desirous to pass from *London* to *York*, or from *York* to *London*, or any other Place on that Road; Let them Repair to the *Black Swan* in *Holbourn* in *London*, and to the *Black Swan* in *Coney-street* in *York*.

At both which Places, they may be received in a Stage Coach every *Monday*, *Wednesday* and *Friday*, which performs the whole Journey in Four Days, (if God permits.) And sets forth at Five in the Morning.

And returns from *York* to *Stamford* in two days, and from *Stamford* by *Huntington* to *London* in two days more. And the like Stages on their return.

Allowing each Passenger 14l. weight, and all above 3d. a Pound.

Performed By { Benjamin Kingman. Henry Harrison, Walter Baynes.

Also this gives Notice that *Newcastle* Stage Coach, sets out from *York*, every *Monday*, and *Friday*, and from *Newcastle* every *Monday*, and *Friday*.

Rec'd in pt. 05-00-0 of Mr. Bodington for 5 70 ld. for Monday the 3 of June 1706

Advertisement for a stage coach, 1706

> 1 When was the London to York service scheduled to begin? How long did it take to cover the journey of 336 km? What other connection could travellers make at York?

Hogarth print of passengers at a coaching inn in about 1740

2 *How were passengers warned when the coach was about to leave?
How did they get into the coach? Where was the luggage carried?
How did poorer passengers travel?*

3 *What was the average speed of the London to York coach? What
modern road takes a somewhat similar course from London, by-
passing Huntingdon and Stamford?*

By 1840, there were over 35,000 km of turnpike roads in Britain and
about 8,000 toll bars and turnpike gates. McAdam's smooth road
surfaces had at last made long journeys by coach tolerable, if not always
comfortable. The demand for effective road transport had grown with
the needs of landowners and industrialists during the busy years of the
Industrial and Agrarian Revolutions.

During the Golden Age of Coaching, in the 1820s and 1830s, there
were over 3,000 daily coach services in Britain, and half of them started
or ended their journeys in London. To maintain each coach, 50 horses
were needed to pull it, and ten men were needed as coach drivers, guards
and hostlers (to look after the horses). Every day 50 coaches left London
for Manchester and Liverpool, 40 for Birmingham and Brighton and 30
for Edinburgh, as well as others to every important town in Britain.

They were called stage coaches because they ran in stages – from one coaching inn to the next. At each new inn, fresh horses were harnessed to the coach whilst the passengers took refreshment or had a meal. Coaches travelled at night, as well as during the day, even though the carriage lamps they carried were nothing like as bright as the headlights on a modern car.

In addition to passengers, they carried newspapers, letters and parcels. Coaches first brought the good news about the battle of Waterloo to people throughout the country The arrival of a coach was an event in the life of many a sleepy village.

Timings for stage coach and mail coach services to or from London

1658: Exeter (274 km) 4 days
1706: York (336 km) 4 days
1754: Edinburgh (652 km) 11 days; Manchester (320 km) 4½ days
1757: Liverpool (338 km) 3 days
1784: Edinburgh 2½ days
1797: Exeter 25 hours
1825: Edinburgh 43 hours; Liverpool 27 hours
1836: Exeter 17 hours; Manchester 19 hours; Holyhead (430 km) 27 hours

---

4 *Name one coach on which you would have travelled on a road built by Thomas Telford.*

5 *What improvements in journey times were there between London and:*
(a) Exeter
(b) Edinburgh
(c) Manchester
(d) Liverpool
in the period covered by these dates?

6 *Work out the average speed taken by each coach service.*

7 *Use these average speeds to work out the typical speed of a stage or mail coach service:*
(a) before 1720
(b) between 1740 and 1760
(c) between 1780 and 1800
(d) between 1820 and 1840.
How do you account for the differences?

The Royal Mail

In 1720, Ralph Allen of Bath was granted the right to operate a postal system, using post boys mounted on horseback. In 1784, John Palmer persuaded the Government to grant him a contract to carry the royal mail in special post or mail coaches, at the same rates as those paid by the Post Office to the post boys.

The first of these black- and maroon-coloured mail coaches, pulled by four smart horses, was introduced into service on 2 August, 1784. The mail coaches were manned by a coachman and a scarlet-coated guard, armed with a blunderbuss to deter highwaymen. He carried a long horn – his 'yard of tin' – to sound a signal, warning the turnpike keeper to open the gate. The mail coaches carried the Royal Mail and went through free of charge. Woe betide the pike-keeper who delayed them! They could travel at an average speed of up to 15 kph, but it was claimed by some people that deaths had been caused to travellers – due to the rapid motion of the coach through the air!

The guard carried a waybill, or time sheet, together with an accurate clock. In those days, of course, there was no way of knowing what the exact time was in the country. So the Post Office gave every mail coach a clock to record times of arrival and departure. As a result country people began to set their clocks by the arrival of the mail coach.

The mail coach was easily distinguished from a stage coach, because it had the royal coat of arms on the door. The towns served by the coach were printed in gold below the windows and the number of the coach could be seen on the guard's seat at the back.

In a mail coach four passengers sat inside and three on top, together with the coachman at the front and the guard behind, who sat on a box holding the luggage. Stage coaches, which were privately run and in competition with the mail coaches, carried as many as six passengers inside, and as many as twelve people on top, all precariously perched on ledges rather than seats and with shallow supports for their backs.

'Quicksilver' passing the Star and Garter Inn near Kew Bridge in 1835, contemporary print

1 *How can you tell that 'Quicksilver' was a mail coach?*
2 *What can you see awaiting travellers on Kew Bridge in the distance? Apart from the fact that the coach is not travelling in that direction, how can you tell that 'Quicksilver' was not expected to cross Kew Bridge?*
3 *Why do you think it was called 'Quicksilver'?*
4 *Imagine you are one of the passengers, the coachman or the guard on this coach. Write an imaginative description of the first ten minutes of a journey, starting from the Star and Garter Inn.*
5 *Study the sources which follow and look at the pictures in this chapter.*

Source A

'The Public is respectfully informed, that a NEW DAY COACH called the TALLY-HO! has commenced running to and from the NELSON HOTEL Birmingham and the GOLDEN CROSS, Charing Cross, London; leaving both houses at six o'clock in the morning and arriving precisely at half past seven the same evening, through Coventry, Daventry and intermediate places. 30s [£1.50] INSIDE – 15s [75p] OUTSIDE; Parcels 1d per lb.'

Advert in the *Birmingham and Lichfield Chronicle* 1822

Source B

'The pavement ceases, the houses disappear; and they are once again dashing along the open road, with the fresh air blowing in their faces, and gladdening their very hearts within them.'

Pickwick Papers, Charles Dickens 1837

Source C

'Nothing more bleak, chilling and miserable, than starting at daybreak of a cold frosty morning, the roads hard and slippery and the cold penetrating through every pore.'

John Cabbell's private diary 1833

Source D

Norwich [185 km] 'new safety daytimes post coach (in 14 hours and driven through by one coachman only) at five in the morning.' Cambridge [96 km] 'Tally-Ho! fast coach (in five hours), at a quarter past two o'clock every afternoon.'

Advert for Royal Mail coaches in *The Age* 1825

Source E

'As the coach rattles through the village every one runs to the window, and you have glances on every side of fresh country faces and blooming giggling girls.'

Washington Irving 1819

Source F

'From Harborough to Leicester I had a most dreadful journey, it rained incessantly; and as before we had been covered with dust, we now were soaked with rain.'

C. P. Moritz (traveller) 1782

Write an essay describing what it was like to travel by stage coach or mail coach in about 1820. Your essay should say what comforts, dangers and discomforts the traveller experienced, how the coach journey was organised, how much it cost, and what benefits it brought the wealthy traveller over 150 years ago. Quote the sources you use in your essay.

6 *Look at Source D. What feature about the 'safety' post coach to Norwich would not be regarded as a safety feature today? How fast was the 'Tally-Ho!' to Cambridge?*

Other travellers

The coaching inns also served private travellers. The most usual form of transport other than stage coach was by post chaise, carrying up to three people. A post chaise was a light four-wheeled carriage pulled by horses and driven by a post boy (or postilion) who rode on one of the horses, instead of in the chaise. On a long journey the horses were changed at posting inns and new post boys took over.

It was a very expensive method of transport however. Bills, receipts and diaries show how much it cost. One traveller from London to Newcastle paid £40 on a journey in 1825, including £24 for horses, £2 8s 0d [£2.40] at turnpike gates, £5 12s 0d [£5.60] for postboys and £8 to innkeepers.

Poor people travelled by stage wagon if they had to go any distance. These huge vehicles with their large wheels, were pulled by teams of eight or ten horses, and lumbered their way slowly through the countryside at walking speeds of about 5 kph. They also carried parcels, packages and heavy items which could not be taken on the stage coach. The people who ran them were called carriers.

In a diary entry in 1793, a Norfolk country parson, called James Woodforde, recorded an accident he had been involved in when visiting relatives in Somerset:

'Going up Frome Hill we met with a large tilted London Waggon with eight horses in it and very heavily loaden, and it being very narrow where we met it, the driver of the chaise in backing his horses to avoid being drove over overturned the chaise.'

From *Diary of a Country Parson* edited by John Beresford

Monument to a carrier in a churchyard, near Diss, Norfolk

1 Describe the stage wagon shown in the photograph.
2 What form of transport was Parson Woodforde using when involved in an accident?
3 Why do you think there were many accidents on the roads, even though the average speeds that vehicles were capable of was usually little faster than that of a bicycle?
4 How much would it have cost to travel from London to Newcastle (450 km) by stage coach, if it cost the same per kilometre as in the Tally Ho! from London to Birmingham (190 km) shown in Source A on page 111? How many times more expensive was the journey by post chaise?
5 How many weeks would a farm labourer (earning the equivalent of 35p a week in 1830) have had to work, in order to travel from London to Newcastle (a) inside a stage coach, (b) by post chaise? Was it expensive? How many weeks would a farm worker have to work today to do the same journey by train?

Decline of the turnpike system and the last days of coaching

The railways eventually brought about the decline of the coaching system, but did not kill off the turnpikes completely. As late as the 1850s, travellers complained about toll gates. A writer in 1845, said that 'the whole road system of Great Britain, with its universal network of toll-bars, is, without exception, the most awkward and absurd institution on the face of the earth'.

The turnpikes, for all their faults, were an indispensable asset in the early days of the Industrial Revolution. Canals and rivers were incapable of providing the swift means of communication required by the people who ran the thriving and rapidly growing industries of the late eighteenth and early nineteenth centuries.

IMPROVING THE INTERNAL WATERWAYS

Navigable rivers

Map of inland waterways in England and Wales in 1760. Which parts of England and Wales were a long way from inland waterways? Why was this a disadvantage?

In the early eighteenth century the only economical way to transport heavy goods was by water – either along the coast or using rivers. Coastal navigation could be hazardous. Storms dashed flimsy sailing boats on the rocks, and enemy privateers (small warships) preyed on unarmed vessels at time of war. As you have already seen many roads were in an appalling condition.

This is why, at the start of the eighteenth century, a substantial amount of river-borne trade was carried on in Britain. Ports, like King's Lynn, at the mouth of the Great Ouse, owed much of their importance to inland waterways.

KING'S LYNN

'The Goodness of its Situation affords a great Advantage to Traffick and Commerce, having a commodious large Harbour, capable of containing 200 sailing ships and several navigable Rivers by which Peterboro, Ely, Stamford, Bedford, St.Ives, Huntingdon, St.Neots, Northampton, Cambridge, Bury St.Edmunds, Thetford are served with Coals from Newcastle, Salt from Lymington, Deals, Fir Timber, all sorts of Iron, Wines, etc. imported hither from beyond the sea; and from these parts Great Quantities of Wheat, Rye, Oats, Cole-feed and Barley are brought down these rivers.'

Benjamin Mackerell 1738

---

1 *What were King's Lynn's advantages as a port?*
2 *What goods would you have expected to see loaded and unloaded in King's Lynn in 1738?*
3 *How big an area was served by King's Lynn in 1738?*
4 *Look at the map and make a list of the principal rivers and their tributaries, which were used as navigable waterways in the eighteenth century.*
5 *Write a brief essay, explaining some of the main disadvantages of rivers as inland waterways. Write about rivers you have seen: their width, narrowness and depth; width and frequency of bends and meanders; mud, sand, pebbles or boulders on river beds and along river banks; speed or sluggishness of flow; strong currents; effects of floods and periods of drought; destruction of river banks.*

The first canals

Using river systems as methods of transport had various drawbacks. The areas with the most navigable rivers, such as the Fenland area of East Anglia, were not necessarily those which most needed effective means of inland transport. Ships carried coal from Newcastle-upon-Tyne to London, but they could not reach places like Oxford, which were too far inland. Coal from the Midlands coalfields was very expensive in London, much more so than Newcastle coal which came by boat.

The improvements to roads in the eighteenth century mainly benefited passengers rather than merchants sending goods. Some attempts had been made to improve the navigability of rivers by widening the banks in places, digging artificial rivers to cut off wide meanders or deepening the river bed. But suitable rivers were not always located where trade and industry could use them for transport.

Canals had already been constructed in Europe (such as the Canal du Midi in France in 1681) and, in 1757, the 13 km-long Sankey Brook

Navigation, near St. Helens, was opened. It had been built by the Liverpool town authorities, to supply Merseyside with cheaper coal.

However, as so often happened, the credit for being the first canal builders went elsewhere. The Duke of Bridgewater and his canal engineer, James Brindley, came to be regarded as the fathers of canal-building in Britain by building the Bridgewater Canal (1761). The Duke owned coal mines at Worsley in Lancashire, but the only way he could get his coal to Manchester was along the improved navigation of the River Irwell. This was not only inconvenient, it was expensive. The Duke decided to build a canal from Worsley to Manchester and chose James Brindley (see below) as his engineer.

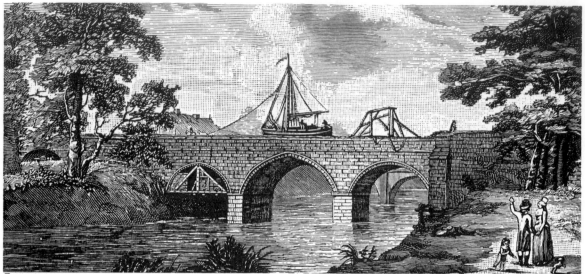

Contemporary engraving of Barton Aqueduct over the River Irwell (1763)

'It is as high as the tops of trees. Whilst I was surveying it with a mixture of wonder and delight, four barges passed me in the space of about three minutes, two of them being chained together and dragged by two horses. I durst hardly venture to walk, as I almost trembled to behold the large river Irwell underneath me, across which this navigation is carried by a bridge, which contains upon it the canal of water, with the barges in it, drawn by horses, which walk upon the battlements of this extraordinary bridge.

This navigation begins at the foot of some hills, in which the duke's coals are dug. In some places, where Mr. Brindley has been forced to carry his navigation across a public road, being obliged to keep the water on a level, he has sunk the road gradually, so as to pass under his canal, which forms a bridge over the road.'

From a letter in the *Annual Register* in 1763

1 *What was the writer describing? What goods was the canal designed to carry?*

2 *What was the name used by the writer to describe the canal? How was it later shortened and used as the general name for workmen who dug canals and did other heavy manual jobs?*

3 *What problems did the engineer meet in constructing the canal? How did he solve them?*

4 *Why was the engineer 'obliged to keep the water on a level'? How were the later canal-builders able to do this in places where there were slopes and valleys? Name three features you might expect to see on such a canal.*

James Brindley (1716–72)

James Brindley was born in Derbyshire and began his engineering career as an apprentice to a millwright. His interest in water wheels led him to experiment with steam engines as well.

The Duke of Bridgewater, having heard of his talents, employed him to survey the ground on which he proposed to build a canal to cover the 11 km or so from his coal mines at Worsley to his customers in Manchester. There were to be no locks on the canal. Brindley astounded everyone by building the Barton aqueduct to carry the canal over the River Irwell. Spectators saw ten men struggling to pull a barge on the Irwell below the aqueduct, and two men pulling a similar barge on the canal above!

There were many other canal-builders in the next eighty years, some as great, or even greater, than Brindley himself, such as John Smeaton (Forth and Clyde Canal), Thomas Telford (Caledonian Canal and Shropshire Canal), John Rennie (the Kennet and Avon Canal) and William Jessop (the Grand Union Canal). But James Brindley was, undisputedly, the first successful canal-builder and went on to build or design some 500 km of canal.

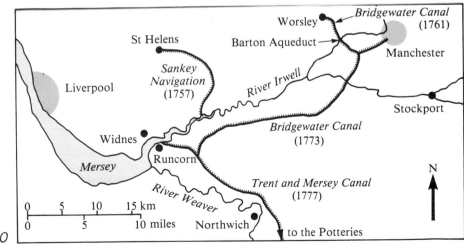

Canals in Lancashire and Cheshire in 1780

The growth of the canal network

The success of the Duke of Bridgewater's canal was such that it began a canal boom in Britain. Very soon afterwards, in 1762, the Duke made plans to extend his canal to Runcorn, in order to connect Liverpool directly with Manchester (via the Mersey, see map). This was welcomed by merchants, traders and residents but opposed by the proprietors of the Mersey and Irwell Navigation and some of the landowners, whose land would be affected by the new canal.

Despite many difficulties, the canal from Worsley to Manchester was extended by another 40 km in length (as you can see on the map on page 117). It needed locks, aqueducts and bridges but proved a resounding and highly profitable success.

Brindley and the Duke, between them, had halved the cost of transporting coal from the Duke's Worsley Colliery to Manchester. Before the canal was built, coal carried over land by pack horse cost £2 a tonne. This was not surprising, since at least four horses were needed to carry a tonne of coal. The coal was held in panniers on either side of the saddle. Coal carried by barge on the river cost 12s 0d [60p] a tonne. But when the canal was opened the cost of the Duke's coal in Manchester dropped to 6s 0d [30p] a tonne and the service offered was quicker than that by land.

Canals were even competitive when compared with the horse-drawn railways, which were being built in Northumberland and Durham at that time. A writer, in 1810, claimed that:

> 'a good horse on a level railway can draw only about eight or ten tons, whereas on a canal a very indifferent horse can draw fifty tons in a clumsy ill-constructed boat; but in a well-constructed iron boat it can draw sixty-five tons in addition to the boat.'

1 *How much more coal could one horse draw on a canal compared with:*
   (a) a packhorse, (b) a horse-drawn wagon on a railway?
2 *Why were the new and improved turnpike roads unable to compete with the canals for this trade?*
3 *What disadvantages did the canal have compared with the horse-drawn wagon?*

   In 1777, a newspaper published these figures comparing the cost of transporting goods by the tonne:

	By road	By water
From Liverpool to the Potteries	£2 10s 0d	£0 13s 6d
From Liverpool to Birmingham	£5 0s 0d	£1 5s 0d
From Manchester to Leicester	£6 0s 0d	£1 10s 0d

4 *What was the average reduction in cost per tonne, carrying goods by water rather than by packhorse on the roads?*

Other industrialists saw the potential benefits a canal could bring to their industries. One of these businessmen was Josiah Wedgwood, then beginning to make a name for himself in the pottery industry (see page 70). He was a leading light in the planning of the Grand Trunk (Trent and Mersey) Canal, which eventually linked the Trent, Mersey and Severn inland waterway systems. It was begun in July 1766, when Josiah Wedgwood dug the first sod of earth at a ceremony in Burslem. The section linking the Potteries to the Mersey was opened in 1770, although the full length of the canal was not opened until 1777.

Brindley was again chosen as the canal engineer and employed a huge army of labourers as 'navigators' (named after navigation), to dig the canal. The canal later linked up with the Grand Junction Canal and the Birmingham and Worcester Canal, joining the four great ports of Britain – London, Liverpool, Hull and Bristol to one another. The pottery industry could then transport china clay by boat from Cornwall and have it delivered cheaply to the quayside on the canal in Stoke-on-Trent. The savings in transport costs were enormous, as on average it cost three or four times as much to transport the clay by road as by the Grand Trunk Canal.

Many other new canals were built in the following forty years, including the spectacular Leeds and Liverpool Canal, which was over 200 km in length. It was started in 1770 but took 46 years to complete.

The canal-builders faced many problems. Apart from the technical problems, such as how to keep the canal level, whether to build tunnels, aqueducts, bridges or cuttings; there was also opposition from local people whose livelihood was threatened (such as owners of stage wagons and packhorses), and the owners of the land on which the canal was to be built. They had to be compensated for loss of land.

The canal had to be supplied with a reliable and constant source of water to keep it at the required level. Reservoirs and pumping stations had to be built. The canal had to be lined with clay to stop the water leaking out. The workmen employed, the navigators, had to be fed and housed. There were 50,000 of them in the 1790s and they had a reputation for being wild and lawless!

Canal mania

Thriving industries on the banks of canals, clearly demonstrated that canal building was a profitable business to be in (at first) and that enormous profits were to be made from canals. Some canal shares yielded huge dividends, sometimes paying a bigger profit each year than the actual value of the original shares. In time all the major industrial towns were linked to one another by inland waterways.

The prospect of huge profits excited the speculators and in the 1790s the boom in building new canals got out of hand. This 'canal mania', as it was called, resulted in new and over-ambitious schemes to build canals between places, where no such canals were needed. Often, there was insufficient trade in heavy goods, to bring in enough revenue to pay back the money borrowed to dig the canal. No fewer than 122 special Canal Acts were passed by Parliament between 1790 and 1796 authorising the construction of new canals.

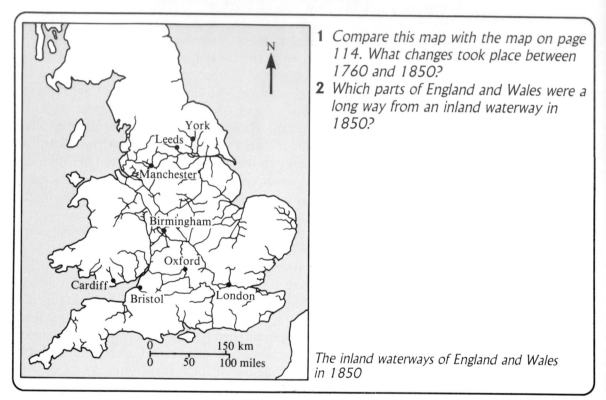

1 Compare this map with the map on page 114. What changes took place between 1760 and 1850?
2 Which parts of England and Wales were a long way from an inland waterway in 1850?

The inland waterways of England and Wales in 1850

Effects of the changes to the inland waterway system

By 1830 there were 6,400 km of navigable inland waterway in Britain and no place in England and Wales was no more than a short distance from a canal or river. The canals were vital to the industries growing in the years before the coming of the railways. Without them there would have been little industrial growth.

(a) Canals provided a safe method of transport for breakable goods, such as pottery, which would have been difficult to deliver by packhorse, or stage wagon, on the bumpy roads of the eighteenth century.

(b) They provided cheap transport for goods. In particular, they provided industries with cheap fuel at a time (before the steam railway) when the steam engine began to transform almost every industrial process.

(c) They gave industrialists access to raw materials (such as the china clay used by Josiah Wedgwood in the Potteries), and they provided markets for goods which would have been too expensive for people to buy if they had been taken over land.

(d) They employed thousands of workers, required huge sums of capital and generally stimulated trade and business on a scale not seen before in Britain.

Unfortunately, there was no national scheme for building canals. No one company was ever involved in canal building on a national scale. As a result the canal system which developed had many faults.

Decline of the canal system

The disadvantages of a canal system, in a small narrow island like Great Britain, were not apparent in the eighteenth century. During the heyday of the inland waterways, from 1760 to 1840, they were the only means of transporting goods cheaply. But when the railway network began to expand from 1840 onwards, canals could not compete with speed of delivery, or convenience to the manufacturer and the customer. The main disadvantages which led to the decline of the canal system were:

(a) Canals differed in the way they were built. They varied in length but most were very short. The largest canals were three times the width and depth of the smallest, so it was not always possible to send a load all the way from its starting point to its destination in the same barge. Unloading and reloading into another barge cost money. There was no standard type of canal lock or towpath. The height and width of bridges and tunnels varied.

(b) Since there were scores of canal companies, several different payments often had to be made for just one journey. A barge going from Liverpool to London, for instance, travelled on nine separate waterways. It was not possible to buy a 'through ticket'.

(c) The canal companies varied in the maintenance of their canals and in the facilities they provided. Locks and canal banks, damaged by the wash from boats, deteriorated. Canals sometimes leaked and the water level dropped.

(d) Many industrial areas in Britain are hilly. Canals in those areas tended to have many locks, which caused long delays. Canal transport was also slow (5 kph). This was relatively fast, in the eighteenth century, compared to the pack horse and the stage wagon, but not when compared to the speed of the railway in the nineteenth century. This explains why the canals were successful until about 1840-50 and then started to decline.

(e)   Competition from the railways halved the income of some canals within the space of two or three years. By 1844, the Grand Junction Canal had lost half its freight traffic to the London and Birmingham Railway (opened in 1838). Yet the decline in traffic was often slow, as many railways concentrated on passenger rather than freight traffic at first. Some canal companies collaborated with the railway companies in fixing freight rates. Many canals were taken over by the railways, in order to monopolise freight services in the area. The Duke of Bridgewater's canal even made higher profits after the opening of the Liverpool and Manchester Railway than before. Despite their many disadvantages, some canals were still profitable at the end of the nineteenth century. But others had closed and some had even been converted into railways!

Contemporary illustration, c. 1840

> **1** How does this picture sum up the changes which took place in the transportation of heavy goods between the early eighteenth century and the middle of the nineteenth century? Write a short essay explaining the significance of this picture.

THE COMING OF THE RAILWAYS

Early wagonways and methods of locomotion

The origins of the railway are found in two quite separate developments:
(a)   the use of wooden rails to move coal wagons and
(b)   the invention and development of the steam engine.

'The coal wagon roads from the pits to the water, are great works, carried over all sorts of inequalities of ground, so far as the distance of nine or ten miles [14–16 km]. The track of the wheels are marked with pieces of timber let into the road, for the wheels of the wagons to run on, by which means one horse is enabled to draw, and that with ease, 50 or 60 bushels [about 2 tonnes] of coals.'

Arthur Young 1769

1 *Which building material were the railways made from?*
2 *What did Arthur Young call the railways?*
3 *Why had they been built?*
4 *Why were they more effective than packhorses or wagons on a road?*

Some of the earliest wooden railway lines in Britain were in use at Wollaton coal mine in Nottingamshire at the start of the seventeenth century. A hundred years later, wooden railways had been so successful that in 1727, Ralph Wood even built a tall viaduct (the 30 m long Causey Arch), to take a wooden railway across the steep gorge lying between the Tanfield coal mines (in County Durham) and the River Tyne. There were few railways outside the coalfields, although Ralph Allen did build wooden wagonways to carry stone from his quarries near Bath.

In the 1720s coal cost only 4s 0d [20p] a tonne to produce at the pithead on Tyneside, but it cost £1 4s 0d [£1.20] in London due to the cost of transport. No other industry in Britain stood to gain as much from big improvements in methods of transporting heavy goods as the coal industry.

Iron railways

In 1767, the Coalbrookdale Ironworks began to make cast iron rails. Laden wagons running on iron rails were easier for horses to pull. By 1775, underground cast iron railways had been installed in a colliery in Sheffield. In 1788, flanged wheels were introduced, since some method was needed to keep the wagon wheels on the rails. An earlier solution had been to fit flanges to the rails instead of to the wheels. These were called plateways. By 1820, wrought iron railway lines were being made.

All the early railways were used by trains or wagons pulled by horses. In 1801 an Act of Parliament authorised the construction of the first public railway - the Surrey Iron Railway from Wandsworth to Croydon, in south London, and in 1806, the first public passenger service, the Oystermouth Railway, was opened at Swansea in South Wales. By 1825, there were nearly thirty of these railways in different parts of Britain.

The first steam locomotives

The Coalbrookdale Ironworks was also the setting for another vital development – that of adapting the steam engine for use as a 'steam horse'. The pioneer engineer who first built a steam locomotive which could move under its own steam, was Richard Trevithick, an engineer from Cornwall. His first engine ran on iron rails at Coalbrookdale in 1803. His second was used at the Pen-y-Darren Ironworks, in South Wales, in 1804. In 1808, he raced his 'Catch Me Who Can' locomotive against horses on a round track on the site of what is now Euston Station in London.

The problem he, and other engineers, had to overcome was one of building an efficient steam engine working under higher pressure than the stationary engines then in use in industry. The heavier the engine, the greater the horsepower needed just to move it. Increasing the horsepower only made it heavier. In these early experimental stages there were frequent breakdowns. Luckily, developments in precision engineering (see Chapter 2), and in iron-making, meant that it was feasible to build more complex steam engines.

In 1812, John Blenkinsop and Matthew Murray used steam locomotives at the Middleton Colliery in Leeds, running on a special 'rack' railway in which the locomotives had cog wheels with teeth which fitted corresponding teeth on the railway track.

In 1813, William Hedley ran his locomotive, 'Puffing Billy', at Wylam Colliery, 12 km to the west of Newcastle-upon-Tyne. A year later, on 25 June 1814, George Stephenson (see page 128) demonstrated his first steam locomotive at Killingworth Colliery, also close to Newcastle-upon-Tyne. He proved its usefulness to the colliery owners when his engine pulled 30 tonnes of coal at a speed of 6.5 kph.

Replica of George Stephenson's steam locomotive, Locomotion, *at Beamish Open Air Museum, County Durham*

The Stockton and Darlington Railway

It was obvious to the farsighted, that a railway system could be built to carry passengers and freight over much greater distances than those to be found within the confines of a colliery. In 1821, a group of business people in the Teesside region persuaded Parliament to authorise a new 43 km railway line linking Witton Park Colliery, near Darlington, with the coal wharves on the river Tees at Stockton. In 1823 they appointed George Stephenson as their chief engineer and in 1825 opened the Stockton and Darlington Railway – the first public transport system in the world to use steam locomotives.

On 27 September 1825, George Stephenson's *Locomotion*, pulled the first train with its 553 passengers and eleven wagons laden with coal. A newspaper report spoke of the astonishment of both spectators and 'the

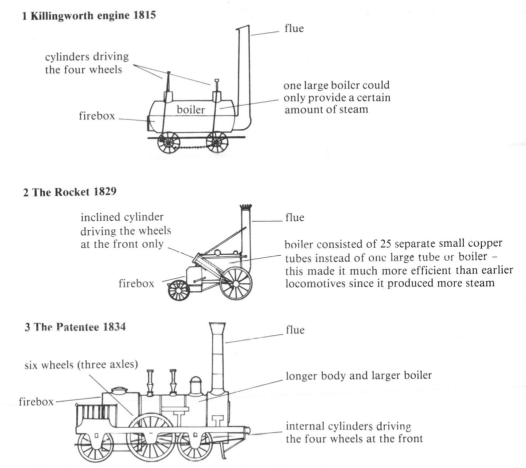

1 Killingworth engine 1815

flue

cylinders driving
the four wheels

one large boiler could
only provide a certain
amount of steam

firebox   boiler

2 The Rocket 1829

inclined cylinder
driving the wheels
at the front only

flue

boiler consisted of 25 separate small copper
tubes instead of one large tube or boiler –
this made it much more efficient than earlier
locomotives since it produced more steam

firebox

3 The Patentee 1834

flue

six wheels (three axles)

longer body and larger boiler

firebox

internal cylinders driving
the four wheels at the front

How the Stephensons developed the steam locomotive

beasts of the field' as the train moved at about 16–20 kph. In fact, some
of the wagons were only fitted with seats for the opening and after the
ceremony, the steam locomotives were only used for the carriage of
freight. Passengers were taken in special coaches, running on rails but
pulled by horses. In places fixed steam engines pulled the wagons up an
incline. But Stephenson had proved that steam locomotives could take
the place of horses and that passenger traffic could be a significant use
for the new steam railways.

The first passenger railways

In 1824, the first steps were taken to build a railway from Liverpool to
Manchester, then the two largest cities in England outside London. This
was because the canal owners refused to lower their freight rates, which
many industrialists thought too high.

The people who stood to lose most, the canal companies, turnpike

1 Look at the first picture below, showing a scene at the opening of the Stockton and Darlington Railway in 1825. Imagine you are a spectator. Write an account of what you see and add the sort of comment you think somebody like yourself might make about the future prospects for railways.

2 Look at the diagrams of the development of the steam locomotive on page 125. Why was the Rocket a more efficient steam locomotive than the Killingworth engine?

3 Study the photograph of the replica of Stephenson's railway engine, Locomotion. Compare it with the diagrams. Which of the other three Stephenson locomotives does it most closely resemble?

4 Draw a diagram of Locomotion, like those shown here, and label these features: (a) flue, (b) boiler, (c) cylinders and pistons driving the four wheels.

Contemporary illustrations

Opening of the first English railway between Stockton and Darlington, 27 September 1825

Race of locomotives at Rainhill, near Liverpool, in which George Stephenson's Rocket won, 1829

A first-class train on the Liverpool and Manchester Railway, 1833

A second-class train on the Liverpool and Manchester Railway, 1833

trusts and landowners, successfully stopped an Act of Parliament going through in 1825, which would have authorised the building of the new railway. But they were defeated the following year when Parliament gave the railway company the authority it needed to go ahead.

About half a million pounds was raised as capital to pay for the railway. Investors bought shares worth £100 each. Even this was not enough, they underestimated the cost and the total bill came to £740,000 by May 1830.

The obstacles to the building of a railway seemed formidable to people at the time. The railway company had to build 63 bridges and a tunnel underneath part of Liverpool to link the two cities. A large number of embankments and cuttings and viaducts were needed. The greatest difficulty of all was presented by Chat Moss, an area of soft bogland, a part of which was drained and made solid with hundreds of tonnes of earth. In addition the railway company laid railway lines and built stations and warehouses.

In order to get the best possible steam locomotives for their new service, the Liverpool and Manchester Railway Company held a competition for steam locomotives, for a prize of £500, at Rainhill, near Liverpool (shown in the second picture on page 126). A large crowd turned up to see the contestants race their engines on a 3 km length of track. The competition was won by George and Robert Stephenson (see below) with their new locomotive the *Rocket* – capable of speeds of almost 50 kph.

On 15 September 1830, the Liverpool and Manchester Railway was opened by the Prime Minister, the Duke of Wellington, accompanied by Robert Peel (a future prime minister) and William Huskisson, a distinguished politician. They set off in the first train, consisting of 33 carriages, containing elegantly dressed ladies and a number of musicians. When the train stopped to take on water, Mr Huskisson was knocked over and killed by a train coming in the opposite direction on the other line.

Within a month of opening, the railway carried over 1,200 passengers a day, which was 500 people more than the mail and stage coaches had managed to carry between them. In December the railway company began to carry merchandise, coal, timber, cattle, sheep and pigs. In 1831, they carried 445,000 passengers and in 1835, the railway was taking over £200,000 a year in receipts. Investors were getting a dividend of £10 a share in 1835. (This was much more than they would have got if they had put their money in a bank.)

The journey between Liverpool and Manchester, at an average speed of 40 kph, took 90 minutes. Despite the fatal accident on the opening day, it was claimed, in an article written in 1836, that 'the risk by the railway is only a hundredth part of the risk by a common coach'.

> **1** _Look at the pictures on page 126. How did the first-class train differ from the second-class train on the Liverpool and Manchester Railway?_
>
> **2** _Write two or three sentences to describe the competing locomotives at the Rainhill Trials. Which is Stephenson's_ Rocket?
>
> **3** _How can you tell that, in these very early days of the railway, the influence of the stage coach was still very strong?_
>
> **4** _Make a list of the people and organisations, such as the canal companies, which you think would be most likely to oppose the building of new railways._
>
> **5** _Why do you think investors rushed to put money into the new railway companies?_

George and Robert Stephenson

George Stephenson

George Stephenson (1781–1848) was born at Wylam, near Newcastle-upon-Tyne. His father was a miner and George was also employed in the pits, first at Wylam and later at Killingworth. When he successfully repaired the steam-pump at Killingworth, he was made engineer, in 1812.

In 1821, he became the engineer responsible for building the Stockton and Darlington Railway and, afterwards, for the Liverpool and Manchester Railway. In later years he was a consultant to many foreign companies, and was involved in the construction of new railways in Belgium, the Netherlands, Italy, Germany, France and Spain.

His son, Robert (1803-59), was also a brilliant railway engineer. He assisted his father with the Stockton and Darlington Railway, became manager of the family locomotive works on Tyneside and later built several important bridges, including the High Level Bridge in Newcastle-upon-Tyne and the tubular bridge at Conwy in North Wales. He was also the chief engineer on the important London and Birmingham Railway, which opened in 1838.

The expansion of the railways

The railways proved to be very popular and most people in Britain wanted them in their area. Wealthy people wanted to invest their money in enterprises as profitable as the Liverpool and Manchester Railway. By 1836, moves were already under way to link many of the towns of northern England to the railway, including Leeds and Sheffield. In 1837, the Grand Junction Railway linked the Liverpool and Manchester Railway to Birmingham and the Midlands. In 1838, the London and Birmingham Railway was opened, followed in 1841, by the Great

Western Railway, from London to Bristol. Isambard Kingdom Brunel was the chief engineer of the Great Western Railway (see below). He was one of the greatest of the Victorian civil engineers.

Isambard Kingdom Brunel (1806–59)

Plaque on The Royal Albert Railway Bridge at Saltash in Cornwall, to commemorate its builder – Isambard Kingdom Brunel

Brunel was the son of a French engineer, Sir Marc Isambard Brunel, who fled from France in 1793 and eventually settled in Britain, where he built the Thames Tunnel.

Isambard Kingdom Brunel grew up to become an even more remarkable engineer than his father. At the age of 23 he designed the Clifton Suspension Bridge in Bristol and at the age of 27 became the engineer to the company building the Great Western Railway, generally regarded as the finest railway line built in Britain during the boom years of the railways.

In total he laid over 1,500 km of railway track and insisted on using a broad-gauge track, unlike that used by all the other companies. Brunel's gauge (i.e. width between the tracks) was 2.1 m whilst the gauge used on all the other railways was the same as Stephenson's – 1.4 m. Brunel felt that the wider gauge made his trains safer, more stable and more comfortable to travel on.

In 1837, he built one of the first transatlantic steamers, the *Great Western*. At the age of 37 he built the first steamship to be powered by a screw propeller, and from 1853–8, he built the world's largest ship, the *Great Eastern*.

Opposition to the railways

At first there was considerable opposition to the new railways from a variety of interested parties. They included people who stood to lose money if the railways proved successful; such as shareholders who had already invested money in canals; proprietors of stage coaches, owners of coaching inns; people involved in the running or financing of the Turnpike Trusts; together with all the road engineers, 'pike-keepers', ostlers, bargees and other workers employed in coaching inns and on the turnpike roads and canals.

Opposition came, too, from landowners opposed to the very idea of a railway and from those who tried to get more money for their land than that offered by the railway companies. Even so they made a huge profit from the sale of land for the railways. They, and many farmers, were to benefit from the opportunities the railways later provided for the sale of farm produce in distant markets.

Huntsmen claimed that railways ruined their sport, since they could not chase the fox across embankments, cuttings and viaducts. Country people complained of fires started by the sparks from a locomotive and feared that their cattle and sheep would be frightened by the noise, shape, smoke and appearance of the first trains. People in villages, and in town suburbs, complained of being cut off from their close neighbours on the other side of the track. Yet, on the whole, the railways put an end to isolation.

You can see the rapidity with which the new railway lines were opened, by looking at these statistics and at the maps.

The growth of the railways

Date	Length of line	Passengers carried
1842	3,000 km	18 million
1847	6,400 km	51 million
1852	11,800 km	89 million
1857	14,600 km	139 million
1862	18,600 km	180 million
1867	22,900 km	288 million
1872	25,500 km	423 million

1 Use the statistics in the table to draw:
(a) a graph showing how the number of passengers carried by the railways grew between 1842 and 1872;
(b) a graph to show how the length of railway line increased during the same period.

2 In which five-year period did the number of passengers carried, and the length of railway line, increase by 100 per cent or more?

3 Did the number of passengers carried for every kilometre of railway line increase or decrease between:
(a) 1842 and 1852
(b) 1852 and 1862
(c) 1862 and 1872?

4 Write a short essay explaining the growth of the railway system shown by these maps and statistics. What do they tell us about the building of the railways in Britain?

5 In 1844, a journalist wrote:

'In planning a new railway, two great considerations operate; the first, to direct it through the most level parts of a tract of country, so as to avoid expense arising from excavating, tunnelling and

1845   N   **1851**   **1872**

0   150 km

0   50   100 miles

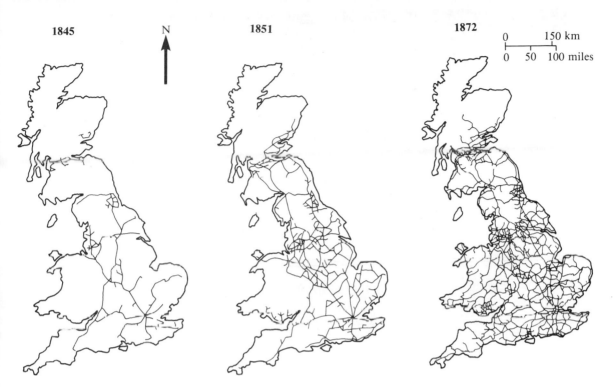

The railway system in Britain in 1845, 1851 and 1872

embanking; and the second, to make it near to the greatest number of populous places, so as to secure a profit: the question is of certain expense on the one hand, and of probable profit on the other.'

(a) What did he mean by 'certain expense on the one hand' and 'probable profit on the other'?

(b) Look at the maps. Were the new railways always near to the 'greatest number of populous places'?

(c) Why is it often cheaper, in the long run, to construct an expensive tunnel, instead of taking the railway on a detour?

(d) How does an engineer take a railway (i) across a deep valley, (ii) over land likely to flood, (iii) through undulating and hilly country?

Railway mania

The worst problem caused by 'railway mania' was the duplication of services. Railway companies sometimes built lines linking towns which were already well-served by rival companies, or where the potential freight and passenger traffic was insufficient to allow the companies to show a profit for the money spent on building the railway.

Railway mania, The Illustrated London News, *1845*

When investors (people and organisations with money to put into new ventures) saw the huge profits being made by the first railway companies, they rushed to buy shares in new companies. By this time (the mid-1840s) much of the original opposition to the railways had disappeared, as people could see the benefits the railways provided.

1 *How is the period of railway mania illustrated by the figures in this table?*

	Number of new Railway Acts submitted to Parliament	Length of the proposed new railway lines	Cost of the proposed new railway lines
1844	49	1,300 km	£20 million
1845	94	4,350 km	£59 million
1846	219	7,300 km	£133 million

2 *What happened between 1844 and 1846?*

3 *How does the picture support the idea that there was railway mania at this time? What do you think the businessmen are holding in their hands? What do you think they were doing?*

George Hudson was an important figure during the railway boom. He was a ruthless man who eventually controlled 1,600 km of railway track in the north of England and was known as 'the Railway King'. He was a Member of Parliament, director of many railway companies and chairman of the powerful York and North Midland Railway Company, which swallowed up several rival companies, merging them into the Midland Railway. Other mergers followed. In 1843, there were over 200 small railway companies. In 1850, there were only 22 large companies and a few smaller ones. The railway companies building the new lines had been amalgamated into different regional areas.

Hudson's efforts, undoubtedly, did much to expand the railway system in Britain but he was corrupt and in 1849 fell from power as the Railway King, accused of fiddling the books.

Not all of the railway tycoons were as unscrupulous as Hudson. Thomas Brassey (1805–70) was by far the biggest railway contractor of his day, building a third of Britain's railways and a large number of foreign railways as well. He was highly regarded by his workmen, looked after their interests and offered living proof that a businessman could amass a large fortune without necessarily grinding his workers into the ground.

Many investors lost money at the time of the railway boom and there was strong criticism of the railway companies and the ways in which they operated. They were accused of taking insufficient care of their customers. Railway accidents were frequent and the humorous magazine *Punch* savagely attacked the railway companies in a series of macabre cartoons.

Parliamentary legislation

Dissatisfaction with the organisation of the railway system led to two important laws being passed in Parliament. There was a feeling in the country that the railway system was not just a means whereby private companies and their shareholders could make large profits. It had to offer a service to the public as a whole and not just the wealthy people who travelled first class. Millions of working-class people travelled third class in very poor carriages which often consisted of open wagons.

The 1844 Railway Act laid down that each railway company had to run at least one train service in both directions, along each of its lines every day. This was called the 'Parliamentary Train' and it was required to stop at every station on the line, charge a maximum rate of one penny per mile [roughly equivalent to 0.25p per km] and travel at a minimum speed of 12 mph [19 kph]. Even so, it was often extremely slow and regarded as a train to be avoided by the passenger in a hurry.

In 1846, the Broad Gauge Act made 4 ft 8½ ins [1.4 m] the standard gauge for all new railways to be built in future in Britain. This was the Government's solution to the 'Battle of the Gauges'. The Great Western Railway, with its 7 ft [2.1 m] broad-gauge railway lines, had been threatening to absorb other railway companies, which used Stephenson's gauge of 4 ft 8½ ins [1.4 m].

It was ridiculous to run train services on two different gauges, since through-passengers often had to change trains to make journeys of only moderate length. The Broad Gauge Act ensured that, in future, through-trains would be able to travel on lines operated by different railway companies. This was further facilitated by Cardwell's Railway Act of 1854, which made it compulsory for railways to make facilities available

This Punch *cartoon was published in June 1892. Write a brief note of explanation of what the picture is about.*

THE BURIAL OF THE ''BROAD-GAUGE''.

for any rival company wishing to run through-trains on lines other than their own.

The Broad Gauge Act also helped to lower the cost of running the railway companies, since locomotives and railway lines could now be built to the same standard gauge. Nonetheless, Brunel's Great Western Railway continued to operate broad-gauge railways, until 1892, by which time it had converted all its railway track to standard gauge.

The economic effects of the railways

'The railways transport goods at much lower rates than any of the former carriers. Coal, for instance, is carried at an average of a half-penny per ton per mile [0.13p per tonne per km]; while the old charge by the canals was three half-pence. With all their faults, these iron roads have promoted the wealth of the people of this country. They save the public two-thirds of their time in transit, and two-thirds in fares and tolls; they have given us the penny post, which could not have existed without them; they have intersected the country with telegraph-wires; they have reduced the cost of many articles of general consumption. Railways bring to London upwards of 80 million pounds of killed meat [36,000 tonnes], more than half her fish; and milk by millions of quarts [litres] in the year.'

Chambers's Journal 1856

1 *What did the writer say were the main economic benefits brought by the railways?*
2 *How did they benefit the factory-owner?*
3 *How did they benefit the worker?*

The economic effects of the railways were felt throughout the rest of the nineteenth century and remained unchallenged until the 1920s, when use of the motor vehicle became widespread.

(a) The most dramatic change was the immediate decline of the stage coach and mail coach – as you can see in the picture at the start of this chapter. As soon as a new railway link was opened, the corresponding coach services were drastically reduced. In 1829, there were 29 stage coaches each day between Manchester and Liverpool. In 1832, there were two. Turnpike roads fell into disuse and grass began to grow in the roadway. Proprietors of coaching inns went bankrupt. But some business people moved with the times. William Chaplin, who owned 2,000 posting horses in London, sold many of them before they lost their value, and became a carrier, instead, for the London and Birmingham Railway. He later became involved with the London and South-Western Railway, and became its chairman in 1842.

(b)   The decline of the canals was also inevitable, although not as dramatic as that of the stage or mail coach. In any case, the reasons for this decline were not entirely the work of the railways – as shown in this chapter.

(c)   The railways created a huge new demand for coal, machine tools, iron rails, steel plate, steam engines, timber planking, bricks, stones and mortar. This stimulated almost every branch of industry.

(d)   Proximity to a railway became an essential requirement for new factory sites, as shown on page 82, when Titus Salt built his new textile mill at Saltaire. Factories using steam engines could now be built well away from the coalfields, since fuel could be taken there cheaply and quickly by rail.

(e)   Passenger and cargo ports, such as Southampton and Liverpool, thrived on the railway. So did ferry ports like Dover, and fishing ports, such as Grimsby and Fleetwood. Seaside resorts also developed.

(f)   Manufacturers found that it paid to advertise branded goods, since their products could now be sold anywhere in Britain. In the past the market for most products had been limited to the local region.

(g)   Hundreds of thousands of new jobs were created by the railways – engine-drivers, railway guards, station-masters, cleaners, porters and engineers. Some jobs were lost, such as those of the hostler, coachman and turnpike-keeper. But, on the whole, the railways created far more jobs than they destroyed.

Victoria Station, The Illustrated London News, *4 May 1861. How did the building of new railway stations affect the everyday life and the livelihoods of the people of a town? How does this railway station differ from a modern station? What are the similarities?*

(h) Farmers benefitted in many ways, as shown in Chapter 1. They could buy coal cheaply for use in their steam engines, to make work easier. They could send farm produce all over Britain to fetch the best prices. This gave them an incentive to grow more and to make their farms more productive. Cheaper and more plentiful food was the result. Some historians even believe that the coming of the railway was a more important turning point in the history of farming than the enclosure of the open fields.

The social effects of the railways

Read the following extracts from an article, entitled *Social Effects of Railways*, which was published in *Chambers's Journal* on 21 September 1844.

'The most important of these changes is the springing up of new towns. On the Birmingham railway, a station was made at Wolverton, about midway from London, the company erecting a refreshment room and a few sheds for their engines. Around these buildings a town has rapidly sprung up, and is so well populated, that the railway directors built a church.

Not the least important effect is the facilities they have afforded to the humbler classes for recreation. Short trips give the working classes the opportunity of seeing that which they would never have been able, under the old stage-coach and wagon dynasty, to behold. The artisan, cooped up, and constantly breathing bad air, has now the opportunity, on every available holiday, of making excursions into the country.

A railway train takes masses of people of all ranks and conditions. The rich are brought into contact and converse with the poor. Nothing opens men's minds, so much as seeing a variety of things, of places, and of men. The greater the number of travellers, then, the greater the social improvement.'

---

1 *Which was the most important change? How and why was it caused by the coming of the railways?*
2 *What did the writer mean by these phrases:*
   (a) 'social effects'
   (b) 'humbler classes'
   (c) 'stage-coach and wagon dynasty'
   (d) 'people of all ranks and conditions'?
3 *Name five of the social effects listed in the article.*

In 1844, it was really too early to say how far-reaching the eventual social effects of the railways would be. It is almost impossible to give an adequate indication of the hundreds of different ways in which the railways affected the everyday lives of people in Britain and the rest of the world.

The railways brought the penny post, the electric telegraph and helped the spread of newspapers. Theatre companies toured the country, sports teams travelled further afield, and people could attend meetings in different parts of the country, for example those arranged by the Anti-Corn Law League (see Chapter 1).

One of the most important social effects was the rapid growth of the seaside resorts. Members of the working classes could now afford to take their families to the seaside on a cheap day excursion. In 1830, it cost £1 4s 0d [£1.20] return, to travel by stage coach as an outside passenger from London to Brighton (a five hour journey). In the 1840s, it cost 8s 0d [40p] by train, third-class return, for a journey taking half that time. Hotels, boarding houses, cafés, piers, promenades, theatres and winter gardens were later built to cater for the holidaymaker.

Some middle-class commuters lived at a distance from their places of work. Suburbs grew up around the railway stations on lines leading to London and other big cities. In time even workers were able to live at a distance from the factories where they worked and the railway companies ran special workmen's trains.

The appearance of many towns was substantially altered, as the railway companies wanted to build their stations as close to the centres of towns as possible. In many cases this was not possible and they had to build on the edge of the existing town. So in older towns, like Norwich, Cambridge and Ipswich, the railway stations were built one or two kilometres away from the town centre.

Towns and cities grew even bigger, because people from outlying districts could now afford to shop there. This helped to stimulate the building of department stores in the cities.

The Great Exhibition of 1851 (see page 83) was visited by over six million people, many of whom travelled to London from all over Britain on cheap day excursions. The Exhibition made a profit – something it would not have done had it been held ten years earlier when only a few railway services were in operation.

---

4 *What people are shown in the picture opposite?*
5 *Which parts of the article* Social Effects of Railways, *published in 1844, are illustrated by this cartoon?*
6 *Why do you think the cartoon is called* THE POUND AND THE SHILLING?

Public schools began to thrive because pupils could travel there by rail from any part of the country. Many new public schools were founded in the 1840s and 1850s. Government inspectors were able to visit schools receiving grants from public funds (see Chapter 9).

This Punch cartoon shows the Duke of Wellington, and other members of the upper classes, mingling with the crowd at the Great Exhibition in 1851

THE POUND AND THE SHILLING

"Whoever Thought of Meeting You Here?"

Policemen and soldiers could be rushed by train to break up disturbances in distant parts of Britain. But criminals also used the railways. The first great train robbery took place on 15 May 1855, when Agar, Pierce and Burgess, stole £12,000 worth of gold bars from the guard's van of a train travelling between London and Folkestone.

7 *Which of the social effects do you think was the most important? Give reasons for your answer.*

8 *How did the railways play a part in politics?*

9 *How did the railway affect your town? Are there any Victorian buildings in the vicinity of the nearest railway station to your home? Is there a Victorian 'Station Hotel' or a Victorian railway station building?*

SHIPPING

The China clipper Spindrift – *first home with the new spring teas,* The Illustrated London News, *19 September 1868*

For much of the first half of the nineteenth century, steamships and sailing ships were rivals. There was no sudden decline of the wooden sailing ship and no sudden rise of the iron steamship.

The China tea clipper

In 1800, almost all the ships afloat in Britain, and off the coasts, were wooden sailing ships. But Britain's supplies of oak timber used for shipbuilding were rapidly dwindling. In the United States, by contrast, there were unlimited supplies of good shipbuilding timber and, by 1800, American shipping was already beginning to rival that of Britain. American ships were faster and cheaper.

When the Anglo-Chinese agreement of 1842 opened up Chinese ports for trade with the West, fast new sailing ships called clippers, were built to bring tea back from China to Britain. These were American-built at first. In the 1860s and 1870s, many people followed with interest, the progress of the annual race between the China tea clippers bringing the new tea harvest back to Britain.

> 'The 16,000 mile [26,000 km] race between some of the finest clipper-ships in the world with the new spring teas from China has this year been watched with more than ordinary interest. In all, about forty sailing ships were engaged in the contest. The race was won by the *Spindrift*. She carried a cargo of 1,306,836 lb of tea [nearly 600,000 kg]. She started on May 29 and on September 2 got into the East India Dock, having accomplished the run from China in little more than ninety-four days.'
>
> *The Illustrated London News*, 19 September 1868

> **1** *Why do you think the captains of the clipper ships wanted to be first back to Britain with their cargo of tea? What was the hurry?*
> **2** *On average, how many kilometres did the* Spindrift *travel each day? What was the ship's average speed in kph?*

Wooden ships versus iron ships

The first iron ship was built in 1785 by John 'Iron-mad' Wilkinson but wood continued to be a popular shipbuilding material, long after the merits of iron had been demonstrated.

The first sea-going iron ships, in 1822, were built with timber structures covered with iron plates. They were called ironclads. One of their disadvantages was that it cost twice as much to build an ironclad as an ordinary wooden ship. In any case some people still had doubts – how could iron be made to float? The ships had other disadvantages as well. They were easily corroded by the salt in sea water and soon became encrusted with barnacles. This reduced the speed of the ship and affected its handling and its ability to carry loads. Shipowners soon realised that regular maintenance was essential and boats were repainted and coated with preservatives at regular intervals.

But wooden ships also had many disadvantages. They were more easily damaged in a gale, and wrecks around the coast were a common sight in Victorian times. Wood was an unsuitable building material for large ships, since it was not strong enough to support the hull of a long vessel.

Sailing ships versus steamships

The transition from sailing ship to steamship was equally slow, even though William Patrick Miller and William Symington had made a small steamboat, capable of 6 kph, as early as 1786.

Sailing ships had a number of disadvantages compared to steamboats. For one thing, they were much more difficult to control, particularly when the wind was too strong or, conversely, when it was too calm. A steamboat was easier to steer, particularly in a crowded dock or shipping lane. It could be steered in a straight line, rather than being tacked from side to side, so journey times tended to be shorter, even when speeds were otherwise the same.

Sailing ships were also notoriously unreliable time-keepers, since their speed was controlled by the direction and speed of the wind. In 1837, it took one ship a hundred days to sail from Liverpool to New York instead of the thirty-two days it usually took for the transatlantic crossing.

The first steamships

One of the first steamships in Britain, the *Charlotte Dundas*, was launched in 1801. The ship was powered by a single paddle wheel operated by a steam engine. On the trial voyage up the Forth and Clyde Canal, the ship steamed into the wind, pulling two barges of 70 tonnes behind it. Unfortunately, the wash from the ship started to erode the sides of the canal and the idea of using a steamboat on a canal was abandoned – for a time.

> **1** What great advantage of the steamboat over the sailing boat is illustrated by the information on the Charlotte Dundas?
>
> **2** What big advantage did sailing ships have over steamships?

Henry Bell's Comet, *from a Victorian engraving*

In 1812, Henry Bell of Glasgow, launched the *Comet*, the first British steamboat to operate a passenger service. Three times a week, the *Comet* took passengers from Greenock to Glasgow, and back again. The ship steamed at a speed of 12 kph and covered the 35 km up the Clyde estuary in 3 hours.

In 1815, the *Margery*, another steamer (of 70 tonnes) which had been built on the Clyde, began a passenger service on the Thames from London to Gravesend. Shortly after that there were steam packet boats crossing the Channel.

Disadvantages of steamships

At first, there were no long distance journeys because steam engines in ships made inefficient use of coal as a fuel. Shipbuilders and owners discovered that the biggest single disadvantage was the constant necessity to carry huge quantities of coal to fuel a ship's boilers. This had the effect of limiting the steamship's usefulness to short journeys only, such as the cross-Channel route.

Another disadvantage was the fact that the first steamboats were powered by paddle wheels. The boats were difficult to manoeuvre in a confined space, because of the position of the wheels. They were also ineffective in high seas, since the paddles kept coming out of the water when the ship rolled.

Steamships also needed a constant supply of fresh water to top up the boilers. At sea the only water available was salt water which corroded the boilers. So large quantities of fresh water had to be carried on long oceanic voyages as well as fuel. A condenser system was introduced in 1843, which caught the steam and converted it back into water.

Coaling station at Singapore, The Graphic, *4 November 1876. What was meant by the term 'coaling'? Where do you think the coal had come from?*

One solution to these problems was to establish coaling stations, like the one shown in the picture, where steamers could take on fresh supplies of coal, water and food. Britain's growing empire proved invaluable in this respect and enabled the shipping companies and the Royal Navy to sustain a large number of these coaling stations throughout the world.

The most effective solutions came with the improvements made to the steam engine in the nineteenth century. The two major advances in this period were the invention of the steam-powered screw propeller in about 1836 and its subsequent use in Brunel's ship the *Great Britain*, which was launched in 1843. The second important invention was that of the compound steam engine in 1854, which cut the amount of coal needed by a steamship in half.

> **1** *Why was the compound steam engine so important?*
> **2** *What were the chief advantages of having a ship fitted with a screw propeller at the stern?*

Development of the steamship

At first, steam ships were also fitted with masts and sails. These provided the main method of propulsion at sea. Steam engines were only used when in harbour and when the ship was becalmed, such as when the *Savannah* made the first voyage by a steamship across the Atlantic, in 1819, and on the pioneer voyage of the steamship *Enterprise* to India, in 1825.

In 1837 Brunel launched one of the first transatlantic steamers, the *Great Western*, with a wooden hull, a full set of sails and a paddle engine. Its successor, six years later, was the *Great Britain*. This had an iron hull, a screw propeller and a full set of sails. In the same year the *Colombia* steamed from Halifax in Canada to Liverpool in just under ten days – compared to twenty-six days in the *Savannah* (part steam, part sail), in 1819, or the thirty-two days taken by a fast sailing ship.

The Great Eastern, The Illustrated London News, *13 June 1857*

The most remarkable ship to be launched in the middle years of the nineteenth century was Brunel's *Great Eastern* – far and away the biggest ship of its time. It was over 200 m long, 25 m wide and 18 m high. It could carry 4,000 passengers or 10,000 soldiers and was so large that it had to have an electric telegraph system to link the engineers in the engine room with the captain on the bridge. It even had its own gasworks to supply lighting and a farmyard to provide fresh lamb, beef and poultry! There were seven masts carrying 5,500 m^2 of canvas; two huge paddles, 17 m in diameter, on either side of the ship; and a giant screw propeller, 8 m across.

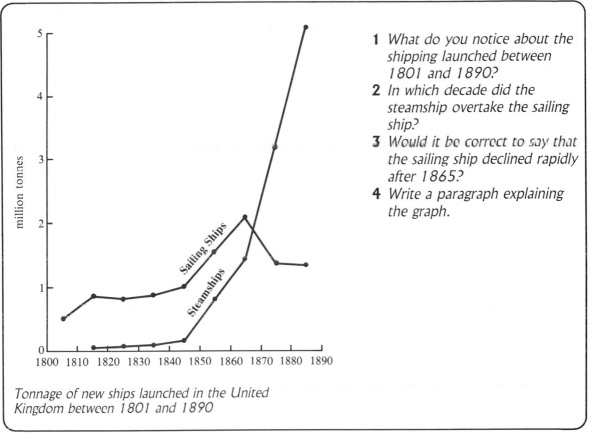

million tonnes

Sailing Ships

Steamships

1800 1810 1820 1830 1840 1850 1860 1870 1880 1890

Tonnage of new ships launched in the United Kingdom between 1801 and 1890

1 *What do you notice about the shipping launched between 1801 and 1890?*

2 *In which decade did the steamship overtake the sailing ship?*

3 *Would it be correct to say that the sailing ship declined rapidly after 1865?*

4 *Write a paragraph explaining the graph.*

Social and economic effects of the changes in sea transport

Improved and swifter sea transport had an important effect on agriculture and industry in the nineteenth century. Ships brought guano from South America to fertilise British fields in the 1840s. Later, in the 1870s and 1880s, they brought frozen meat from Argentina and New Zealand, and grain from the prairies of North America. The cost of shipping wheat across the Atlantic eventually dropped from £2 a tonne in the middle years of the century to 6s 0d [30p] a tonne, fifty years later. The improvements in sea transport in the nineteenth century, indirectly helped to hasten the decline of British farming in the face of competition from cheap American corn.

Improvements in shipping also opened up new markets for British industry and made the export of heavy goods, such as coal and iron, possible. They also played a large part in ensuring the supremacy of the British Empire in the nineteenth century. Ships took troops, guns, farmers, miners and settlers to the colonies.

The numbers of people travelling overseas increased dramatically, partly because ships were now much bigger and much more comfortable, and partly because they were also much quicker and much safer. Safety at sea increased when Samuel Plimsoll got Parliament to pass a law in 1876, limiting the amount of cargo a ship could take on board. A line was painted on the hull of the ship and called the Plimsoll Line. This line had to be above the water level when the ship was loaded.

FURTHER QUESTIONS AND EXERCISES

1 *Describe the work and achievements of:*
   (a) *Thomas Telford*
   (b) *James Brindley*
   (c) *John Loudon McAdam*
   (d) *George Stephenson*
   (e) *Isambard Kingdom Brunel.*

2 *To which features of the Transport Revolution do we owe these words or phrases:*
   (a) *first class*
   (b) *tarmac*
   (c) *navvy*
   (d) *getting up steam*
   (e) *going off the rails*
   (f) *guard?*

Extract from John Cabbell's diary 26 November, 1833

3   Look at the extract from the diary of a young Scotsman, called John
Cabbell, who travelled in Europe, in 1833. He arrived back in
Edinburgh on 26 November and travelled to his home in Glasgow in a
stage coach.

(a)   The stage coach arrived in Glasgow at 16.00 hours. How long did
the journey take?

(b)   What did he think about the countryside between Edinburgh and
Glasgow?

(c)   How can you tell the coach was unlikely to have been a mail
coach?

(d)   Use an atlas to find out the distance between Edinburgh and
Glasgow. What was the average speed taken by the stage coach to
cover the journey? What stops would the stage coach have made
on the journey?

(e)   Is this a primary or secondary source of information?

4   Write a short essay explaining the development of the railway system.
Mention the early tramways, the experiments of Trevithick and
Blenkinsop, George Stephenson, the Stockton and Darlington Railway,
the Rainhill Trials, the opening of the Liverpool and Manchester Railway,
railway mania, the Parliamentary Train and the battle of the gauges.

5   Imagine you have been working on the construction of one of these
projects:

(a)   the Liverpool and Manchester Railway,

(b)   the Duke of Bridgewater's canal in 1761,

(c)   the Great Eastern.

Describe your experiences and say what effect you, and your fellow
workers, think it will have on the lives of people in Britain, in the future.

6   What reasons help to explain the following developments:

(a)   the formation of the Turnpike Trusts,

(b)   the rapid rise and decline of the canals,

(c)   the slow evolution of the steamship?

7   In The Mikado (written in 1885), W. S. Gilbert specified the
punishment for:

> 'The idiot who, in railway carriages,
> Scribbles on window-panes,
> We only suffer
> To ride on a buffer
> In Parliamentary trains.'

Why do you think Victorian audiences found this funny? What were
Parliamentary Trains? Why did Gilbert think it a punishment to travel on
them? What was particularly hazardous about 'riding on a buffer' on
Victorian trains?

8 *Study this route, compiled from a road book of 1811.*

LONDON to DERBY

km from London	Towns and inns supplying post horses
18	**Barnet**: Green Man, Red Lion
24	**South Mims**: White Hart
34	**St. Albans**: Angel, White Hart, Woolpack
47	**Market Street**: Sun
54	**Dunstable**: Crown, Sugar Loaf
69	**Brickhill**: George, White Lion Cross the Grand Junction Canal
84	**Stoney Stratford**: Bull, Cock Cross the River Ouse, and the Grand Junction Canal
106	**Northampton**: Angel, George, Peacock
134	**Market Harborough**: Three Swans
158	**Leicester**: Blue Bell, Crane, Three Crowns
175	**Loughborough**: Anchor, Bull's Head
191	Cavendish Bridge Cross the River Trent, and enter Derbyshire Near Derby cross the canal
203	**Derby**: Bell, George, King's Head, New Inn

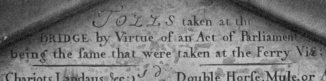

Tolls which were charged in the eighteenth century for crossing Cavendish Bridge in Leicestershire

(a) *The tolls on Cavendish Bridge are given in old shillings (s) and in pence (d). One shilling was equal to 5p, and 1d was roughly 0.4p. What tolls, in modern money, did the following pay: (i) a pedestrian, (ii) a woman in a two-wheeled chaise, (iii) a stage coach? What difference did it make if your carriage, cart or wagon had two wheels instead of four? Which animals cost most to drive across the bridge – sheep, cattle, pigs, mules? Which cost least?*

(b) *Using the information in the table work out the distance between each successive pair of places with post horse inns. Which was the longest distance you would have had to travel between inns? What was the average distance between post horse inns? Look at a modern road book and see if you find out whether any of these inns can still be used by a traveller today.*

(c) *Which river did Cavendish Bridge cross? How did people cross the river before the bridge was built? Why was a toll bridge built there? What legal right had the tollkeeper to charge a toll for crossing the bridge?*

9 *Look at the following situations. Choose one and note the possible risks involved; decide what you will do and explain fully the advantages of the course of action you propose to take.*

(a) *You are a ship owner in 1860, debating whether to replace a wooden sailing ship with an iron steamship.*

(b) *You are the owner of a large number of stage coaches in 1835 and are thinking of selling them to another coach proprietor, but for less than you think they are really worth. If you do decide to do this you intend to join other business people in forming a railway company.*

(c) *You are the most influential member of a Turnpike Trust in 1825 and you are proposing to build a new road. You have decided to choose either Mr Telford or Mr McAdam as your road engineer.*

10 *Read the following extract from a letter published in the* Birmingham and Lichfield Chronicle *on Thursday 24 October, 1822:*

CANAL PROFITS

SIR, The Birmingham Canal Company derives an income amounting to nearly £80,000 a year, which is principally drawn from the trade and industry of Birmingham and its neighbourhood. The original shares in this concern it is well known cost only £100 each, but their shares are now currently selling in the market at £2,500 or £2,600 each.

A friend, has been visiting the collieries of the North of England, and inspecting the steam rail-roads which are used there. He informs me that steam engines work there upon rail roads so as to carry coal eight or ten miles, at only 5d per ton [2p per tonne], which is about the distance that the coals are brought to Birmingham upon the canal.

The engines or machines are said to cost but £150 or £200; and travelling upon small carriages by means of small cog wheels, draw 15 or 20 coal carriages after them, carrying about three tons each, say from 40 to 60 tons in the whole. If such steam roads were established between Birmingham and Wednesbury, it would compel the Canal Company to make a reasonable reduction in their tonnages, and would prove an incalculable advantage to the town of Birmingham.

I am, Mr. Editor, yours,
VERITAS

(a) What evidence does this letter provide to show that some canals were highly profitable?

(b) What proposal did the writer make to lower the cost of transport in the Birmingham area? When it did come was its effect to prove of 'incalculable advantage to the town of Birmingham'? What happened to the canals then?

(c) Which of the different 'steam rail-roads' in the north of England had the friend visited?

(d) How was the complaint made in the letter written in 1822, echoed by the business interests who promoted the Liverpool and Manchester Railway in 1825–6?

(e) Imagine you are a large shareholder in the Birmingham Canal Company. Write a letter to the Birmingham and Lichfield Chronicle *replying to VERITAS.*

11 Describe and account for the changes which took place between 1700 and 1870 in either:
(a) road
(b) canal
(c) rail
(d) sea transport in Britain.
What were the principal economic and social effects of these changes?

Chapter Four

Trade and Economy

INTRODUCTION

Cartoon in Punch in 1856 – provoked by the failure of the Royal British Bank

THE BRITISH BRIGANDS' BANK.

'In the case of the Northumberland and Durham District Bank, which failed in 1857, and which had a capital of about £600,000, there was one company among its debtors, the Derwent Iron Company, which owed the bank £947,000 – a circumstance which found a somewhat sinister explanation in the fact that the managing director, who was the moving spirit of the whole bank, was also largely interested in the Derwent Iron Company.'

Magazine article 1893

1 What did the writer mean when he wrote that the Bank had 'failed in 1857'? Who could be hurt by such a failure?
2 To whom had the Bank granted a huge loan? Why would they need such a loan? What would they use it for?

3 What was 'sinister'? Why?

4 What was the attitude of the Punch cartoonist to the failure of the Royal British Bank, a year earlier, in 1856? Whom did he think had been hurt by the Bank's failure? Whom did he blame?

5 How could the Northumberland and Durham District Bank make a loan of £947,000 if its capital was only £600,000?

There were many bank failures in the eighteenth and early nineteenth centuries. A sudden lack of confidence, such as the threat of war or the failure of a neighbouring bank, sometimes started a panic with people trying to withdraw their savings, or cash their banknotes, before the bank closed its doors. The large number of failures was partly a result of the fact that there were hundreds of small banks.

Banking, insurance, trade and finance all grew rapidly during the period of the Agrarian, Industrial and Transport Revolutions. Without loans from private investors and banks there would have been a lack of capital to finance the building of new factories; the construction of canals and railways; or the purchase of the latest farm machinery. In this chapter you will see how and why the financial world developed rapidly during this period.

BANKING AND FINANCE

Goldsmiths as bankers

Banks and banknotes, as we know them, developed in the eighteenth and nineteenth centuries. Before that time, people who wanted to keep their

Goldsmiths at work, from an invitation to a meeting of the Goldsmiths' Company in 1707

money safe sometimes left it in the hands of a goldsmith. The goldsmith gave them a receipt promising to pay the bearer of the note the sum specified. These promissory notes, as they were called, were often made out for set sums of money. People later found it easier and less risky to exchange these pieces of paper when they did business, rather than go to the goldsmith's vaults to collect the gold in person. Sometimes they just wrote a letter to the goldsmith authorising the payment of a sum of money.

At first, depositors paid the goldsmith to keep their gold in his strongroom. But in time, the goldsmiths paid the depositors interest instead. They found they could make money by lending gold to people who needed a loan and who were prepared to pay a high rate of interest.

Governments also borrowed money, especially at time of war. Taxes were usually insufficient to meet the cost of keeping a large army. So they borrowed the necessary money from rich merchants and goldsmiths, and repaid the loan (with interest) out of taxes collected in succeeding years.

The Bank of England

In 1689 individual merchants and goldsmiths were not rich enough on their own to find the huge sums of money needed by the Government when war broke out with France. So Parliament authorised the setting up of the Bank of England in 1694, to enable the Government to borrow £1.2 million 'towards the carrying on the war against France'.

A group of financiers founded the Bank of England for this purpose. They acted together (jointly) to put up the cash (the stock) which was required. This is why it was called a joint-stock bank. Joint-stock banks or companies are those with many shareholders. So, if there are losses, there are many stockholders to support the bank or company until it begins to make profits again. The Bank of England was also allowed to buy and sell gold, and to lend money.

> 1 *How did the idea of the cheque and the banknote begin?*
> 2 *How did the Bank of England and the goldsmiths make their money?*
> 3 *Are all modern British banknotes issued by the Bank of England?*

The loan which started the Bank of England, led in 1696 to the beginning of the National Debt. This is the system, in which the Government borrows money from investors, paying them interest on these loans every year out of taxation. Financiers and merchants know the government can always repay the loan, since it controls taxes. Secure government stocks like these are called gilt-edged securities.

From the Government's viewpoint, the National Debt was an effective way of raising large loans and by the time of the battle of Waterloo, in

1815, the National Debt was over £800 million. At various times attempts had been made to pay back the money, but there were too many wars in the eighteenth century for this to happen.

In 1708, Parliament helped the Bank of England to become even stronger, when it passed a law which effectively prevented rival banks from setting themselves up in competition. The Act prevented all larger banks (those with more than six partners) from issuing banknotes. As a result, the Bank of England became the only joint-stock bank in London to issue banknotes.

In what ways is this banknote, issued in 1699, similar or dissimilar to a modern banknote?

The clearing banks

The new regulations restricted the freedom of financiers and goldsmiths to set up new banks, although it did not stop them from accepting money deposited by their customers, nor did it prevent their customers from writing cheques. So the banking system continued to develop.

In London, in the middle of the eighteenth century, the private banks were receiving hundreds of these cheques every day, many of them drawn on the other banks, requesting that a sum of money be paid into a customer's account. In the crowded, dangerous streets of Georgian London, it was inconvenient and unwise to send clerks round to collect large sums of money from each of the other banks in turn. In any case it was unnecessary, since the clerks from the other banks usually came round with similar cheques for similar sums of money, also seeking payment in cash.

By the late eighteenth century, the clerks began to meet each day in a chop house (an eating place) called the Five Bells, in the City of London. There they totalled up the sums of money payable on each cheque, worked out the differences between them, and settled these with cash. This was the beginning of the London Clearing House system.

Financing the Industrial Revolution

In the early years of the Industrial Revolution, financial backing for industry often came from private sources rather than from banks. Indeed, many small manufacturers financed the expansion of their businesses and the purchase of new machinery, from the profits they earned, rather than from loans. Even large companies, such as Josiah Wedgwood's, were built up in this way, by ploughing profits back into the business.

Local merchants and landowners were often willing to invest in the new, expanding business enterprises, which were stimulated by the coming of the machine in the eighteenth century. Sometimes, they lent money (and received interest on their loan) in exchange for a mortgage on the property. If the loan was not repaid they were then entitled to take over the mortgaged buildings.

Money to finance major projects, such as the turnpikes, canals and railways, often came from people who bought shares or stock in a company, in return for dividends (a share in the profits). The brokers (dealers), who dealt in stocks and shares, met in Jonathan's Coffee House in the City of London, not far from the Five Bells Chop House (where the bankers met) and Lloyd's Coffee House (where the insurers met). In 1773, trade had expanded so much that the stockbrokers did their business, instead, in the newly-built Stock Exchange. Public interest in holding shares mounted with the boom in new canals in the 1790s and with the extraordinary rush of investors, in the 1840s, seeking to put money into the new railway companies (see Chapter 3).

The growth of banking

Many banks were started throughout Britain in the late eighteenth and early nineteenth centuries. These small private banks issued their own banknotes and outside London this was the paper money normally used for payment, since the Bank of England largely confined its banking services to London.

Lack of adequate banks hampered merchants, farmers and industrialists, since they needed cash to pay wages and to buy machinery and equipment. Some even paid their workers with tokens. In addition, many of the landowners and farmers, who prospered after the enclosures, wanted to put their profits in banks where they could earn interest. Much of this surplus money from the land was eventually deposited by the small country bankers in accounts with the larger London banks. The London banks, in turn, lent some of the money to industrialists in the North and Midlands. So, indirectly, the farmers and landowners helped to finance new industry.

Between 1750 and 1815, hundreds of small country banks were founded. Many of them were offshoots of some other business, such as when a corn merchant agreed to provide banking facilities for his customers or suppliers. By 1810, there were 721 of these private banks in England and Wales with a very large number of different bank-notes in circulation. The drawbacks to the system were numerous.

(a)   It was relatively easy for criminals to forge the many different banknotes and so deceive the public. Some of the small private bankers were fraudulent and spent their customers' money or absconded with the cash.

(b)   The law did little to protect the customer, since the Act of 1708 prevented the establishment of large joint-stock banks with many backers. Many small banks had insufficient funds to tide them over difficulties. They were at risk, if they lent a large sum of money to a company which later went bankrupt. They lost their money and so did their creditors.

(c)   It was too easy to print paper money! As already shown, even the small banks could issue their own banknotes. In theory, these were backed by cash, but most banks issued more banknotes than they had cash in their vaults. They got into difficulties, if a number of customers suddenly demanded cash instead of banknotes, or wanted to withdraw the money they had on deposit. In time of war there were frequent 'runs' on banks and many failures, such as in 1793 and between 1814 and 1816. Even in peacetime there were bank crises when people lost confidence in banking, as in 1825, when sixty banks failed.

The 1825 crisis forced the Government to take action and in 1826 they made it possible for new joint-stock banks, backed by large groups of shareholders, to be established outside a 100 km ring round London. The new banks could issue banknotes and, being larger, were better able to meet unexpected demands on the bank's funds. As a result, many of the small private banks closed down, or merged with the larger banks. The Birmingham and Midland Bank, for instance, which was founded in 1836, had nine branches in 1891 when it merged with another bank to become the London City and Midland Bank. In 1833, the law was also clarified, to allow joint-stock banks to be established in London itself, although they were not allowed to issue banknotes.

The Bank Charter Act of 1844

In 1844, the Government decided to restrict the issue of new banknotes and to tie the value of those issued by the Bank of England, to actual deposits of gold. There had been a big argument in the early 1840s as to whether or not banks should be able to back every banknote they issued with an equivalent sum of gold.

The Government said they should and, in the 1844 Bank Charter Act, took steps to try to ensure that, in future, paper money was backed by gold sovereigns (the standard unit of currency).

The Bank Charter Act separated the Bank of England, which was still basically a privately-owned, and not a public, bank into two departments – the Banking and the Issue Departments. The Issue Department could only issue banknotes backed by gold in the bank's vaults plus an additional sum of £14 million in Government securities.

The Bank Charter Act also prevented all new banks from issuing banknotes and if they merged with other banks then all lost the right to issue banknotes. Sooner or later, this was bound to affect every bank in England and Wales, since big banks were safer than small. Fewer banks issued their own banknotes and Bank of England notes eventually came to be regarded as the normal standard currency. In Scotland the banking system was different, which is why some Scottish banks still issue their own notes to this day.

The private banks in England and Wales expanded the cheque system of payment as an alternative to the banknote. This was a highly effective method of transferring funds from one bank to another and, also, of granting credit to finance new projects.

Even so, at a time when industry and transport were growing rapidly, the curb on the issue of banknotes could have had a serious effect on the economy. Luckily, Californian gold (after 1849), and Australian gold (after 1850), ensured a steady increase in the supply of gold to the Bank of England – as the pictures on this and the next page from *The Illustrated London News* for 22 January 1853 show.

Landing Australian gold at the East India Dock in London in 1853

Carrying Australian gold to the Bank of England in 1853

1 *How was the gold carried from Australia to the East India Dock in London, and thence to the Bank of England? How was it protected in London?*
2 *What do you think happened to the London City and Midland Bank? When did it celebrate its 150th birthday?*
3 *Charles Dickens first used the phrase 'as good as gold' in* The Old Curiosity Shop, *published in 1841. Suggest a possible historical explanation for this phrase.*

Insurance

In 1726, Cesar de Saussure visited Britain and wrote in a letter that, in London:

'Every person has the facility of insuring his house against fire. There are in London two or three companies of insurance who for a small sum paid yearly, according to the value of the house, are bound to pay for it, or to rebuild it, should it be burnt down. These companies pay a considerable number of men to run and extinguish a fire as soon as signalled. All insured houses have on their fronts placards or slabs of metal, on which their number and also the mark or sign of the company is engraved.'

1 *What does the photograph show? To which part of the extract does it relate?*
2 *Do any of the buildings in your town have similar plaques on the walls?*

London grew rapidly in the eighteenth and nineteenth centuries, to become not only the largest and richest city in the world, but also the centre of the world's largest empire. As a result, many other important financial institutions flourished, besides the Bank of England and the London Clearing Banks. These included the Stock Exchange, the great finance houses and the commodity markets, specialising in goods such as tea and tin. London became the centre of world finance. The effect of this financial growth on the Industrial Revolution was immense, since loans, banking facilities and insurance could always be found in London. For instance, the Victorian successors to the traders who met at Lloyd's Coffee House in the eighteenth century accepted all types of insurance risks, from ships to steel-works.

> **3** What are the insurers, whose predecessors once did business in LLoyd's Coffee House, known as today?

TAXATION

The Government used the National Debt to raise loans, on the strength of its ability to increase taxation to pay the interest on the loan. In the early eighteenth century various methods were used to increase taxation:

> 'Beer pays three different taxations, every pack of playing cards pays sixpence [2.5p], and silver plate and goldsmith's work sixpence in the ounce [28 grams]. Householders pay taxes on windows and on chimneys, but you hear no complaints, and life is extraordinarily easy and comfortable.'
>
> Cesar de Saussure in 1729

In fact, so many goods were taxed, that people from all walks of life thought nothing of buying smuggled goods. Smugglers were not regarded as real criminals and even James Woodforde, a Norfolk country clergyman, used to have his gin delivered by the local smuggler. Many of the taxes were ridiculous, not least the iniquitous tax on windows, which only made householders brick them up to save paying more tax than they needed. This tax was eventually repealed in 1851.

> **1** What were some of the taxes which had to be paid in 1729?
> **2** What was the point of taxing windows and chimneys?
> **3** If you saw a house with bricked-up windows today, what might this tell you about the age of the house?

In 1799, William Pitt the Younger introduced a temporary tax on people's incomes. Those with an income of more than £60 a year had to pay a percentage of this in tax. The maximum was 10 per cent on all incomes of £200 or more. This was the first time that British taxpayers had to pay income tax, and the money (£6 million) was used to pay for the war against Napoleon. In 1802, the income tax law was repealed during a brief period of peace but re-introduced in 1803, when war broke out once more.

Income tax was abolished again in 1816, at the end of the Napoleonic Wars, but by then a very wide range of new taxes had been imposed on different types of goods and these brought in the revenue required by the Government. But the burden of taxation did not fall evenly on everyone. Income tax and the old taxes on land had previously been paid by those best able to afford them. Taxes on drinks, tobacco and household goods hit the poorest people hardest of all and contributed to the distress and unrest at this time (see Chapters 7 and 8).

Income tax was re-introduced, by Sir Robert Peel in 1842, at the rate of 7d in the pound [roughly 3p per £1]. Peel said it was for a period of three years.

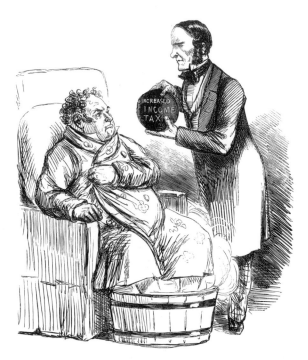

PEEL'S BANE AND ANTIDOTE.

SIR ROBERT (*loq.*) "Come, JOHNNY, be a good boy; take it like a Man and I'll give you a little bit of sugar."

THE GLADSTONE PILL.

DR. GL-DST-NE. "THERE, MR. BULL—SWALLOW IT AT ONCE, AND IT WILL RELIEVE YOUR CHEST DIRECTLY."

Punch *cartoons on income tax in 1845 (left) and 1860 (right)*

4 *Look at the cartoons from* Punch. *What happened to income tax in 1845, when the original three-year period expired?*

5 *When Gladstone became Chancellor of the Exchequer he also promised to abolish Income Tax. But he actually raised it to 9d in the pound [nearly 4p in the £1]. In which year?*

6 *In what ways are the two cartoons very similar? What do they tell you about popular attitudes to taxation in the nineteenth century?*

OVERSEAS TRADE

The Chartered Companies

Britain's trade with the rest of the world greatly increased during the Industrial Revolution. The growth of trade kept pace with industrial expansion, helped by the various wars in which Britain took a leading part in the eighteenth century. The navy gradually took command of the seas, giving protection to British merchant ships, whilst the development of a large empire provided Britain with huge sources of raw materials, such as wool from Australia, and huge new markets for goods such as cotton textiles.

Much of the credit for this expansion of trade must go to the merchants and seamen of the Chartered Companies who helped to create a demand for British products and opened up the areas with new sources of raw materials.

The Chartered Companies, founded in Tudor and Stuart times, had been given exclusive trading rights. For example, the Hudson's Bay Company traded in Canada whilst the Baltic Company traded in Russia. The most important organisation, however, was the East India Company, which originally traded in the East Indies but eventually came to control trade with India and China.

Many fortunes were made by the merchants and adventurers who traded overseas in the eighteenth century. Tea and silk from China were highly prized luxuries, as were the spices of the East. The East India Company became very powerful; so much so that it became the virtual ruler of a large part of India, with the aid of its own private army.

The South Sea Bubble

Fortunes were sometimes lost by the Chartered Companies, as well as won, and in 1720 there was a huge scandal, the South Sea Bubble, in which a large number of investors lost most of the money they had put into the South Sea Company.

The South Sea Company had been founded in 1711 to raise money for the Government. In return the Government agreed to pay interest on the capital and granted the new company a monopoly of trade with Central and South America, and the Pacific coast of North America – an area controlled by the Spanish and known as the South Seas. The South Sea Company later got the sole benefit of the trading rights in the Spanish Indies which were conceded to Britain at the Treaty of Utrecht in 1713. In particular, they secured the Asiento contract to supply 4,800 negro slaves a year to Spanish America.

In 1720, the South Sea Company even agreed to take over part of the National Debt, and investors were so impressed by the scale of this proposal, that they kept on buying its shares. A merchant with £77 worth of South Sea stock in 1711, saw his shareholding rise in value to £290 on 7 April 1720 and soar to £890, two months later, on 2 June. But people began to sell their shares, the 'bubble' burst and the value of South Sea Company stock fell dramatically, losing large sums of money for many of its foolish investors.

Hogarth satire, c. 1720 – the South Sea Bubble

You can see what one critic, the artist William Hogarth, thought in this picture. 'Honesty' is being broken on the wheel, 'Honour' is flogged by a ruffian armed with a pistol and dagger, whilst a bedraggled 'Trade' lies on the ground (in the bottom right-hand corner).

---

1 *Which two famous London landmarks are shown in this picture?*
2 *What does the inscription on the monument say? What disaster does the real monument commemorate?*
3 *Which characters represent the directors of the South Sea Company (Hogarth thought they had taken people for a ride)? Where are the investors?*
4 *Where and why are people shown doing business with the devil? What has happened to honest business, to trade and to honour? Why are religious leaders shown gambling? Write a short essay saying what you think Hogarth thought about the South Sea Bubble.*

The Triangular Trade

'To be sold, a negro boy, aged eleven years. Enquire of the Virginia Coffee-house in Threadneedle Street, behind the Royal Exchange.'

Advert in the *London Daily Journal* 1728

'1751 John Norton, in company with Francis Jerdone, purchases a store-house in York Town with the river at one door and the street at the other. The young men of the town are grouped in various "adventures". Messrs Norton, Thruston & Co. have bought up a consignment of Tobacco. Messrs John Norton, David Anderson and Francis Jerdone, one third each, buy 32 negroes imported by Messrs. Rootes & Hill. They pay £1037 8s 0d [£1,037.40] for the lot. The duty thereon is £47 17s 8d [£47.88]. Their net profit each is £65 17s 5d [£65.87]. Norton and Jameson also speculate in this commodity.

From *John Norton and Sons, Merchants of London and Virginia*, edited by Frances Norton Mason, 1937

---

1 *Where is Virginia? How were John Norton's premises ideally suited for his business as a merchant? What did he trade in? What connections are there between this item and the advertisement in 1728?*
2 *What did the writer mean by the phrase 'Norton and Jameson also speculate in this commodity'? What was the commodity? In what other ways was 'this commodity' spoken of, as if it were just a commercial product like tobacco?*
3 *Why does the writer refer to these trading activities as 'adventures'? What was an 'adventurer' and a 'business venture'?*

4 *On average, how much did the slave dealers have to pay for each slave? What was the duty on each slave? Why did they have to pay a duty? To whom was the duty paid? What did they sell their 'lot' of slaves for, if each made a profit of £65 17s 5d [£65.87]? What was the average cost of each slave to the plantation owners who bought them?*

PLAN OF THE LOWER DECK OF THE SHIP *VIGILANTE*

Plan of a slave ship

5 *Write two or three sentences describing the conditions in which the slaves travelled across the Atlantic.*

Slavery was an infamous trade. Yet many respectable merchants in Britain and America grew rich on its profits. The slave trade had been organised since 1672 by the Royal African Company. Slaves were purchased from dealers trading in West Africa and then shipped across the Atlantic to work on the plantations in the Caribbean and in the colonies of North America.

The traders had devised a very profitable trade route, known as the 'Triangular Trade' route. Ships set out from Liverpool or Bristol, on the first stage of the journey, bound for West Africa, carrying trinkets, badges, buttons and other cheap goods to be exchanged for slaves.

The slaves had often been captured in battle and, yoked together, were driven in chains to the coast by African or Arab slave dealers. There they were packed on to slave ships for the 'middle passage' across the Atlantic. For six weeks or so, they lay shackled together on the decks, scarcely able to move, subject to the miseries of storms at sea, ravaged by hunger and disease. It was hardly surprising that barely half survived the journey from their homes in Africa to the alien plantations of America.

The proceeds from the sale of the slaves were re-invested in plantation products, such as sugar, rum, tobacco and cotton, which were in great demand in Britain, and sent on the third and final leg of the Triangular Trade route back to Bristol or Liverpool. In this way a small investment in cheap manufactures on the first leg of the journey could pay eventually for a valuable cargo on the return journey to Britain, and could provide huge profits when the ship returned to port.

The slave trade was abolished in Britain in 1807, largely as the result of William Wilberforce's crusade in Parliament against the evils of slavery. In 1833, slavery itself was abolished throughout the British Empire.

Overseas investment

The City of London helped to finance trade overseas, and, in the nineteenth century, substantial sums of money were invested in government stocks, railways and other projects in Europe, the United States and South America, and later in the territories of the Empire. These investments earned interest which also went back to Britain. In addition, the money invested was usually spent on British machinery and equipment.

FREE TRADE

British Exports 1700–1850
The sizes of the circles are in proportion to the total export trade (excluding re-exports of colonial products)

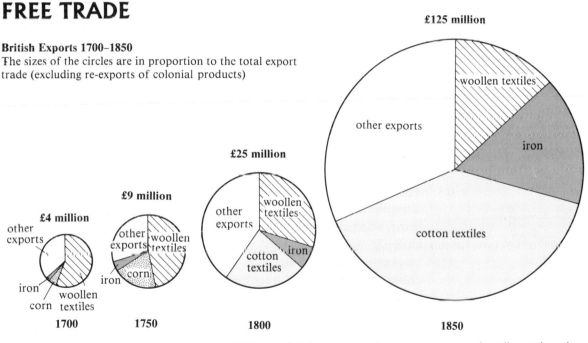

British exports 1700–1850. Write two or three sentences to describe and analyse these graphs.

Mercantilism

There were many opportunities for overseas business 'adventures' in the seventeenth and eighteenth centuries. Yet British governments exercised tight control over this trade, mainly by charging customs duties on goods imported from foreign countries, making them more expensive than those made in Britain.

This tight control of trade was part of the Mercantilist System. This was the general trading policy in the era before Free Trade. Its main features were as follows.

(a)   The encouragement of exports and the discouragement of imports, in order to ensure that the balance of trade was always in Britain's favour. Otherwise gold and silver would leave the country and it was thought that this would weaken Britain. Tariffs, or duties, on foreign imports 'protected' the British manufacturer. Protection was a key feature of Mercantilism. Exports were encouraged by giving bounties (payments of money) to exporters of British goods. In addition, restrictions were put on workers who wanted to get jobs abroad, since it was feared they might pass on industrial secrets to foreign competitors.

(b)   The encouragement of trade in order to expand and develop the merchant navy. This was done so that there would always be a large number of trained merchant seamen who could be recruited into the navy to defend Britain in time of war. This is why the Navigation Act of 1660 began as follows:

'An Act for the increase of shipping and encouragement of the navigation wherein the wealth, safety and strength of this kingdom is so much concerned.'

The Act went on to prevent foreign ships trading with British colonies in Asia, Africa and America. Only British or colonial ships could export or import goods from the colonies.

(c)   The granting of trading monopolies to the great Chartered Companies, such as the East India Company, to further trade and bring additional wealth to Britain.

(d)   Colonies were to be used to supply raw materials for the home market. Many 'enumerated goods', such as tobacco, sugar and indigo dyestuff, could only be exported to Britain. They could not be sent directly to merchants in Europe. Many of these goods were later re-exported from Bristol and Liverpool.

(e)   Regulations were also made to prevent colonial manufacturers from competing with those in Britain. For instance, the felt hats, ploughs and woollen cloth they used had to come from Britain.

These regulations on trade relating to the treatment of colonies were known as the 'Old Colonial System' and they were a constant source of grievance to settlers, particularly the colonists of North America, who resented the imposition of controls designed to benefit people living 5,000 km away.

In practice, the trading regulations were often ignored or evaded since they were difficult to enforce. Smuggling was common. Ordinary people bought tobacco, spirits and tea, knowing they had been smuggled into the country without payment of Customs and Excise duties. The serious Porteous Riot in Edinburgh, in 1736, even had its origins in a public demonstration at the execution of a smuggler. Captain Porteous fired on the crowd and was later lynched by the mob.

'The Wealth of Nations'

In 1776 the American colonists signed the Declaration of Independence asserting that 'liberty' was one of their fundamental rights. In the same year Adam Smith's book *The Wealth of Nations* was published. Smith was a Scottish economist. Like the American colonists he also preached liberty. His book made a deep impression on the British Prime Minister, William Pitt, and on hundreds of other influential people in British affairs.

In his book Smith said there should be freedom for manufacturers, farmers, merchants and financiers to do their work with a minimum of government interference. There should be Free Trade – no customs duties, no restrictions on trade, no attempt by government to control the economy.

Adam Smith was opposed to monopolies, such as the exclusive trading rights enjoyed by the East India Company in India and China. He wanted free enterprise – competition between businesses. Products should be sold at whatever price people were prepared to pay for them. Adam Smith said governments should leave trade alone and, in time, the French phrase '*laissez-faire*' (meaning 'leave it alone') was used to describe this policy.

Laissez-faire was later used to justify non-interference by the government in many other matters as well as trade, such as whether legislation should be passed to prevent factory owners from making their employees work long hours.

---

1 *Which of the following is an example of Free Trade?*
   (a) *Smugglers landing rum and tobacco in Cornwall.*
   (b) *The abolition of the Corn Laws in 1846.*
   (c) *Lower duties on Portuguese wine imported into Britain in return for lower duties on British textile exports to Portugal (1703).*
2 *In what ways was Free Trade the opposite of the Old Colonial System and the ideas of Mercantilism?*

The change from Mercantilism to Free Trade

Adam Smith's arguments were so compelling that, in time, government policy changed from one of regulation and restriction to one of Free Trade. Four government ministers, in particular, brought about this conversion.

William Pitt the Younger

(a) **William Pitt the Younger** was a staunch admirer of Adam Smith. Pitt reformed and simplified the system of duties imposed on foreign goods entering the country. But he was severely restricted in what he could do to bring about Free Trade, since for most of the time he was in government the country was at war. His most successful trading agreement was with France in 1786, in which Britain agreed to lower duties on French wines and other goods, in return for lower duties on British exports to France. But three years later, the French Revolution rendered the agreement useless.

Britain was changing rapidly. The steam engine, better communications, the Napoleonic Wars, the growth of the Empire, poverty and rioting at home, were all factors which had an effect on government attitudes to trade. Reform was in the air (as you will see in Chapter 8).

(b) In the 1820s, **William Huskisson**, as President of the Board of Trade, modified the Navigation Acts but they still gave preference to British merchants. Even Adam Smith thought the Navigation Acts were wise, since they strengthened British naval defence. However, in 1823, Huskisson did allow British colonies to trade directly with Europe, and he also gave preference to colonial imports by charging lower ('differential') duties than those imposed on similar imports from elsewhere. Thus, wool from Australia was charged a lower rate of duty than wool from Europe.

Huskisson lowered the duties payable on many imported raw materials, such as tin, and negotiated agreements with other European trading nations, whereby each side agreed to lower its tariffs in order to encourage freer trade. The Government was given the power to do this by the Reciprocity of Duties Act in 1823.

---

1 *How did ordinary people stand to gain or lose by the lowering of customs duties on imports?*

2 *Which of the measures introduced by Pitt and Huskisson could actually be called* laissez-faire*?*

(c) In 1841, **Sir Robert Peel** became Prime Minister, and eventually abolished the Corn Laws which restricted the entry of foreign corn into Britain. A substantial campaign was waged by the Anti-Corn

Law League, with the active support of the manufacturers, who stood to gain most from the abolition of the restrictions on grain imports (see page 32).

This was one of the most important Free Trade measures of the nineteenth century, but it was not the only improvement to be made by Peel. He re-introduced income tax in 1842 because his budget in that year reduced many customs duties. He followed this in the next few years by abolishing customs duties on over 600 types of goods and reducing duties on another 1,000 items.

In 1853, the restrictions on foreign shipping, imposed by the Navigation Acts, were finally abandoned. By this time the new Tory government, with Disraeli as one of its leading members, had already abandoned the idea of protection and was now converted to the idea and benefits of Free Trade.

Sir Robert Peel

A DIP IN THE FREE TRADE SEA.
"THERE, TAKE OFF HIS COAT LIKE A GOOD LITTLE BEN,
AND COME TO HIS COBDEN."

Write two or three sentences commenting on the underlying significance of this cartoon, published in Punch *in 1852.*

(d) The final abandonment of 'protection' was masterminded in 1853 by **William Ewart Gladstone** the new Chancellor of the Exchequer, when he abolished duties on many articles, such as soap, and drastically lowered them on others, such as tea. In 1860, he completed the transformation by abolishing almost all the remaining duties apart from the few commodities which brought in the greatest revenue, such as wine, tobacco, tea and spirits. From that time onwards, until the 1930s, Britain traded freely with the rest of the world. The duties which remained were designed, not to discourage foreign competition, but simply to earn revenue to pay for government expenditure.

FURTHER QUESTIONS AND EXERCISES

1 *Read these extracts from the diary written by James Woodforde, a Norfolk country parson.*

1 September 1784   *Mr.Hardy and Boy fastened up 3 Windows with Brick for me.*

13 December 1794   *Busy all the Morning almost in bottling two tubs of Gin, that came by Moonshine this Morn' very early.*

31 January 1799   *Paid Js Pegg this Morning a Quarters Land-Tax £3 0s 0d.*

19 April 1799   *I delivered this Morning my Income Tax-Paper to Js Pegg in which I have charged myself £20 per Annum.*

13 April 1802   *To James Pegg paid £3 6s 8d [£3.33] being two Months Income Tax – at twenty Pounds per Annum – Valued at £200 per Annum. The above Tax to be repealed this Month – it being universally disliked.*

(a) *What jobs were done by Mr Hardy and James Pegg?*

(b) *What did Parson Woodforde mean when he talked of gin having come 'by Moonshine'?*

(c) *How do these diary extracts support the view that all taxes, not just income tax, were 'universally disliked' at this time? How many different taxes did Parson Woodforde mention? (N.B. one tax is not directly stated but it can be deduced from a diary extract.)*

(d) *What was Parson Woodforde's annual income in 1802? How many times better off was he than a farm labourer earning 7s 0d [35p] a week?*

(e) *What was the rate of income tax at that time? Was it (i) 5 per cent, (ii) 10 per cent, (iii) 20 per cent, or (iv) 30 per cent of a person's annual income? When, why, and by whom had it been introduced?*

2 Draw a graph to show the following average yearly figures:

	British exports (including re-exports)	British imports
1720s	£7.5 million	£7.0 million
1760s	£15.0 million	£10.5 million
1800s	£37.5 million	£28.5 million
1840s	£141.5 million	£79.5 million

(a) In which 40-year period did trade grow at the fastest rate?

(b) How do these figures reflect the growth of industry during the period 1720 to 1840?

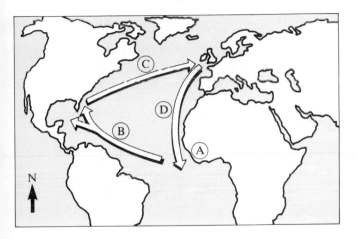

3 What trade route is illustrated by the map?

(a) What dealers were to be found at A in the eighteenth century?

(b) What was route B called?

(c) What products were shipped along each of the routes marked B, C, D?

4 Describe and account for the growth of banking and finance in the eighteenth and early nineteenth centuries.

5 Comment on the significance of each of the following items of Parliamentary legislation:

(a) Navigation Act of 1660,

(b) the Bank Charter Act of 1844,

(c) Bank of England Act of 1694,

(d) Abolition of the slave trade in 1807,

(e) Reciprocity of Duties Act of 1823,

(f) Peel's Budget of 1842.

6 What were the advantages and disadvantages of Free Trade?

7 Define and explain the importance of each of the following:

(a) Mercantilism,   (d) Laissez-faire,

(b) the South Sea Bubble,   (e) Protection.

(c) the Old Colonial System,

Chapter Five

Population

INTRODUCTION

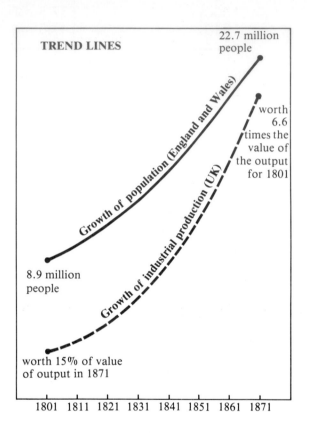

TREND LINES

22.7 million people

Growth of population (England and Wales)

worth 6.6 times the value of the output for 1801

Growth of industrial production (UK)

8.9 million people

worth 15% of value of output in 1871

1801 1811 1821 1831 1841 1851 1861 1871

Trends in population and industrial growth in the nineteenth century

---

Look at the graph above.

1 By how many times did:
  (a) the population of England and Wales,
  (b) United Kingdom industrial production,
  grow between 1801 and 1871? What does the graph suggest?

2 How could population growth affect the growth of industry; or industrial expansion affect the growth in population?

3 Why is the graph on its own not enough to prove that there is any connection between population growth and industrial expansion?

This chapter will show how the population of Britain grew rapidly at the same time that agricultural and industrial production rose sharply. This is why some historians used to think that industrial growth was the cause of the rapid rise in population. However, the population of other much less industrialised European countries also grew rapidly, though not as fast as that of the UK, during this period.

Industrial and agricultural growth undoubtedly played an indirect part in stimulating the rapid growth of population in Britain as a result of improvements in living standards and better, cheaper, more plentiful food.

Other historians thought it was the other way round; that population growth helped to stimulate the growth of agricultural and industrial production; by creating more mouths to feed, more bodies to clothe, more people to employ. It was not the only cause of industrial and agricultural growth however. If it had been, then Finland would have experienced a similar Industrial Revolution at the same time. Like England and Wales, the Finnish population also doubled in size between 1801 and 1851.

Nowadays, most historians admit they cannot be absolutely certain why there was a sharp growth in population at the time of the Industrial and Agrarian Revolutions. Some of the different factors, which may have had some effect on population growth, are discussed in this chapter. But they made their effect at different times and their real significance is often hard to determine.

CHANGES IN THE METHODS OF MEASURING POPULATION GROWTH

Estimating population before 1801

The first official census in Great Britain was held in 1801. Before that date we have no way of accurately knowing the size of the population and instead have to rely on estimates. One of the earliest of these estimates, based on tax records, was made by Gregory King, in 1695. He calculated that the population of England and Wales at that time was 5.5 milllion. Modern estimates of the population of England and Wales in 1700 more or less agree – and put it at 5.8 million.

When the first census was organised in 1801, details of baptisms in the eighteenth century were also collected, and John Rickman, who prepared the first four census reports, worked out past populations of England and Wales from these records.

He calculated the average number of annual baptisms in England and Wales in the late 1790s and divided the 1801 Census population by this number. He worked out that, on average, there was one baptism a year for every 36 people. Since he had records of baptisms throughout the

John Rickman's estimates of the population of England and Wales

1700	5.5 million	1740	6.1 million	1780	8.0 million
1710	5.2 million	1750	6.5 million	1790	8.7 million
1720	5.6 million	1760	6.7 million	1800	9.2 million
1730	5.8 million	1770	7.4 million		

eighteenth century, he used this ratio to estimate the size of the population of England and Wales.

Rickman's method of calculating the population was ingenious, but unfortunately the records of baptisms cannot be relied upon. Modern historians, who have studied parish registers, have found that there are frequent gaps; some even miss out a whole year and there are careless mistakes.

Bills of Mortality have also been studied. These provide birth and death statistics for the bigger towns. In a newspaper printed in mid-July 1721, London was said to have christened 306 babies and buried 421 people in the previous week.

The first accurate birth-rate figures in England and Wales only became available after 1836, when new legislation made it compulsory to register births, marriages and deaths. The Factory Act of 1833 (see Chapter 8) prohibited the employment of children under nine years in textile mills, so it then became necessary to have an official register of births. The official records in 1838 show that, on average, there was one birth for every 31 people. By the end of the century the ratio had slightly widened to one birth for every 34 people.

---

1 Did London's population rise or fall in mid-July 1721?
2 John Rickman calculated that there were 152,540 baptisms in England and Wales in 1700. What was his estimate of the total population for that year?
3 Why was Rickman unwise to assume that the ratio of baptisms to numbers of people would always be the same throughout the eighteenth century? How could a rise or fall in the numbers of babies dying at birth affect his estimates of population?
4 Write two or three sentences to say whether you think John Rickman's method of estimating population was likely to be reliable or not.

As the table shows, Rickman estimated that the population of England and Wales rose slowly from 5.5 million in 1700 to 6.5 million in 1750 and then, more rapidly, to 9.2 million at the time of the first census. Modern estimates, on the other hand, tend to put the population of

England and Wales at about 5.8 million in 1700 and about 6.4 million in 1750, whilst the figure quoted for the 1801 Census gives a population of 8.9 million.

> **5** What was the percentage increase in population between 1700 and 1750, and between 1750 and 1800:
> (a) using John Rickman's estimates,
> (b) using modern estimates of the population?
> Is there any significant difference between these figures?

The official Census of 1801

Since 1801, the census has been taken every ten years, the only exception being 1941 (during World War II).

On the first census forms only simple questions were asked, so the range of data published in the Census Report was fairly limited. Even so, it meant that people could now know accurately the populations of the different countries of Great Britain and those of the separate counties and towns. In 1811, people could compare the 1801 figures with those compiled for the new census. They could see which areas were growing fast and which, if any, were decreasing in size. The information was essential, not only for governments, but also for people with business interests. Reformers could demonstrate the glaring injustice of large cities unrepresented in Parliament (see Chapter 7).

> **1** Draw three graphs to show the population figures in England and Wales, Scotland and Ireland, using the statistics listed in the table below.

Year	England and Wales	Scotland	Ireland
		(millions)	
1801	8.9	1.6	5.2 estimate
1811	10.2	1.8	6.0 estimate
1821	12.0	2.1	6.8
1831	13.9	2.4	7.8
1841	15.9	2.6	8.2
1851	17.9	2.9	6.6
1861	20.1	3.1	5.8
1871	22.7	3.4	5.4

2 By which year had the 1801 population of England and Wales more than doubled in size? By which year did the 1801 population of Scotland do the same? What happened to the population of Ireland during this period?

3 Which was the greater percentage increase in population in England and Wales:
  (a) from 8.9 to 10.2 million (1801–11), or,
  (b) from 20.1 to 22.7 million (1861–71)?

4 Assuming that modern estimates of the population of England and Wales are correct for 1701 (5.8 million) and 1751 (6.4 million), work out the percentage increases between 1701 and 1751, 1751 and 1801, 1801 and 1851, 1851 and 1901 (32.5 million). Which fifty-year period saw the steepest percentage rise in population? Write a short paragraph commenting on these figures.

The census after 1801

The censuses from 1841 onwards give a much fuller picture of the population of Britain. In 1841, for instance, the Census Report listed 377,662 people employed in the cotton industry – 48 per cent of them female and 135,000 of them under twenty years of age. It also recorded a total of 908,825 female servants and 256,408 male servants. The Census Commissioners thought this especially worthy of comment and suggested that it was a matter for congratulation, that so large a number of women:

> 'should be comprehended in a class in which habits of steady industry, of economy, and of attention to the maintenance of a good character, are so necessary as that of domestic servants'.

1 What did they mean by this?
2 What do you think the Census Commissioners thought the role of a working-class woman ought to be?

The census of 1841 also recorded the birthplace of everyone living in Britain at that time, showing for example the number of people from Ireland who had moved to England. These statistics have enabled historians to examine the extent to which people migrated from one area to another.

The extra details given in the 1841 and following censuses were made possible by enlarging the size and scope of the forms. The forms were delivered by enumerators who each had about 200 homes to visit. It was their job to see that the forms were completed properly.

In 1881, for instance, householders had to fill in the following details for each resident on census night; a) name and surname, b) relation to head of family, c) whether married, d) sex, e) age last birthday, f) rank, profession or occupation (e.g. farmer, scholar, dairymaid), g) where born, h) whether handicapped. Since many householders were illiterate (see Chapter 9), enumerators often spent much of their time before Census Day explaining how to fill in the form.

When the forms were collected many were found to be incomplete or inaccurate, householders excusing themselves on the grounds that they were 'no scholars'. One enumerator at the 1871 Census said that:

> 'in the column for age it is not uncommon to find "306" for "36"; and the geography of place of birth needs a little attention, hazy notions being entertained as to the counties. The "occupation" is very often given in technical phrases that need a little more light. In ship-building towns "holder-up" will at times imply a riveter's labourer; in mines there are "spraggers", "trappers", "callers" and others.'

The enumerator collected the missing information – sometimes having to rely on 'the memory of the mother supplying all the details with tolerable accuracy'. All these details were later re-classified by a huge army of clerks at the Census Office. Totals were compiled for different categories and for different areas (e.g. wards, parishes, towns, counties). At each stage the copying was checked and double-checked. One clerk invented 'averages for himself, and filled his next sheet with marvellous rapidity. He was, however, promptly detected and dismissed'.

---

3 Make up a census form along the lines of the questions asked in 1881. Complete the form for the people living in your home today. Would you have needed the help of the enumerator to fill in the form?

4 Why do you think it may be necessary to treat nineteenth-century census statistics with a certain amount of caution?

5 Do you think that modern census statistics are likely to be more or less accurate than the 1871 Census statistics? Give reasons for your answer.

Causes of the changes in population size and rate of growth

Basically there are only four factors which cause the rise or fall of the population of a town, county or country. These are increases, or decreases, in:

(a) the birth rate,

(b) the death rate,

(c) the rate of immigration,

(d) the rate of emigration.

If the number of births keeps pace with the number of deaths, then the population remains static. But if there are more deaths than births, the population falls. Similarly, if there are more emigrants (people leaving the country) than there are immigrants (people coming into the country), then this also causes the population to fall.

---

1 *What will happen to the population figures if the number of births exceeds the number of deaths?*

2 *What will happen to the population figures if the number of immigrants exceeds the number of emigrants?*

3 *To what figure will the population of a country of 10 million rise or fall, if the number of emigrants in one year is 100,000; the number of immigrants is 150,000; and there are 250,000 births and 200,000 deaths?*

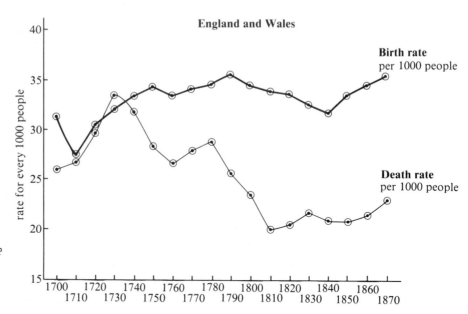

The rise and fall of the birth and death rates in England and Wales (1700–1870)

The graph shows the fluctuation in the birth and death rates in England and Wales between 1700 and 1870. The figures from 1700 to 1840 are only estimates, based on local records. As late as 1860 the official figures (based on compulsory registrations of births, deaths and marriages) are thought to underestimate the actual numbers involved.

As you can see, the death rate usually (but not always) followed the same trend as the birth rate. This was caused by the high level of infant mortality in the eighteenth and nineteenth centuries.

The important thing to note was that between 1730 and 1870 the birth rate remained fairly constant, the figure fluctuating between about 31 and 36 births per 1,000 people. The death rate, on the other hand, is estimated to have fallen from a maximum of over 33 per 1,000 people (in 1730) to 20 per 1,000 (in 1810), and then to have risen slowly to about 23 per 1,000 (in 1870).

---

4 *Look at the graph. When would you have expected the total population of England and Wales:*
(a) to have fallen,
(b) to have remained steady,
(c) to have risen?
Compare your answers with John Rickman's estimates and the census figures for 1801–71.

5 *Use a ruler to measure the gap between the birth rate and death rate for each of the years shown on the graph. In which year was there the widest difference between the birth rate and the death rate? When was the biggest percentage increase in population in England and Wales? Write two or three sentences commenting on these facts.*

6 *Which was the most important single reason for the rapid growth of population in England and Wales between 1750 and 1870:*
(a) a rise in the birth rate,
(b) a fall in the death rate?

REASONS WHY THE BIRTH RATE ROSE AND FELL

The birth rate was high throughout the eighteenth and nineteenth centuries. This high fertility was due to a number of factors.

Age and sex of the population

The population as a whole was young. In 1851 roughly half the population of England and Wales was under 23. As the overall death rate fell (see page 182), so the number of women able to bear children increased. In those parts of the country where the number of older people was above the national average, the birth rate tended to be lower than normal, since they had fewer women of child-bearing age.

In general, the growing industrial towns had a higher proportion of young people than the rural areas did. This was partly because many young people left the countryside to work in the towns where there were more jobs. Having a job meant they could settle down earlier and get married. The large mill or factory, employing hundreds of hands, offered far greater opportunities to find a partner than the country village did.

As a result the factory towns of the North and Midlands had a higher than average birth rate. This, coupled with the general lowering of the death rate, was one of the main reasons why they grew more rapidly than the country market towns.

Family size

In the eighteenth and nineteenth centuries, there was little incentive to practise birth control. Women continued to produce children during their child-bearing years, one reason being that many infants died at birth or in the first five years of childhood. As a result large families with as many as ten children were normal. In the agricultural counties, large families, together with a healthier rural environment, made it possible for the population of the counties to continue to grow, despite the movement to the towns.

Marriage and employment

The earlier people married, the earlier they would start a family. In the eighteenth century, however, many young men had to undertake long periods of apprenticeship. This meant that it was a long time before they could settle down and raise a family. Apprenticeship began to decline during the Industrial Revolution with the fall in the number of craftsmen and the rise of the factory worker. A greater proportion of young workers could marry earlier than had been the case in the past. Some historians used to believe that this was one of the main reasons for the high birth rate in the eighteenth and nineteenth centuries. However, this could only have had a slight effect as the changeover from domestic to factory industry took place mainly in the period after 1790.

> **1** *Look at the graph on page 178. Does it support the theory that the decline in apprenticeship helped to cause a rise in the birth rate?*

Farmworkers were also said to have married earlier, since the old practice of the hired hand living on the farm with the farmer's family had declined. The Speenhamland System (for full details see page 267) may have helped to accelerate this process, since it gave a farm worker with a large family a much greater income than that of the single man. This too used to be thought of as one of the most important causes of the growth in population, since the Speenhamland System (which was mainly confined to the rural counties of southern England) was only effective between 1795 and 1834. This was when the sharpest rise in population occurred.

> **2** *Why do modern historians think that the Speenhamland System could only have had a slight effect on the population growth of the country as a whole?*
>
> **3** *Does the birth-rate graph on page 178 support the suggestion that the Speenhamland System was a contributory cause of population growth in the early nineteenth century?*

Similarly, historians also used to think that the widespread employment of children in the factories of the North encouraged parents to have large families. The more members of a family earning a wage, the greater was the family income. But (as you will see in Chapter 8) Parliament introduced the first effective Factory Acts, to curb child employment in mines and factories, in 1833, 1842, 1844, 1847 and 1850.

> **4** *Does the birth-rate graph on page 178 support the suggestion that the employment of child labour in factories could have been a contributory cause of population growth in the early nineteenth century?*

Infant mortality

A high birth rate in itself does not mean that the population will rise. What is significant is the number of children who survive the perils of infancy, as you can see if you compare the following Sources A, B, C with the graph of birth and death rates.

Source A

Percentage of infants in LONDON who died before the age of five

1730–1749 74.5%	1770–1789 51.5%	1810–1830 32.0%
1750–1769 63.0%	1790–1809 41.5%	

Dr Andrew Combe's estimates 1840

Source B

1880: 23.8% of infants in ENGLAND AND WALES died before the age of five years

Dictionary of Statistics 1899

Source C

Infant mortality rate (deaths under 1 year) in ENGLAND AND WALES

1841–50 15.4%	1851–60 15.3%	1861–70 15.4%

European Historical Statistics 1750–1975, B. R. Mitchell 1981

1 *Draw a graph to show the percentage of children surviving the first five years of childhood, in London, during the period 1730–1830 (according to Dr Combe).*
2 *If Dr Combe's figures for infant mortality are reliable, what do they tell us about London between 1730 and 1830? What was one of the basic reasons for the growth in population?*
3 *Why can Dr Combe's figures not be directly compared with the other infant mortality statistics?*
4 *What do the statistics for England and Wales between 1841 and 1870 suggest? Compare these figures with the graph of birth and death rates beween those dates. Why did the population continue to rise?*

REASONS WHY THE DEATH RATE ROSE AND FELL

The rise and fall of the death rate has been attributed to a number of different factors. Some can be proved (such as statistics showing the numbers of people who died in the major cholera epidemics). The effects of other factors, such as better and more plentiful food, are almost impossible to prove.

At different times, and in different parts of the country, for a variety of reasons, the death rate fluctuated. But overall, it was always substantially lower than the birth rate and as a result the population grew.

In looking at the causes of the rise or fall in the death rate, we can see that some were positive causes such as improved diet which helped to promote or preserve good health. Others were negative, such as alcoholism which only did good when it was not present.

Diet

The Agrarian Revolution brought substantial improvements in the production of food in Britain. Excellent harvests in the 1730s meant cheaper bread. The use of roots and green fodder crops in the eighteenth century meant that animals could be kept through the winter, and therefore there was less need to salt pork or beef for winter storage. In theory, people in Britain now had the opportunity to enjoy a better, healthier diet – eating more grain, potatoes, meat, dairy products, fresh vegetables and fruit. They not only got enough to eat, they also consumed the protein and vitamins which help to give the body resistance to disease. This was one reason why well-to-do families lived longer, on average, than poor families.

Nonetheless, there were often complaints about the quality of the food on sale in the towns. In the novel *Humphrey Clinker* by Tobias Smollett, published in 1771, a country squire complained about the food he ate in London, as a 'tallowy rancid mass, called butter, manufactured with candle-grease and kitchen-stuff'.

---

1 *What do you think he was describing when he referred to: 'a paste, mixed-up with chalk, alum and bone-ashes; insipid to the taste – people prefer it because it is whiter'?*
2 *What was the significance, in 1771, of his comment about 'fresh eggs, imported from France and Scotland'?*

Without improvements in farming and increased output of food, it would certainly have been difficult to sustain the growth in population. In particular, the introduction of the potato provided subsistence farmers, in the poorer, wetter lands of Ireland and western Britain, with a crop which gave them a plain but satisfactory diet. When the potato crop failed in the 1840s, it provoked an appalling famine, which not only directly caused the deaths of up to a million people, but indirectly caused a net loss of population in Ireland, since it was the main reason why a great number of Irish people emigrated to America.

The famine in Ireland – Victorian engraving showing starving people outside the gate of a workhouse

---

3 *How did the Victorian artist try to show the appalling effects of the famine in Ireland in the 1840s?*
4 *Look back at the population statistics for Ireland between 1801 and 1871. What was the net loss of population to Ireland between 1841 and 1871?*

5 *When was the greatest decade of loss:*
(a) 1841–50
(b) 1851–60
(c) 1861–70?

Improvements in transport (mainly the railways after 1840) also helped to make it easier and cheaper for farmers to deliver food to market. People were no longer so reliant on the success of the local harvest and on local farmers for their supply of meat, vegetables and milk. There was less starvation, since food could be taken to stricken areas by rail.

But despite all the improvements in food supply, many poor people still lived close to starvation level. As you will see in Chapter 7, there were frequent riots in protest at high bread prices. There were periods of great distress in mainland Britain as well as in Ireland, particularly in the period between 1811-20, the time when the percentage increase in population reached its peak. Lack of sufficient and adequate food was a contributory cause of ill-health, since people suffering from malnutrition are more likely to catch epidemic diseases.

Alcoholism

In the early eighteenth century large numbers of people died each year from alcoholism, the result of drinking cheap gin, which was available at a ridiculously low price. In the painting *Gin Lane* by Hogarth, painted in 1751, a sign reads 'Drunk for 1d. Dead drunk for 2d'. The poor found it a cheap way to forget their troubles and sink them in oblivion. The boom in gin-drinking began in the 1720s, when the government freed gin from many of the restrictions controlling its sale. But by 1751 they had to take decisive action and restricted its availability and imposed higher taxes.

1 *In which period, between 1700 and 1870, did the death rate exceed the birth rate?*
2 *Why is it wrong to suggest that this was due entirely to the evils of gin-drinking? What other evidence would you need?*

Epidemic disease

In the seventeenth and eighteenth centuries, epidemic diseases were common. Before 1700, bubonic plague, which caused the Black Death in the Middle Ages, was a recurrent visitor to Britain, sweeping through the country killing large numbers of people. As many as 100,000 people were thought to have died in the Great Plague of 1665-6.

The Great Plague was carried by fleas which lived in the hair of the black rat. For some unknown reason, the black rat was ousted by the brown rat in the eighteenth century and the plague ceased to be a major problem.

Smallpox was another epidemic disease which caused many deaths in the seventeenth century. Inoculation helped to prevent the spread of the disease in the early eighteenth century, but it was not until the introduction of vaccination by Edward Jenner, in 1796, that an effective method of controlling the spread of the disease was found (see Chapter 10). In London, in 1730, about 800 deaths in every 10,000 were caused by smallpox. By 1860, the rate had dropped to only 100 deaths in every 10,000.

One of the worst epidemics of the nineteenth century was that of cholera. The first major outbreak began in Sunderland in 1831. It spread like wildfire and eventually caused the deaths of over 50,000 people. In 1849, there was a further outbreak of the disease with 55,000 deaths. Two more cholera outbreaks occurred in 1854 and in 1865. You can find out more about the cholera epidemics in the section on public health in Chapter 6. The epidemics finally galvanised the authorities into doing something positive to improve the living conditions of the poor.

Children's hospital, The Graphic, *1881*

Medical advances

In theory, better, cleaner hospitals (e.g. the use of easily-cleaned iron beds, instead of wooden beds); higher standards of nursing, new drugs and medicines, advances in surgery; a higher proportion of childbirths taking place in hospitals, and other important medical advances should have had an important effect on lowering the death rate (see Chapter 10).

But in the eighteenth century, the imperfect nature of these medical advances may have resulted in higher, rather than lower death rates. Some historians have even said of eighteenth-century medical care, 'not that it did no good but that it positively did harm'. In the Crimean War, conditions were so bad in the hospital at Scutari that more patients were said to have died from diseases caught in the hospital, than from wounds sustained on the battlefield.

Even so, there were good hospitals as well as bad, and it is undoubtedly true that many significant advances in medical care had been made by the 1870s (see Chapter 10). Better infant care, the use of anaesthetics in surgery and the use of antiseptics generally, led to higher survival rates, even though the overall effect on the death rate may only have been slight.

Hygiene, sanitation and public health (see Chapter 6)

Improvements in living conditions probably made the greatest single contribution to the decline in the death rate in the eighteenth and nineteenth centuries. Although by modern standards the towns of Georgian Britain lacked most of the conveniences we take for granted, such as running water, mains drainage and effective heating, they did begin to improve. Francis Place, a noted Radical, gave evidence to a committee in 1835, in which he compared London then with the London he had known fifty years earlier. He was asked if there had been any improvements in the living conditions of the working classes.

> 'Vast improvements. At Lambeth, there is a mean-looking street with pitched pavement; in that street every window was broken and patched with paper or rags; the door-posts of the houses were blacked with dirt; there were no curtains in any of the windows; the women used to come to the doors, and wash their linen in large earthenware pans; they wore coarse black worsted stockings, linsey-woolsey petticoats, no gowns, and no handkerchiefs on their necks; that was the common practice. There is no such thing now; there is not a window without a curtain, nor a door-post that is not clean. Trade is a great deal worse than formerly, yet there is much more decency and comfort among them.'

1 *How could improvements like these have helped to lower the death rate, particularly among infants?*
2 *What was Francis Place relying on for his facts?*
3 *Is Francis Place's evidence sufficient in itself to demonstrate that hygiene had improved in towns in the fifty years before 1835?*
4 *What is wrong with the use of this source as historical evidence? Suggest how and why it could give a misleading impression. What is its value?*

The rapid growth of the towns, however, began to create serious problems (see Chapter 6 for full details). These included the following:
(a) overcrowding,
(b) inadequate drains and lack of main sewers,
(c) lack of adequate means of getting rid of rubbish and filth,
(d) lack of pure water supplies,
(e) filthy, badly ventilated, damp rooms,
(f) conditions in which vermin, such as lice, rats and mice thrived.

Squalid though the living conditions were, they had little effect on the rate of growth of the population as a whole. The slight rise in the death rate between 1850 and 1870 mainly followed the rise in the birth rate. However, there was genuine cause for alarm in some towns. The death rate in Liverpool, for instance, rose sharply from 21 per 1,000, in 1831, to 35 per 1,000, in 1841.

Moreover, the fall in the death rate after 1870 does suggest that the appalling urban living conditions of the early nineteenth century probably kept the death rate at a higher level than it would otherwise have been, had improvements in hygiene, sanitation and public health been made much earlier (see Chapter 6).

Personal hygiene

There were significant improvements in personal hygiene during this period. These were largely the result of advances made during the Industrial Revolution. Francis Place said in 1835 that cotton had produced a revolution in the previous fifty years. 'It superseded the woollen garments, which were seldom or never changed, and seldom or never washed; it brought in a degree of cleanliness which had been increasing continually.' Cotton cloth was also cheap.

1 *Why were woollen garments 'seldom or never washed'? What happens to wool if it is washed many times?*
2 *Why was it possible for poor people to wear cotton clothes in 1835 and not in 1790?*

3 *What health benefits were brought about by cleaner clothes? How was this likely to have an effect on the spread of diseases like typhus (carried by lice)?*
4 *How was cotton of benefit to doctors?*

The advent of cheaper soap paralleled this advance. The development of the early chemical industry led to a doubling of soap output in the eighteenth century. Together with better water supplies and cheaper coal, there was now far less excuse for dirty clothes or dirty bodies. Householders were now much more likely to boil water, to wash clothes and to scrub the home. Cheaper coal also meant warmer, drier homes.

The nineteenth century saw improvements in personal hygiene and better living conditions in which to bring up babies and young children.

CHANGES IN THE DISTRIBUTION OF POPULATION

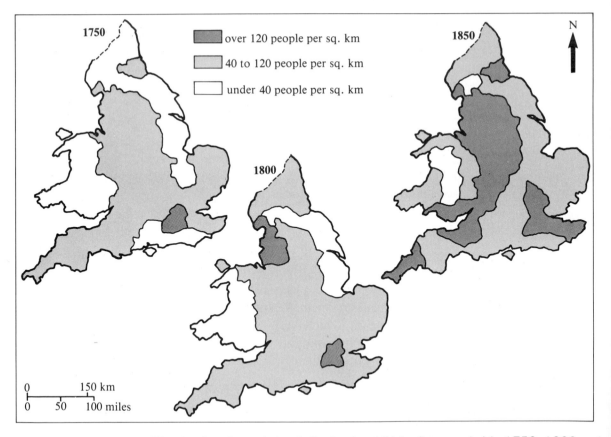

The density of population in England and Wales (by counties) in 1750, 1800 and 1850

The growth of population in Britain was not uniform throughout the country. In 1801, the counties of Suffolk and Warwickshire both had about 210,000 inhabitants. By 1871, Suffolk's population had grown by 66 per cent to 350,000 but Warwickshire's population had trebled to 634,000. Suffolk was still largely agricultural but Warwickshire had become largely industrial. Part of this growth of population was due to internal migration – the flow of country workers into the towns, for instance, but part was also due to the higher rate of fertility in the towns. By the 1850s, there had been a substantial change in the distribution and density of population in Britain.

Look at the maps opposite showing the density of population (number of people per square kilometre) in England and Wales in 1750, 1800 and 1850.

---

1 Which areas were most densely populated in 1750? Why?
2 Name an area of England and Wales, in which the density of population more than trebled between 1750 and 1850.
3 Which areas were most densely populated in 1850? Why?

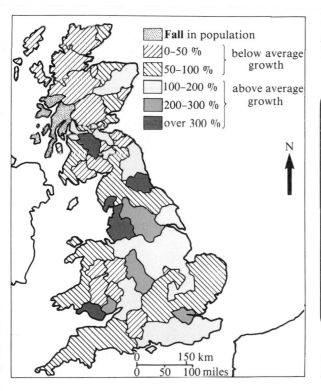

Fall in population
0–50 % } below average growth
50–100 % }
100–200 % } above average growth
200–300 % }
over 300 % }

N

0   150 km
0   50   100 miles

Look at the map showing the percentage growth of population in Britain between 1801 and 1871.

---

4 Which areas grew most rapidly between 1801 and 1871? Which grew least rapidly? What factors (studied in Chapters 1 and 2) help to explain these differences?
5 In which county did the population actually fall? Can you think of a reason to explain this?
6 Write a short essay analysing what can be learned about the population of England and Wales, from 1750 to 1871, using the maps.

Growth of population in the British counties between 1801 and 1871

EMIGRATION AND IMMIGRATION

Population change in the nineteenth century had two particularly significant effects. These were:

(a) on the growth of the towns (see Chapter 6),

(b) on the rate of emigration.

In the nineteenth century, rural depopulation became a serious problem in Ireland and in parts of western Scotland. These areas saw a decline in population at a time when other areas were growing rapidly. Much of the movement away from the land was internal migration to the towns of Britain but emigration overseas (to North America, Australia and other parts of the British Empire) also played an important part in population change. Over six million people from Ireland, Scotland, England and Wales emigrated overseas during the 1840s, 1850s and 1860s.

	Number of people who emigrated from Britain			
	TOTAL	**England and Wales**	**Scotland**	**Ireland**
1815–34	560,000	110,000	30,000	420,000
1835-50	1,809,000	320,000	80,000	1,409,000
1851-60	2,054,000	640,000	183,000	1,231,000
1861-70	1,675,000	650,000	158,000	867,000
1815-70	6,098,000	1,720,000	451,000	3,927,000

Compare these statistics with the table of population on page 175.

---

1 What percentage of the total emigrants, in each period, came from (a) England and Wales, (b) Scotland, (c) Ireland?

2 What percentage of the 1851 populations of England and Wales, Scotland and Ireland, emigrated in the period 1851–60?

3 What would have been the effect on population growth in Britain, had emigration not been possible at this time?

Many people from Ireland settled in mainland Britain in the nineteenth century, but immigration from outside the United Kingdom was not an important factor in population growth in the period up to 1871.

Factors which stimulated emigration

The reasons for the rise in the numbers of people emigrating, in the nineteenth century, were partly 'push' and partly 'pull'. Distress at home, notably after the Irish famine in the 1840s, pushed people out of Britain. At the same time, the attraction of 'a better land overseas' pulled them away from their roots. The discovery of the Californian and Australian goldfields (1849–50) were further incentives to emigrate.

Emigration was deliberately encouraged by the authorities, as you can see in the sources which follow. Emigration societies and cheaper fares made it easier for poor people to leave Britain. Improvements to sailing ships and to steamships (see Chapter 3) made their journeys safer, quicker and easier, although they still endured terrible hardships on the long voyages.

Emigrant ships and societies

Look at Sources A, B, C, D, E, F, G, H which follow.

Source A

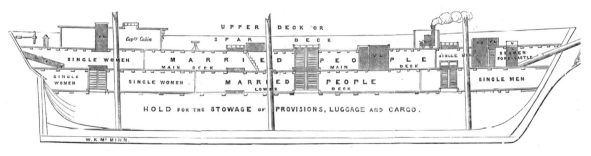

Arrangements made for Government passengers on the emigrant ship Bourneuf *which sailed to Australia in 1852,* The Illustrated London News, *10 July 1852*

Source B

'FREE EMIGRATION to SOUTH AUSTRALIA, via Southampton. First class SHIPS of large tonnage, with the best arrangements and equipment, will embark passengers in the Docks, at Southampton, on the 28th May, for Adelaide, South Australia; subsequently on fixed days in each month. The undersigned are authorized by Her Majesty's Colonial Land and Emigration Commissioners, to grant a free passage by these ships to this healthy and eminently prosperous colony, to agricultural labourers, shepherds, male and female domestic and farm servants, miners, and mechanics of various trades, of good character. The demand for labour in the colony is urgent, with remuneration ensuring the comfort of every well-conducted man and his family.'

Advert in *The Northampton Herald* 1846

Source C

'We had been longing for the hour of sailing; and now, when it arrived, we would have delayed it if possible; and when the after-noon came, how we strained our eyes to catch a distant glimpse of the Welsh coast, perhaps for the last time in our lives.'

The emigrants spent seven weeks at sea on the *Julius Macgregor*, sailing from Liverpool to New York, for £2 15s 0d [£2.75], until eventually they caught sight of the United States.

'The sun was shining brightly on the dazzling white farm-houses and prim churches of Long Island; the country was chequered like a piece of patchwork with fields of every colour. It was a very cheering sight; and a stout farmer standing by me, dressed in his Sunday clothes, rubbed his hands joyfully together, and chuckled out, 'Ah, this will do; this is something like.'

A young emigrant from Manchester in 1844

Source D

'We are told that there are a hundred thousand people, less or more, starving in wretched mud hovels on the barren sea-shores of the Highlands and Islands. We would press upon the attention of persons in authority, the propriety of forming some regular system for the gradual removal, under humane regulations, of the Highlanders to the great seats of industry.'

Chambers's Journal 1837

Source E

An Irish home in the nineteenth century, The Illustrated London News, c. *1885*

Source F

'EMIGRATION FROM THE ISLE OF SKYE

It was for the purpose of aiding the Highlanders, that the Highland and Island Emigration Society was formed. The emigration will be conducted, as much as possible, by entire families. The emigrants will be required to repay to the society the whole of the sums advanced to them, which will again be applied in the same manner as the original fund.

His Royal Highness Prince Albert has become Patron of the undertaking. Subscriptions to a considerable amount have been received; and since the end of May 1852, when the society commenced its operations, it has sent to Australia from the distressed districts in the Highlands about 3000 persons.

HMS Hercules is now in the harbour of Campbelton, receiving emigrants by an arrangement with the Admiralty and the Colonial Emigration Commissioners. A measure made conducive to the relief of distress in the islands of Scotland caused by the excess of population, and at the same time, the relief of distress, hardly less urgent, in Australia, caused by a deficient supply of labourers.'

The Illustrated London News, January 1853

Source G

HERE AND THERE;
Or, Emigration a Remedy.

Cartoon in Punch *15 July 1848*

Source H

In 1849, 'The Female Emigration Fund' began to sponsor young women from London who wanted to emigrate to Australia. By March 1853, they prided themselves on:

'a grand total of 1071 young women rescued from the brink of starvation in London; and now – at least the vast majority of them – comfortably settled in marriage, or service, amid the plenty of Australia. The gold fever has attracted a vast male emigration, and the balance of sexes in Australia is more uneven than ever.'

The Illustrated London News, March 1853

1 *Imagine you are emigrating from Britain to Australia in 1852 – either as a member of a family from Northamptonshire, Ireland or the Isle of Skye, or as a poor working girl from London. Describe your decision to apply for help in order to emigrate. What are your feelings before, during and after the voyage?*

2 *What different ways of meeting the cost of emigration are illustrated by these extracts?*

3 *Two in every three emigrants from the British Isles went to the United States. How do you think you could use a New York telephone directory to show the extent of emigration from Scotland and Ireland to North America in the nineteenth and twentieth centuries?*

4 *Why were free passages offered to South Australia in 1846? What sort of settlers were they trying to attract? What were the attractions of emigration to Australia and North America in the late 1840s and early 1850s? What were the advantages to the British Government? What arrangements did they make for emigrants who wanted to go to Australia?*

5 *Look at the statistics in the table on page 190. Which accent would you have expected to predominate on board an ordinary emigrant ship?*

6 *What different solutions were suggested in these extracts for the relief of poverty in the Scottish Highlands in the middle of the nineteenth century? Look at the statistics on page 190 and at the map on page 189. Was Scotland an area of growing, declining or static population? Which other area endured great suffering in the 1840s?*

7 *Write a short essay on emigration in the middle of the nineteenth century using Sources A, B, C, D, E, F, G, H and the maps, graphs and pictures in this chapter as your sources of information.*

FURTHER QUESTIONS AND EXERCISES

1. *Look at the above picture by George Cruikshank. Does it illustrate a major or minor cause of the decline or growth in Britain's population between 1700 and 1870? Write an explanatory caption for the picture.*

2. *Why must population statistics be treated with great caution before 1801, and with a certain amount of care thereafter? In what ways might the census reports be inaccurate?*

3. *Write a short essay, saying which of the following reasons you think best explain the rapid growth in population, in England and Wales, in the eighteenth and early nineteenth centuries:*

   (a) *use of cotton cloth,*
   (b) *better diet,*
   (c) *decline in apprenticeship,*
   (d) *cheaper soap,*
   (e) *better medical care,*
   (f) *rapid growth of industry,*
   (g) *immigration,*
   (h) *control of the sale of gin,*
   (i) *better drains,*
   (j) *purer water supplies,*
   (k) *use of child labour,*
   (l) *cheaper coal.*

4 Look at this picture from The Illustrated London News. What aspect of population history do you think it illustrates? Write a detailed explanatory caption for this picture, explaining who you think these people are, what you think they are doing, and why.

5 Write a short essay about the census in the nineteenth century. How are the census reports useful to people studying social and economic history?

6 How and why did the geographical distribution of population in Britain change between 1801 and 1871?

7 Write a reasoned account, describing and explaining the different rates of population growth in:
(a) England and Wales,
(b) Ireland,
in the nineteenth century.

8 Why is it so difficult to get a convincing and definitive explanation of why the population of England and Wales grew so rapidly in the eighteenth and nineteenth centuries?

Chapter Six

Urban Problems

INTRODUCTION

London Bridge, The Illustrated London News, *16 November 1872*

> 1 *How many different types of vehicle or other forms of transport can you see in this picture? Roughly how many people crossed the bridge on foot compared with those in horse-drawn vehicles? In what ways is this scene different from what you could expect to see on London Bridge today? In what ways is it similar?*
>
> 2 *Imagine you are one of the people on the bridge. Write a vivid description of the sounds and smells and excitement you experience, and the people you can see.*

In 1852, a traffic census showed that over 13,000 vehicles crossed
London Bridge between 08.00 and 20.00 hours.

Start of hour	08.00	09.00	10.00	11.00	12.00	13.00
Number of vehicles	680	1,128	1,332	1,124	1,094	1,048

Start of hour	14.00	15.00	16.00	17.00	18.00	19.00
Number of vehicles	1,101	1,180	1,344	1,308	962	798

3 *When was the peak flow of traffic across London Bridge in 1852?
Is this what you would expect today? What was the average flow of
vehicles per hour during the course of the day? Was the traffic flow
controlled in any way in 1872? Did traffic keep to the left? How
many lanes of traffic were there across the bridge?*

In the first five weeks of 1869, a total of 21 people died in road accidents
in London: 5 killed by horses; 1 by a carriage; 2 by omnibuses; 2 by cabs;
5 by light waggons and vans; 6 by heavy carts.

4 *What would have been the annual number of road deaths in
London, if accidents had continued at this rate? London's
population then was about 3.8 million. Work out the rate per
1,000 people. Compare this figure with statistics for the present
day (in 1985 there were 5,200 road deaths in the UK which had
a population of approximately 55 million people). Were road
accidents a problem in 1869?*
5 *In what ways do you think the flow of traffic contributed to
London's problems in the nineteenth century?*

Towns had grown rapidly since the start of the eighteenth century, when
even Liverpool and Manchester had fewer than 10,000 inhabitants. As
shown in the earlier chapters, the population of Britain rose rapidly at
the time of the Industrial and Agrarian Revolutions, but the sharpest
rises of all were in the towns.

Glasgow had a population of 24,000 in 1755, when Elizabeth Gray of
nearby Edinburgh was two years old. When *The Illustrated London
News* announced her death in 1856, the population of Glasgow was just
under 400,000. If she had visited Glasgow as a child, she would have seen

'one of the prettiest towns in Europe'. As an old lady, she could only have been horrified by Glasgow's teeming tenements and its smoking chimnies – said to be 'possibly the filthiest and unhealthiest of all the towns of Britain at this period'.

The problems of rapid growth, appalling slums, pollution and disease, which plagued Glasgow and many other towns in Britain, are the subject of this chapter.

CHANGES IN URBAN GROWTH

Distribution of towns

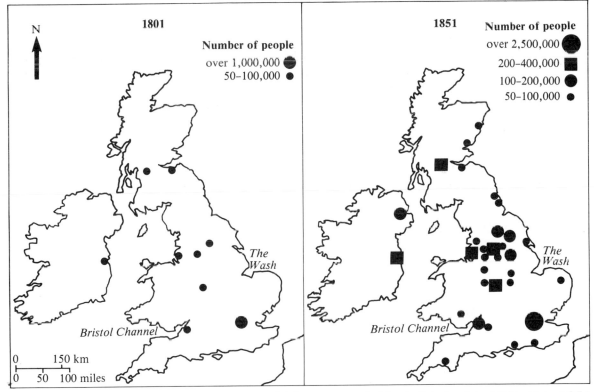

Major towns and cities in Britain a) in 1801, b) in 1851

Look at the maps showing the distribution of the major towns and cities of Britain in 1801, compared with those in 1851.

1 *How many towns were there in Britain with more than 50,000 inhabitants in 1801? By how many times had that number grown by 1851?*
2 *How many towns, with more than 50,000 inhabitants, were situated to the north and west of a line drawn between the Bristol*

Channel and the Wash, in 1851? How many were to the south and east? Does this support what you know about the distribution of population at this time (see Chapter 5)?

	Population figures				
	1701	**1751**	**1801**	**1831**	**1871**
London	500,000	750,000	1,100,000	1,900,000	3,900,000
Liverpool	5,000	35,000	82,000	202,000	493,000
Manchester	9,000	45,000	75,000	182,000	351,000
Norwich	25,000	35,000	36,000	61,000	80,000

3 *By how many times did the population of London grow between 1701 and 1871? Which of the other towns grew at a faster rate than this? Why? Which town grew at a slower rate than London? Why?*

4 *Write a short paragraph commenting on the facts you can deduce from these maps and from the table of statistics. In what ways did the distribution of large towns in Britain change in the nineteenth century? How and why did the towns grow?*

Suburban growth

The rapid growth of the towns created many problems. One of the most difficult to solve was that of finding space in the towns to accommodate everyone who wished to live there. Nowadays many people live a long way from a town centre or from their place of work. But in the middle of the nineteenth century there was no cheap public transport and so people had to live near to their place of work.

In the industrial towns of the North, terraces of back-to-back houses were built in the shadow of the great chimneys of the textile mills or within sight of the pit winding gear. In London, because of its great size, many people working in the City lived at a much greater distance from their work, as you will see later (Further questions and exercises on page 225).

Large houses with gardens were cheaper in the suburbs than in the City, so more and more middle-class families moved out there from the 1820s and 1830s onwards, attracted by the cleaner air and the healthier environment. Business people commuted to work by carriage or bus.

Horse-drawn cabs and private carriages were strictly for the well-to-do, whilst horse buses (which were first introduced into London in 1829) were usually too expensive for the ordinary worker. In 1850, a bus journey of 5 km cost 3d [about 1.25p] – as much as most ordinary workers earned in an hour. A railway journey cost about the same. So for most people, as you can see in the picture of London Bridge, the usual way to get around a large city was on foot.

Cheap public transport only made its appearance in the 1860s, when horse-drawn trams came into service. 'Workmen's trains' were introduced on the railways in the 1880s. By 1900, the electric tram further helped ordinary workers to live at a distance from their places of work. The opening of the first London Underground Railway line in 1862 also paved the way for the rapid growth of the London suburbs in the early twentieth century.

Different types of towns

Before 1700, most towns in Britain were known chiefly for their markets rather than for their industries. The right to hold a market was a much sought-after privilege. Throughout the eighteenth and early nineteenth centuries, most of the towns in the shire counties retained their rural character. Thomas Hardy described Dorchester in the 1840s, when on Saturday afternoons:

> 'field labourers and their wives and children trooped in from the villages for their weekly shopping, and instead of a rattle of wheels and a tramp of horses, there was nothing but the shuffle of many feet'.

With the spread of industry, many old market towns, such as Huddersfield, became business centres for the new manufactures. In Halifax, for instance, a large and splendid Piece Hall was built in 1775, where 'pieces' of cloth were sold by the local clothiers.

Although London was by far the most important business centre in Britain (see Chapter 4), each industrial area had its own local centre as well, such as Manchester for the Lancashire cotton industry, Leeds for the Yorkshire woollen industry, and Birmingham for the metal-working industries of the Midlands.

Meanwhile, the flood of new and expanding factories stimulated the growth of towns, since homes had to be built for the rapidly increasing numbers of extra workers near to the factories.

Some towns, such as Wolverton, Crewe and Swindon, grew rapidly as railway junction towns (see Chapter 3). Ports, such as Liverpool, Glasgow and Bristol, thrived on the vast increase in trade (see Chapter 4). And by the 1870s, a new type of town, the seaside resort, was beginning to thrive.

Towns as shopping centres

Christmas Shopping,
The Illustrated London
News, *25 December*
1852

---

1 *Which two types of shop are shown in this picture? What did they sell? In what ways are they similar or dissimilar to the shops which sell these goods today?*

2 *Identify a street trader. What is he selling? Identify the sandwich-board man. What was his job?*

3 *What details in the picture do you think were probably made up by the artist? Does this mean, therefore, that the illustration is of little value to a historian?*

As the industrial towns, ports, railway junctions, seaside resorts and business centres grew rapidly, so they developed important shopping centres. New types of shop were pioneered.

(a) In 1844, a new type of store was opened in Rochdale, in Lancashire, where the customers shared in the profits of the business according to the value of the goods they bought during the course of the year.

(b) In 1848, William Henry Smith, a London newsagent, took advantage of the coming of the railways, to open a bookstall on Euston Station, and in 1863 Jesse Boot took over his father's shop in Nottingham, which sold herbal remedies, and studied to be a chemist in his spare time.

(c) In the same year, 1863, William Whiteley opened a new store in London, which he called 'The Universal Provider'.

> **4** *What type of shop was opened in Rochdale? What was its importance to the working classes? What would we call William Whiteley's 'The Universal Provider' today? What type of shop eventually developed out of the pioneer trading activities of Jesse Boot and William Henry Smith?*

LIVING CONDITIONS

Look at the following two extracts.

Description of Sheffield

'Perhaps the most hideous town in creation. All ups and downs and back slums. Massive volumes of black smoke veil the sun and the blue sky even on the brightest day. More than one crystal stream runs sparkling down the valleys, and enters the town; but they soon get defiled, and creep through it heavily charged with dyes, clogged with putridity, and bubbling with poisonous gases.'

Charles Reade

Description of Manchester

'Heaps of dung, rubble for buildings, putrid, stagnant pools. A sort of black smoke covers the city. The footsteps of a busy crowd, the crunching wheels of machinery, the shriek of steam for boilers, the regular beat of the looms, the heavy rumble of carts, those are the noises from which you can never escape.'

Notes on England by Alexis de Tocqueville

> **1** *What do these extracts tell you about urban problems in the nineteenth century? What did the writers find offensive about these towns?*
> **2** *Make a list of the urban problems mentioned here, and against each, indicate a possible solution. Why were these problems of much less concern to towns in the eighteenth century – apart from London?*

As you have already seen, London was a huge city of about 750,000 in 1750, when none of the other major towns of Britain had more than 50,000 inhabitants. Most people lived in squalid slums. The death rate was high (about 50 per 1,000 in 1750) and the infant mortality rate was appalling (an estimated 3 out of every 4 infants died before the age of five).

In this drawing by Hogarth, in 1738, you can see a street in the vicinity of what is now Trafalgar Square. It can be identified from the statue of Charles I (seen in the distance).

London Street in 1738,
By Hogarth

3 Draw a rough sketch of this street and label the following features:
   (a) the nightwatchman with his lantern,
   (b) a linkboy with his link (lighted torch) to guide people through
        the dark streets at night,
   (c) a barber's shop – with its advert – 'Shaving Bleeding Teeth
        Drawn',
   (d) a shop sign,
   (e) slops being emptied out of a window into the street,
   (f) a coach accident,
   (g) a poor family living in a cellar,

(h)   a house on fire,
(i)   a tenant with a cartload of furniture fleeing from the landlord by night.
4 *What were some of London's urban problems in the middle of the eighteenth century?*

Pollution

As towns and cities grew larger and more important, they attracted greater volumes of horse-drawn traffic on to the streets and roads. As a result the streets were filled with horse manure. They stank! The horse manure attracted germ-carrying flies and it has been suggested that this was why infantile diarrhoea reached its peak in the hot summer months.

The filth in the streets created a major problem for pedestrians. In about 1700, a Frenchman called Henri Misson noted that London 'women wear pattins or Galoshoes of Iron to keep themselves out of the dirt and wet'. These were rather like bicycle pedals and clipped under the shoes to raise the hem of the skirt above the ground.

In the middle of the nineteenth century, people wanting to cross the street in London could have a clear path swept for them, for a small charge. Crossing sweepers, armed with brooms made of twigs, were a familiar London sight.

Pollution was a serious problem, as you can see from the following picture and extracts.

London street scene, The Illustrated London News, *12 January 1867*

'Above this din and the hum and clatter of thousands of tongues and feet one hears the chimes from church towers, the bells of the postmen, the organs, fiddles, hurdy-gurdies, and tambourines of English mountebanks, and the cries of those who sell hot and cold viands in the open at the street corners.'

Georg Lichtenberg 1775

'Know ye the stream where the cesspool and sewer
Are emptied of all their foul slushes and slimes
Where the gas-works rain down the blackest of soot
Where the air's filled with smells that no nose can define,
And the banks teem prolific with corpses canine.'

'Pride of London' from *Punch* 1852

'Took the children by boat from Vauxhall Bridge to show them the great buildings. The ride on the water was refreshing except for the stench.'

B. J. Armstrong 1855

'Forty years ago good salmon were taken in the Thames. The walks along the Thames were pleasant places in those days. How changed now is the river and its banks! The former has become a filthy sewer, the fish have been destroyed.'

The Illustrated London News 1861

---

1 *What were the authors describing when they referred to:*
(a) mountebanks,
(b) corpses canine?

2 *What was the significance of the salmon in the Thames in 1821 and their absence in 1861?*

3 *What helped to cause London's fog problem? What would we call it today?*

4 *What different forms of pollution made London an unpleasant place in which to live in the nineteenth century?*

5 *What was the 'Pride of London'? How was it polluted? What evidence is given here to show the extent and recent nature of this pollution?*

In 1859, many people hoped that the massive new London Main Drainage scheme, just begun, would clean up the river, and that salmon would once again return to the Thames. In fact, it was well over 100 years (January 1986) before newspapers could announce 'salmon have returned to the river'.

Housing

> **1** *Study the following information on pages 207–12. Use it as your source material to write a report for a Victorian magazine or newspaper, exposing the appalling living conditions endured by the poor who lived in the slums during this time.*
>
> *List the different problems you can identify, such as overcrowding and bad ventilation. Examine each in turn, quoting the evidence you can find to show that this was a major problem.*
>
> *Conclude your report by showing that these problems could be solved, again quoting facts and evidence from the sources to support your case.*

Source A

Cotton worker's home in Manchester, The Illustrated London News, *1862*

Source B

'The courts consist usually of two rows of houses placed opposite to each other, with an intervening space of from 9 to 15 feet [3 to 5 m], which communicates with the street by a passage or archway about 3 feet [1 m] wide, often built up overhead, and the farther end closed by a wall, or other building.'

Report of the Health of Towns Commission 1845

Source C

Samuel Holme (in about 1845) was reported as saying:

> 'that in Liverpool, he had seen a court of houses, where the whole floor of the court was running with sewage, so dreadfully offensive that he was obliged to retreat; yet the whole of the houses were inhabited.'

Source D

The working classes of Liverpool numbered 160,000 people at that time (total population 286,000). Only half lived in acceptable houses, facing the street, whilst 55,534 people were crammed into 1,982 courts containing 10,692 houses. A further 22,158 inhabitants lived in 6,915 cellars.

Analysis of the Census Report for 1841

Source E

DWELLINGS OF THE POOR IN BETHNAL-GREEN

> 'As foul a neighbourhood as can be discovered in the civilised world. The entrance to most of them is by a covered alley not wider than an ordinary doorway. At the end of this blind court there will be found a number of black and crumbling hovels forming three sides of a miserable little square.
>
> The miserable rooms are teeming with inhabitants. The water for some fourteen or fifteen houses is frequently supplied from one tap in a dirty corner, where it runs for only a short time every day; and the places are mostly undrained. Add to this the decay of vegetable matter, the occasional evidence of the presence of pigs and the result will represent a score of places in Bethnal-green.'

The Illustrated London News 1863

Source F

The cellars were 'still more horrible'. They were about three to four metres square, with stone flag or bare earth floors. 'There is often no window, so that light and air can enter only by the door. They are of course dark, and from the defective drainage, are also very generally damp.'

In one group of 26 streets, two-thirds of the houses 'were without yard, ash-pit or other convenience'. The surface of the ground was covered with sewage which leaked into the neighbouring cellars. A pool, over a metre deep, and 'filled with this stinking fluid, was found in one cellar under the bed where the family slept'.

From a newspaper item 1845

Yet some observers thought that the lodging houses were even worse. An eighteenth-century magistrate recalled the London parish of Shoreditch (see Source H).

Source G

NARROW COURT – allowing little sunlight to penetrate

ENCLOSED ON ALL FOUR SIDES APART FROM THE ALLEYWAY AT THE ENTRANCE

BACK-TO-BACK HOUSES (i.e. another court on the other side)

HOUSES TEEMING WITH PEOPLE

NO KITCHENS – if a family could afford a joint of meat it was roasted in the nearest baker's oven or in an oven serving all the people in the block

BADLY FITTING WINDOWS AND DOORS

ENTRANCE THROUGH TUNNEL

SOLITARY STANDPIPE – supplying water to all the houses

NO DAMP COURSE = DAMP HOUSES

COMMUNAL PRIVY (LAVATORY) The cesspit was emptied into large buckets and taken away at night – but the job was often neglected and sewage overflowed into the court

SOME PEOPLE LIVED IN CELLARS

WATER SUPPLY – often contaminated by cesspit if it came from a well

OPEN SEWER OR GUTTER FOR SLOPS – many houses lacked even this

Sketch of a Victorian court

Source H

'Where two little houses were emptied of near seventy men and women; such is the poverty of these wretches, that a single loaf hath supplied a whole family with their provisions for a week. If any of these miserable creatures fall sick (and it is almost a miracle that stench, vermin, and want, should ever suffer them to be well) they are turned out in the streets by their merciless host or hostess.'

From a pamphlet by Henry Fielding 1751

These lodging houses were temporary homes for travellers (particularly Irish immigrants in the 1830s and 1840s) who sometimes paid 1d [0.4p] a night to sleep on straw. Others 'dressed in rags during the day' were provided 'with rags to lie upon during the night' (1844).

Source 1

'Consider a house, with floor above floor, packed as shown in the Engraving; the cellars filled with either refuse or wretched inmates – the ventilation shocking – the drainage bad – the parts adjoining filled with filth and refuse.'

The Illustrated London News, 22 October 1853

Difficult though it may be to believe, living conditions in the nineteenth century were generally an improvement on those which had been commonplace in the eighteenth century. Attention is usually drawn, as here, to the gruesome nature of many Victorian slums, but there were also many sound houses as well, particularly those built towards the end of the century.

Many Victorian houses were built in terraces, back-to-back. In this way a house in the middle of a row shared three of its walls with neighbours, thus reducing building costs but restricting access and ventilation, since outside windows could only be fitted to one wall. This was not necessarily a major problem, since many houses had only two rooms, 'one-up, one-down'.

Although the deficiencies of these houses can only be condemned, it must not be forgotten that wages were so low in Georgian and Victorian Britain, that the ordinary working family could not afford to pay the rent for anything better, even if it had been available. Their only hope was to live in housing subsidised in some way or other by a private charity or by an employer.

Source J

Peabody Square, Islington

The Illustrated London News, 10 March 1866

Source K

'The grand gift of a quarter of a million pounds bestowed on the poor of London by a generous American merchant is applied by the trustees to the building of healthy and comfortable dwellings for working-class families, let at a cheaper rate than the wretched apartments for which exorbitant rents are too often paid in the crowded parts of this city. Peabody-square, Islington, consists of four blocks of buildings, five stories in height, comprising 240 separate tenements of one, two, or three rooms, with baths and laundries, ample supplies of water and gaslight, shafts for the removal of refuse, and perfect drainage and ventilation, at rents of 2s 6d [12.5p], 4s [20p] or 5s [25p] a week.'

The Illustrated London News, 10 March 1866

Compare the rents charged in Peabody Square with the rents of 2s [10p] a week which were charged for a cellar in Liverpool in 1843.

Some factory owners built model housing estates. Sir Titus Salt did so in his new model village of Saltaire (see page 81).

Source L

'Already the architects of Saltaire have instructions to erect 700 dwelling-houses for the operatives to be employed, and they are specially enjoined to make those dwellings replete with every convenience conducive to the health, comfort and well-being of the inhabitants. On no account are they to suffer the air to be polluted by smoke, or the water to be injured or deteriorated by any impurity. Healthy dwellings and gardens, in wide streets and capacious squares – ample ground for recreation – a large dining-hall and kitchens – baths and washhouses – a covered market – schools – mechanics institution – a church: these are some of the characteristics of the future town of Saltaire.'

The Illustrated London News, 1 October 1853

PUBLIC HEALTH

The biggest single problem in the towns in the eighteenth and nineteenth centuries was that of public health. It is a paradox that the improvements in living conditions, which led to the rapid growth in population (outlined in Chapter 5) and which stimulated the rapid growth of the towns, should themselves eventually lead to overcrowding and a deterioration in living conditions in some towns. Water supplies could not cope with the pressure put on them by the rapidity of urban growth. Nor could most towns deal adequately with the problems of the removal of refuse and excreta, pollution, finding land in which to bury the dead, and traffic congestion.

How disease spread

Some diseases, such as typhoid fever, dysentery and cholera, were spread when people consumed drinking water and food contaminated by the excreta of people suffering from, or carrying, these diseases. Some, such as typhus (not to be confused with typhoid fever) and infantile diarrhoea, were carried by the insects and other vermin which thrived amidst filth and rubbish. One virulent strain of typhus was carried by body lice in people's clothes and on their bodies (hence the adjective 'lousy'). Typhus was a killer disease, and accounted for 25 per cent of all deaths in London in 1741.

Tuberculosis, scarlet fever, whooping cough, diptheria and measles could all be spread by droplet infection in the air – from coughing and sneezing. They spread rapidly in overcrowded conditions and all (except tuberculosis) took their toll primarily on young children. Tuberculosis was a terrible wasting disease and took a number of forms, such as scrofula. Bovine tuberculosis was passed to humans via contaminated milk (dairies were far from clean and milk was not pasteurised).

Relatively few children went to school from the slums, so the small cramped homes and dark narrow alleyways and courts of Victorian towns were always teeming with people. Not surprisingly, people who lived in such close contact with one another were much more likely to catch the diseases which are spread by contagion (direct physical touch) or by inhaling other people's germs.

The problems of disease were made worse by poor diet. People suffering from malnutrition were particularly vulnerable to diseases such as tuberculosis. People who were weak or recovering from some other illness were also likely to catch diseases. Damp, dark rooms provided ideal conditions for the tubercle bacillus to thrive – it is killed by sunlight. Inadequate ventilation was another factor which hastened the spread of many diseases. As you have seen, window tax was not repealed until 1851 and until that time landlords sometimes bricked up windows to avoid paying taxes. A writer in 1846 said it was 'darkness forced upon the people by a mischievous window-tax'.

Tracing an outbreak of cholera

On 9 September 1854, *The Illustrated London News* carried the following item about an outbreak of cholera in the Soho district of London:

'The President of the Board of Health has directed special attention to the supply of water in the several localities: the source of supply; whether filtered or not before supply. Inquiry also will be made into the state of the sewers. The inspector is also to report whether in those places which were the seats of disease in former years, the epidemic had appeared in a less virulent form where drainage and general improvements have been carried out. House to house visitation is strongly recommended, and disinfectants are to be used where necessary.'

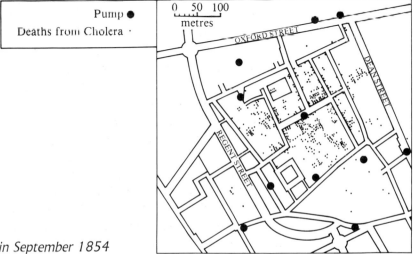

Deaths from cholera in Soho in September 1854

Within the space of ten days – 1 to 10 September 1854 – five hundred people died of cholera in the Soho district of London. John Snow, one of the investigators, discovered a contaminated water pump in the area by plotting all the cholera cases on a map and then locating the pump at the heart of the outbreak. He removed the handle from the pump so that it could not be used and helped to bring the outbreak to an end.

---

1 *Which of the water pumps on the map on page 213 do you think was contaminated?*
2 *Describe and explain the value of the method of investigation adopted by John Snow.*

In 1859, however, *The Illustrated London News* said the cause of the Soho cholera epidemic of 1854 was because 'cesspools and imperfect surface-drains polluted the air, and surely poisoned those who were exposed to the necessity of breathing it'.

At this time, the medical profession still knew very little about the causes of diseases or the reasons why they spread. The work of the scientists, Pasteur and Koch, on microbes and germs was still to come. Some doctors still believed the old theory that fevers were spread by 'miasmas'. These were the noxious vapours, gases, odours and stenches, which they understandably associated with the spread of diseases. The 'deadly effects of foul air' were stressed by the *Report of the Health of Towns Commission* in 1845:

> 'Defective drainage, neglect of house and street cleansing, ventilation, and imperfect supplies of water, contribute to produce atmospheric impurities which affect the general health and physical condition of the population, generating acute, chronic and ultimately organic disease.'

A writer thought this one of the 'gloomiest features of the volume', with its 'startling fact' that 'impure air' was a cause of tuberculosis. And, in 1863, a newspaper reported that a poor shoemaker had 'lost two children by disease which has been directly attributed to the impure air'. Some doctors even thought different miasmas caused different diseases.

---

3 *What was the most obvious 'miasma' to greet any visitor to a Victorian slum?*
4 *Why do you think doctors and public health officials blamed overcrowding, bad drains and impure water as the main causes of these diseases, even though they had no knowledge of germs?*

5 *Does the news item of 9 September 1854 on page 213 suggest that the Board of Health was completely ignorant of the causes of cholera and the reasons for its spread?*

Look at the following cartoons and the extract on page 216.

DIPHTHERIA　　SCROFULA　　CHOLERA

Cartoon from Punch, 1858. The offspring are called 'diphtheria', 'scrofula' and 'cholera'.

FATHER THAMES INTRODUCING HIS OFFSPRING TO THE FAIR CITY OF LONDON.

Cartoon from Punch, 1852

A COURT FOR KING CHOLERA.

'The Earl of Harewood, in his speech of thanks to Mr. Salt, mentioned the fearful ravages of the cholera in Newcastle upon Tyne, which he said was attributable to the overcrowding of cottages, bad drainage, and the want of attention on the part of those who employed the working classes in that town.'

The Illustrated London News 1853

---

6 *(a)* *Explain fully why* Punch *called the cartoon* A Court for King Cholera.

(b) *What type of housing is featured in the picture at the foot of page 215?*

(c) *To what causes did* Punch *and the Earl of Harewood attribute the spread of diseases?*

(d) *Did they correctly identify the causes of cholera, diphtheria and scrofula (tuberculosis)?*

Water supply

London has always drawn its main supply of water from the River Thames, but in the nineteenth century the Thames was heavily polluted. This was a matter of great concern to Londoners at that time, as you can see in the rhyme and illustrations published in 'The water that John drinks', *Punch*, in October 1849. The final verse went as follows:

'This is the price that we pay to wink
At the vested interests that fill to the brink
The network of sewers from cesspool to sink,
That feed the fish that float in the ink-
-y stream of the Thames with its cento of stink,
That supplies the water that John drinks.'

---

1 *What did* Punch *think about the water that 'John' drank?*

2 *What were 'the fish'? Why didn't the cartoonist show ordinary fish?*

3 *Whom did* Punch *blame for the lack of pure drinking water?*

4 *What are 'vested interests'? What other sources of pollution were there, besides the sewers which served people's homes?*

In the towns there were two main sources of water supply:
(a) from wells (an inefficient method of supplying large urban areas),
(b) through pipes installed by a company selling water.

The problem became acute with the rapid increase in town populations in the early years of the nineteenth century. When large towns doubled in population in twenty years (such as Liverpool from 138,000 people

THE WATER THAT JOHN DRINKS.

THIS is the water that JOHN drinks.

This is the Thames with its cento of stink,
That supplies the water that JOHN drinks.

These are the fish that float in the ink-
-y stream of the Thames with its cento of stink,
That supplies the water that JOHN drinks.

This is the sewer, from cesspool and sink,
That feeds the fish that float in the ink-
-y stream of the Thames with its cento of stink,
That supplies the water that JOHN drinks.

to 286,000 in 1821–41), tremendous pressure was put on the water companies to improve not only the quality of the water they supplied, but also the quantity available. Rapid growth in industrial production had a similar effect, since water is one of the most important raw materials used in factories.

In working-class districts, water usually had to be carried from a standpipe or stopcock in the street. It was often dry for most of the time. In 1752, a writer described a scene in London at 4.0 a.m. on a Sunday morning, when people 'who live in courts and alleys where one cock supplies the whole neighbourhood with water, take the advantage before other people are up, to fill their tubs and pans with a sufficiency to serve them the ensuing seven days'.

Similar scenes were common over a hundred years later in many working-class districts, as you read in the description of the tap which served a number of dwellings in Bethnal Green on page 208. Lack of a piped water supply often meant that clothes were washed in dirty water to save going out to fetch fresh water from the tap. Regular baths were a rarity for the same reason. Yet experts told the Health of Towns Commission, in 1843–5, that water closets and piped water could be brought to all working-class homes at small cost – about 1d [0.4p] a week for water and twice that sum for a water-closet. It was emphasised that without adequate water supplies, the sewers would not function properly. An engineer told the Commission that water was the 'moving power or carrier' in the sewer.

The quality of London's drinking water had been suspect long before 1849. The country squire in *Humphry Clinker* complained:

'If I would drink water, I must quaff the maukish contents of an open aqueduct, exposed to all manner of defilement; or swallow that which comes from the river Thames, impregnated with all the filth of London and Westminster. Human excrement is the least offensive part of the concrete, which is composed of all the drugs, minerals and poisons, used in mechanics and manufacture, enriched with the putrefying carcases of beasts and men; and mixed with the scourings of all the wash-tubs, kennels, and common sewers, within the bills of mortality.'

Humphry Clinker by Tobias Smollett, 1771

---

5 *What did he mean by 'concrete', 'defilement', 'maukish contents' and 'open aqueduct'?*
6 *How was the Thames polluted in 1771?*

By 1849, London's population had grown to about 2,500,000 and the growth of the slums had made the water supply problem worse. The sewers were a large part of the problem. The contents of many urban lavatories emptied into cesspits or cesspools. Sometimes these drained into proper sewers and ultimately into the Thames. If they were not connected to the main drains, they were usually emptied by night-soil workers. The stench as the workers slopped pails of raw sewage into their carts was unbearable. This is why they usually did the work at night rather than during the day (hence the term night-soil). Even so, many poor people preferred to put up with their overflowing cesspools rather than pay for them to be emptied.

When cesspools leaked, or overflowed, the sewage which seeped through the ground sometimes contaminated the water drawn from wells. Sometimes it seeped through badly-fitting joints in the water pipes and into the mains water supply itself. Even where the pipes were intact, the water supply was often contaminated, as most of it came from the Thames, which was where most of the raw sewage ended up. There was a limited amount of filtration of the water supply but this did not always remove the contamination. Thus London's major public health problems were correctly identified as stemming from the Thames and from inadequate drains and sewers – even though the Victorian theory that the stench caused disease was not scientifically correct.

The water companies however were constantly expanding. In 1852, the Lambeth Water Company opened a new plant, taking water from the Thames at Ditton and passing it through filter beds, before steam engines pumped it by pipe to the Company's reservoirs in Brixton and Streatham. What was really needed, above anything else, was a cleaner Thames.

Mains drainage

Constructing the Fleet Street sewers, The Illustrated London News, 1844

Although some sewers had been built in towns long before 1800, the rapidity of urban growth in the nineteenth century, and the lack of stringent building controls, meant that by 1840, many town houses were still not connected to a sewer. Half of Manchester and most of Liverpool were without mains drainage in 1830. But by the middle of the nineteenth century, scenes like the one shown in the picture of the construction of the Fleet Street sewer in 1844, were beginning to be commonplace in many towns.

In 1845, a writer in *Chambers's Journal* said that few people in London even knew about 'the vast and wonderful scheme of sewerage that extended underneath. From the remotest district of London, small sewers flow into larger ones; and these again, after a long course and many windings into the Thames.'

Matters began to improve in February 1859, when Joseph Bazalgette, Engineer-in-Chief to the Metropolitan Board of Works, started work on the construction of a massive mains drainage scheme to serve London. It was estimated that it would cost £3,000,000 (at least £1 billion by modern standards).

The object of the London Main Drainage scheme was to intercept London's sewage in its progress towards the Thames and to divert it, by covered channels, to points about 22 km below London Bridge. There the sewage could be emptied into the river at the start of the ebb tide, causing it to be diluted and eventually swept out to sea. The scheme involved the construction of about 80 km of brick-lined sewer underground, together with the pumping works necessary to carry it over rivers, canals, railways and roads. These pumping stations lifted 'whole rivers of liquid sewage from a lower to a higher level'.

CONTROLLING THE TOWNS

Local Improvement Acts

Before 1835, there was no uniform system of local government in Britain. Much of the responsibility for overseeing or initiating necessary improvements was in the hands of the local Justices of the Peace. As shown in Chapter 3, they had responsibility for the maintenance of all the roads which were not run by the Turnpike Trusts. They were also responsible for the upkeep of law and order in their areas and were also required to administer the Poor Law system (see Chapter 8).

Some towns were chartered boroughs (those granted a Royal Charter) but many of the largest towns were not. Towns with a Charter were given rights, such as the right to hold a market or a fair. Town government in these boroughs varied and the officials were often lazy and incompetent. Mayors and aldermen were rarely elected to office. Many were corrupt and more interested in lining their own pockets and protecting the rights of landlords and landowners, than looking after the interests of the townspeople. On the other hand, some towns had progressive leaders who took action through special Acts of Parliament – called Local Improvement Acts. These enabled them to take steps to improve their towns. In 1831–2, for instance, Parliament approved the following Acts:

- 'An Act for lighting with Gas the Town of Saint Helens in the County of Lancaster.'
- 'An Act for better supplying with Water the Borough of Preston.'
- 'An Act for better paving, lighting, watching, cleansing and otherwise improving the City of Exeter.'
- 'An Act for improving and regulating the Township of Chorlton-cum-Medlock in the County of Lancaster.'
- 'An Act for making and maintaining a Reservoir in the Parish of Bolton-le-Moors in the County of Lancaster.'

1 What improvements were being sought for Exeter? What do you think they meant by 'watching'? How were streets lit in the early nineteenth century?

2 Make a list of the various improvements approved by Parliament in 1831–2. Who is responsible for these services today?

The Municipal Corporations Act of 1835

The reform of Parliament in 1832 (see Chapter 7) created a more democratic electoral system, whilst the passing of the Poor Law Amendment Act in 1834 (see Chapter 8) created locally elected Boards of Guardians to supervise the administration of the Poor Law. It was clear that a new and more democratic system of town government was needed to replace the corrupt municipal corporations then in charge of the towns.

In 1835, the Municipal Corporations Act reorganised the existing 178 boroughs of England and Wales, giving them a common system of local government. The ratepayers in each town had to elect a town council, to be responsible for many of the services already authorised by the Local Improvement Acts (such as street lighting, water supply and policing the town). The new councils had to hold public meetings and had to submit their accounts each year to an audit (to check that the rates had been spent properly). The councillors elected the Mayor and appointed the town clerk and the treasurer.

Councillors could only be elected if they owned property, so they usually came from the middle classes. Since they represented electors who were property-owning ratepayers, the councillors were usually keener to save money than spend it on municipal improvements. This is why there was considerable variation in the scale and provision of municipal services in the nineteenth century. Some Municipal Corporations were very progressive, but others fought tooth and nail to keep things as they were. Many used the doctrine of 'laissez-faire' (see Chapter 4) to justify doing nothing.

This is why a doctor, in 1846, said that fever was the 'favourite child of *laissez-faire*', and why, in 1853, *The Illustrated London News* claimed that:

'Neglect, ignorance, and laissez faire prepare the way for a fresh pestilence [cholera]. Most deeply is it to be regretted that at such a time as the present, men should be found to lend the weight of an official position to obstruct endeavours to obtain improvement in the neglected portions of this two-sided metropolis.'

---

1 What did the writer mean by the phrase 'this two-sided metropolis'?
2 Who was being criticised in the extract?
3 To what did the writer attribute outbreaks of cholera?

Chadwick and public health reform

Edwin Chadwick (see page 224) was the power behind the drive to improve public health in the towns. In 1839 he began a massive survey of the living conditions of the working classes. His *Report on the Sanitary Conditions of the Labouring Population of Great Britain* was published in 1842.

In his Report, Chadwick claimed that the average life expectancy for people living in Rutland (which was an agricultural area) was 52 years for a gentleman and 38 years for a working man. But in the towns it was only 38 years on average for a gentleman (35 in Liverpool, 44 in Leeds) and only 17 years for a working man (15 in Liverpool, 19 in Leeds).

1 *How do you think these life expectancy figures were calculated?*

2 *How would a high birth rate help to bring down the average age at which people died?*

3 *Do you think Chadwick took into account the higher birth rates in the towns (see Chapter 5) when he calculated these life expectancy rates?*

4 *How would this distort the comparison between town and country? Would it exaggerate the differences between the life expectancy figures or narrow the gap between them?*

5 *How do you explain the differences which Chadwick noted between the life expectancy of a gentleman and that of a working man?*

Chadwick argued that the spread of a disease like cholera was due primarily to four causes. These were:

(a)   filth and dirt,
(b)   dampness,
(c)   overcrowding,
(d)   lack of pure water.

He blamed dirt, rather than poverty itself, for the spread of disease and blamed the municipal authorities, rather than the working classes, for poor public health. He recommended the following to the municipal authorities:

(a)   cleansing of streets and homes,

    (b)   better drainage,
    (c)   better ventilation,
    (d)   better water supplies.

The Public Health Act of 1848

Chadwick's Report was followed by another massive survey, prepared by a Royal Commission on the 'Health of Large Towns and Populous Districts', which was published in 1844 and 1845.

When Chadwick's research and constant prompting resulted in the passing of the Public Health Act in 1848, it aroused considerable opposition, much of it directed at Chadwick. An article in the *Economist*, in May 1848, even suggested that 'sufferings' were Nature's punishments. In other words, the poor only got what they deserved.

The Public Health Act set up a General Board of Health in 1848, with Chadwick as one of the commissioners, together with Dr Southwood Smith, one of the most able and influential members of the medical profession at that time, and Lord Ashley, the noted philanthropist (see also Chapter 8).

The General Board of Health supervised the setting up of local Boards of Health in the towns. It was compulsory to set up a local Board of Health if the town suffered a death rate greater than 23 people in every 1,000, or if at least 10 per cent of the population demanded it. Needless to say, some towns readily complied with the new regulations, others evaded its provisions.

Those local authorities (about 200 of them), which did establish Boards of Health, were able to enforce a number of new regulations, such as those requiring that all newly built houses in their areas should have proper drains and lavatories. They could request that other houses be linked to a main sewer. They could enforce adequate standards of water supply, cleanse the streets, organise refuse collections and pay for these improvements with the aid of a local rate. In other words, they could introduce most of the improvements which Chadwick had recommended in his Report.

The trouble with the Act was that it was too weak. A modern historian has said its 'main principle was permission rather than compulsion to act'. But some of its achievements were very striking. For instance, the town of Macclesfield reduced its death rate from 42 per 1,000 in 1847, to 26 per 1,000 in 1858. Many new towns installed effective earthenware sewers and improved their systems of water supply. Sanitary inspectors helped to ensure minimum standards for many dwellings.

In succeeding years, other legislation came into force, although too little of it was actually designed to compel local authorities to take action. Liverpool appointed a Medical Officer of Health in 1847 but it was not until 1875 that all local authorities were required to do so by law.

Edwin Chadwick (1800–90)

Edwin Chadwick in 1848

Edwin Chadwick was Secretary to the Poor Law Board in 1834 (see Chapter 8) and had been involved in enquiries into the operation of the Poor Law and into the treatment of children working in factories. He had been disturbed by the high incidence of disease reported in the workhouses by Doctors Arnott, Key and Southwood Smith and this stimulated him to produce his massive 'Report on the Sanitary Conditions of the Labouring Population of Great Britain' in 1842. Unfortunately Edwin Chadwick was, although immensely talented, not a tactful man, and he provoked hostility to his views. He became very unpopular with many of the municipal authorities affected by the 1848 Public Health Act.

At that time no-one knew the real causes of diseases like typhus, typhoid fever and cholera. When these broke out in areas with piped water and new drains, opponents scorned Chadwick and his new-fangled ideas.

In 1854 he was made to retire from the Board of Health on a pension of £1,000 a year. The Board of Health was abolished in 1858, but the local Boards of Health continued to function.

In a newspaper article on the slums, in 1863, a writer said that the continued 'state of extreme filth and squalor may be due to the fact that private moneyed interests have had little to fear from parochial authority. Owners may well believe that neither board, nor commission, nor sanitary officer will trouble them.'

Civic pride

In the middle of the nineteenth century the municipal authorities in the industrial towns took great pride in their achievements, in the rapidity of their growth and in the success of the town's industries. Their success was symbolised by the solid and impressive public buildings which were erected at this time, in the magnificent town halls, the new reservoirs, the mains drainage systems, street lights, shops, and the growing suburbs.

One of the more enlightened civic achievements of the middle years of the nineteenth century was the provision of amenities for the use of the poor people in the town, such as public baths (for baths, not swimming) and public parks.

Three public parks were opened in Manchester and Salford, in 1846, to give working people the chance to enjoy fresh air and exercise, in an area of green space within the city limits. They were financed by public subscription and received a grant from Parliament as well.

A visitor to Peel Park in Salford, in October 1846, said it had an entrance lodge 'resembling the gate of a gentleman's grounds' and areas for bowls and children's games complete with swings, poles and see-saws.

The People's Park in Halifax in 1857 – a gift from a local carpet manufacturer. The Illustrated London News, *22 August 1857.*

FURTHER QUESTIONS AND EXERCISES

1   *Look at the following Sources A, B, C, D, E.*

Source A

'ELEGANT RESIDENCES may be ERECTED on Land adjoining the Spring Grove Station on the Windsor Line. SPRING GROVE ESTATE presents unusual advantages to persons seeking an agreeable and select place of residence. The South-Western Railway, which passes through a portion of the estate and has a station within a few minutes walk of every part of it, admits of hourly communication with town. Residents have the benefit of a large reduction in the price of season tickets.'

From an advert in *The Illustrated London News* 1856

Source B

'The early clerk population of Somers and Camden towns, Islington and Pentonville, are fast pouring into the City, or directing their steps towards Chancery-lane and the Inns of Court. Middle-aged men plod steadily along, apparently with no object in view but the counting house.'

Sketches by Boz by Charles Dickens 1836

Source C

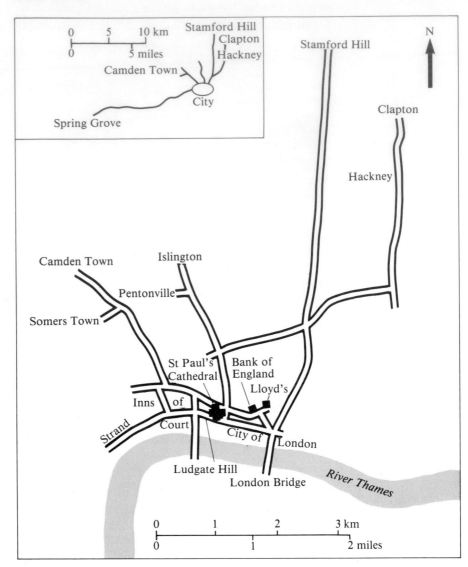

The London suburbs named in the extracts

Source D

'The regular City man who leaves Lloyd's at five o'clock, and drives home to Hackney, Clapton, Stamford-hill, or elsewhere.'

Sketches by Boz by Charles Dickens 1836

Source E

'THE SUBURBS OF LONDON

Here are no pestilent gasometers, nor belching tall chimneys, nor any reeking dunghill and stagnant pools to taint the breeze and offend the nostrils of the passer-by. The houses in the suburbs each possess a small garden. Their occupants are principally superior clerks, heads of firms, or gentlemen who are compelled to visit the City daily, and who reside in the suburbs both on account of its cheapness to themselves, and its healthfulness for their families. Scarcely is breakfast concluded, when the punctual city omnibus, grinding along the newly-gravelled road, draws up.'

Chambers's Journal 1844

(a) Make a list of the London suburbs in which the following lived: the clerks who worked in the counting houses near the Bank of England and in the Inns of Court (Source B), the City men who worked at Lloyd's insurance (Source D), an official of the Bank of England who lived in an 'elegant residence' on the Spring Grove Estate (Source A).

(b) Find these suburbs on the map (Source C). What was the average distance to work travelled by each of these workers?

(c) What different methods of getting to work are indicated in Sources A, B, D, E? What travel bonus was available to the resident of Spring Grove? How long do you think it took the clerks (Source B) to get to work in 1836? What would you say was the furthest distance a factory worker would want to live away from a workplace at this time?

(d) Who lived in the more distant suburbs (Sources A, D, E)? Why did they live there? How can you tell from these extracts that the suburbs were being extended?

(e) To which of London's major problems does Source E relate? Compare the advantages of living in the suburbs with the disadvantages of living in the inner city. Why were the more distant suburbs (Sources A, D, E) occupied by the middle classes?

2 *What were the main provisions of (a) The Municipal Corporation Act of 1835, (b) The Public Health Act, 1848? What were their merits and what were their defects?*

3 *Write a short essay describing the living conditions in a large town in the early nineteenth century. Indicate the different types and quality of the homes which housed the working classes. Why were they built close together in courts and back-to-back terraces? Why were improvements urgently needed, and what hampered their progress?*

4 *Describe and account for the distribution and growth of large towns in Britain in the nineteenth century.*

5 *Explain briefly the importance of each of the following in the improvement of living conditions in towns in the nineteenth century:*
(a)   the Local Improvement Acts,
(b)   the work of Joseph Bazalgette,
(c)   the charity of George Peabody,
(d)   the example of Sir Titus Salt.

6 *Assess the contribution of Edwin Chadwick to the improvement of living conditions in the towns in the nineteenth century.*

7 *Critically analyse each of the statements which follow and say in which respects it is right or wrong.*
(a)   'Typhus fever, a disease generally produced by filth, intoxication and vice.'
(b)   'The highest mortality rates are traceable to poverty, bad ventilation, want of cleanliness, vice and intemperance.'
(c)   'Defective ventilation appears to me to be the principal cause of tuberculosis.'

8 *What were the major problems which arose as a result of London's rapid growth in the eighteenth and nineteenth centuries?*

9 *To what extent were the urban problems of London in the nineteenth century the same as those of London in the twentieth century?*

10 *Look at the cartoon below from* Punch *in 1858. To which project did this cartoon apply? Who was the 'Silent Highwayman'? Explain the significance of this cartoon.*

Cartoon from Punch, *1858*

THE "SILENT HIGHWAY"-MAN.
"Your MONEY or your LIFE!"

Chapter Seven
Working-class Movements

INTRODUCTION

Open-air meeting of mill workers on strike in Preston (The Illustrated London News, 12 November, 1853). The owners of the cotton mills had refused to honour an agreement on pay, and the article accompanying the picture used the terms 'severity', 'stern', 'unbending' and 'oppressive' in the description of the conduct of the Preston mill-owners. It was one of the rare occasions when the newspapers sided with the strikers – unlike the extract at the start of this chapter.

'At this moment, there is not a manufacturing town in South Lancashire in which that trade pest, a strike, does not rage in some form, or that is not in daily fear of contagion. The adjacent counties are no less dangerously infected. Trade in Cheshire, Yorkshire and Derbyshire languishes under the disease; and valleys are once more given up to silence and want, through the errors of the class most interested in the prosperity of the works which they reduce to inactivity.'

Manchester Guardian 1861

1 *How many words or phrases in this newspaper report resemble those used to describe the cholera epidemics between 1831 and 1865?*

2 *Why do you think the writer described a strike in this way? What other evidence shows that he was biased against strikers?*

3 *Why is it important for a historian to find out whether evidence about the past is biased? If it is, does that make it worthless?*

4 *Which of today's newspapers would be most likely to describe:*
(a) a strike as a 'disease',
(b) employers as 'oppressive'?
How do you think The Guardian *(formerly the* Manchester Guardian*) would describe a strike?*

In this chapter you will read about two main types of working-class movement. These were:

(a) **The political struggle** to try to reform the electoral system in order to elect Members of Parliament who would represent the working classes. Only in this way could they hope to see an end to the laws which they saw as oppressive, such as those against trade unions, the Poor Laws (see Chapter 8) and unfair systems of taxation.

(b) **The trade union movement** which tried to protect jobs, raise wages, lower the number of hours at work, increase safety standards and improve living and working conditions.

At some periods political struggles made the headlines, such as those of the Luddites in 1811–12, and the Chartists in 1837–48. At other times trade unions dominated the history of the working-class movement, as in 1825-34 after the repeal of the Combination Acts, and in 1867-8 at the time of the Sheffield Outrages, the *Hornby* v. *Close* trial and the first TUC Congress.

Before 1800, poor communications, small towns and scattered workplaces, made it difficult to organise trade unions and plan political meetings. But the coming of the railway and the rapid growth of factories and towns soon altered that. Large numbers of workers employed in the same factory shared the same resentment against poor working conditions and against low rates of pay. They could see the power they might be able to exert if they combined together to force employers to consent to their demands.

WORKING-CLASS MOVEMENTS BEFORE 1800

Combinations

Before 1800, only a minority of workers were employed in large factories and lived in towns. Most were still craft workers working in small workshops and cottages. It was hard, if not impossible, to persuade all the workers in a particular industry to take action. Not surprisingly, most of the protests took place in London, easily the biggest city in Britain, or on the coalfields, where many workers were sometimes employed by a pit owner. Thus in 1721, the Master Tailors of London complained that 7,000 of their workers had 'entered into a combination to raise their wages, and leave off working an hour sooner than they used to'.

In 1763, Tyneside coal miners had to sign an undertaking, called the Yearly Bond, which stated that 'the parties hired shall continue at work, without striking, combining or absenting themselves'.

---

1 *What do you think was meant by 'combining' or 'entering into a combination'?*
2 *How can we deduce from the Yearly Bond that there had been miners' strikes before 1763? What would such an agreement be called today?*
3 *Look at the picture on page 47 showing a silk-weaving workshop in 1747. Why were strikes ineffective in workshops like this?*

However, most of these strikes in the eighteenth century were small-scale and confined to local rather than national areas.

The corresponding societies

The storming of the Bastille, in 1789, at the start of the French Revolution, made a tremendous impression on people in Britain. If ordinary people could seize power in France, what could stop ordinary people doing the same in Britain? The thought occurred alike to both the ruling and the working classes! The London Revolution Society welcomed the French Revolution and reform societies were formed in several cities.

But the members of 'The Friends of Freedom', who met in Birmingham on Bastille Day in 1791, were themselves the victims of mob violence. A crowd destroyed the homes of local reformers and others thought sympathetic to the French Revolutionaries.

Many reform societies, like the 'Friends', had sprung up at this time throughout Britain. These Georgian reformers wanted to reform the electoral system. They demanded universal suffrage (votes for all) and annual parliaments. In 1792 a group of London working men, under the leadership of a shoemaker, called Thomas Hardy, started the most influential society, the London Corresponding Society, with a membership of over 3,000. They met in 'sections' of 30 members, paid one penny [0.4p] a week subscription and were drawn largely from the working classes, unlike the members of most of the other reform societies who liked to debate issues over dinner! It was called a Corresponding Society because the members corresponded with each other. The Government was alarmed because it wondered whether this was the start of an English Revolution. Pitt's Government tried to suppress the Reform movement, by charging its leaders with rebellion – but they had no evidence of any intention to start a revolution and the courts found Thomas Hardy and others not guilty. By then Britain was at war with France and this helped to dampen enthusiasm for reforms inspired by the French Revolution. The London Corresponding Society was already in decline when Parliament passed new laws curbing the activities of the Reformers and banning the London Corresponding Society.

To all intents and purposes the Reform movement was dead. But the aims of the Reformers were kept alive and you will see them recurring at different times – in 1819, at the time of the Peterloo Massacre; in the early 1830s, before the passing of the Reform Bill; in the 1840s, at the time of the Chartists; and in the activities of the Reform League, in 1865.

Cartoon in about 1830 depicting Reformers attempting to chop down a tree labelled 'rotten boroughs'. Rotten boroughs returned Members of Parliament even though there might only have been one or two people entitled to vote there.

Trade clubs and friendly societies

During the eighteenth century, workers in a number of different industries and occupations had formed friendly societies and trade clubs, which met in inns and taverns. Inn signs, such as the Bricklayer's Arms, are reminders of these clubs and societies.

The main purpose of the trade clubs was similar to that of the Woolcombers' Trade Club in 1794, whose members paid a regular subscription:

> 'to enable the woolcomber to travel from place to place to seek for employment, when work is scarce where he resides; and to have relief when he is sick; and if he should die to be buried by the club.'

---

1 *What three important benefits were provided for the woolcombers?*
2 *Why were they necessary?*

By 1815, there were over 7,000 of these friendly societies and they had the approval of the authorities, since they encouraged the working classes to save money. Some had other aims, besides providing members with burial, sickness and unemployment benefits. They sought to protect their members' jobs, to raise pay levels and to improve working conditions – these are the classic aims of any trade union.

The Combination Acts

Strictly speaking, it was unlawful to organise workers to take action 'in restraint of trade'. But under the existing laws it took a long time to bring offenders to trial. This is why, in 1799, and in 1800, when the government clamped down on the Reformers, it also introduced the Combination Acts, banning trade unions. The Act of 1800 stipulated gaol sentences for workers, who:

(a) attended strike meetings;
(b) **combined** with others to force employers to raise wages;
(c) **combined** to force employers to improve working conditions;
(d) picketed;
(e) helped to finance strikes.

The Combination Acts came into force at a time when the factory system was beginning to grow fast. Undoubtedly it stunted the progress of the trade union movement, since it drove many trade unions to secrecy, although even this did not prevent strike action. The weavers of Preston, for example, went on strike in 1808, 1818 and 1821. Strikes also took place in the context of other protests, such as the Luddite riots of 1811–12.

THE AGE OF PETERLOO

Riots and disturbances

Between 1811 and 1819 there were many disturbances and serious riots. The memory of the French Revolution was still in the hearts of many liberals and in the minds of the governing class. But there was no single reason why there were so many demonstrations, other than the fact that desperate people, driven by poverty, tried to defend their livelihoods and support their families at a time of great change. Some of the most important factors were as follows.

(a) **Rapid change:** As Chapter 2 showed, the pace of industrial change was quickening. Factories, steam engines and machines were replacing small workshops, home industries and handloom weavers. Rural unemployment had also become a serious problem and many farmworkers were seeking jobs in the industrial towns which were growing at a furious pace. In the decade, 1811–20, Britain's population reached its peak period of growth – Glasgow and Manchester grew by nearly 50 per cent.

(b) **Effects of the Revolutionary and Napoleonic Wars:** Although the economy was growing rapidly, it did not do so at a constant rate. The Napoleonic Wars between 1793 and 1815 created many jobs, since the army and navy needed weapons, munitions, food and cloth for uniforms. But the war also cut Britain off from unlimited supplies of foreign grain, so corn prices rose steeply (see the graph on page 26), raising the price of bread which was the staple diet of the poorest people and increasing their hardship.

(c) **Effects of the French Revolution:** The slogan of the French Revolution – 'Liberty, Fraternity, Equality' – and the fact that the Revolutionaries had overthrown their King, still fired the imagination of many Radicals.

(d) **Unemployment:** As soon as the Napoleonic Wars were over, industry slumped. The countries of Europe had been drained by the expense of providing armies to fight for, or against, Napoleon and were unable to purchase British exports. The British army stopped placing orders for uniforms, weapons and munitions. Jobs became scarce. Many factories and workshops in Britain had to close down or sack workers. Many banks collapsed (see Chapter 4). The problem became worse when soldiers and sailors returned from the war.

(e) **The Corn Laws:** Despite the distress caused by unemployment, Parliament approved the Corn Laws in 1815 (see Chapter 1), to protect farmers and landowners, whose living standards might suffer if the price of wheat fell. The Corn Laws helped to keep the price of bread high. This meant that the living standards of the poorest people were lowered at a time of high unemployment, in order to maintain the living standards of those who could best afford to pay.

(f) **Taxation:** During the Napoleonic Wars the Government had raised money by an income tax (see Chapter 4), mainly affecting people who were well-off. In 1816 this was repealed. Taxes were still needed, of course, but the burden of the new taxes fell most heavily on the poor.

The Luddite riots

The distress and turmoil of the years of war and peace at the start of the nineteenth century disrupted life in Britain. Hungry, unemployed people, who had no voice in parliament, took action in the only way which they felt was left to them – by violent protest.

Contemporary caricature of the Luddite riots in 1811–12. Did the artist approve of Captain Ludd?

As Chapter 2 showed, the new inventions of both Kay and Hargreaves, in the 1730s and 1760s, were destroyed by angry workers, frightened they might lose their livelihoods. In 1811, similar anger was aroused, when a stocking frame was widely used in Nottinghamshire:

'whereby a considerable saving of manual labour was produced, and a consequent further diminution of hands. On November the 10th, a number of weavers, assembling near Nottingham, began forcibly to enter houses in which were frames of this kind, and destroy them. The rioters assumed the name of Luddites, and acted under the authority of an imaginary Captain Ludd.'

From the *Annual Register* for 1811

The frames were not actually new at all, just wider than normal. Unscrupulous manufacturers were using them to produce wide cloth which was then cut up into stockings or gloves and stitched.

In 1812 the Luddite riots took a more serious turn, when they broke out in Lancashire against firms using power looms, and in Yorkshire against firms using shearing frames (for trimming woollen cloth). The Yorkshire Luddites used a heavy hammer, made by Enoch Taylor, to smash the hated machines. A manufacturer was murdered near Huddersfield and a factory near Wigan was burned down.

Some of the Luddites died in attacks on textile mills, such as at Middleton in Lancashire, where five hand loom weavers were killed, and at Liversedge, near Leeds, where two men died in a night attack on William Cartwright's Rawfolds Mill. Others died later on the gallows or were transported to Australia for the part they played in the riots.

---

1 *In what ways did the Luddite riots resemble the later riots by farmworkers in 1830–1?*
2 *What do you think this Luddite rhyme was about? 'Great Enoch still shall lead the van, Stop him who dare! Stop him who can!'*
3 *Why was the Luddite movement doomed to failure?*

Further demonstrations

In London, in March 1815, mobs roamed the streets, protesting against the effects the Corn Laws would have. So violent was the popular opposition to the new measures, that a rioting crowd broke into the home of the government minister responsible. They broke windows, knocked down the front door, smashed furniture and ripped up valuable paintings.

A meeting at Spa Fields in London in 1816, called to protest against the Corn Laws, was addressed by Henry 'Orator' Hunt – a radical speaker. It turned into a riot, and had to be put down by soldiers. The authorities were seriously disturbed when some of the workers broke into a gunmaker's premises. The French Revolution was still in people's minds.

In 1817, unemployed workers from Pentrich in the Midlands tried to march on Nottingham but were forced to turn back when soldiers blocked their way. The same thing happened to the Blanketeers, a group of Manchester weavers, who tried to march to Derby and London in the same year.

The Peterloo Massacre

The Peterloo Massacre, 1819, contemporary print by George Cruikshank

On Monday, 16 August 1819, a huge crowd of 60–80,000 people gathered at St Peter's Fields, in Manchester, to hear another speech by Henry 'Orator' Hunt. This time the protest ended in tragedy, when thirteen people were killed and hundreds wounded in a cavalry charge.

You can read about the Peterloo Massacre on the following pages, with sources extracted from a round-up of the news, published in *The Times* on 19 August 1819. In the days before the telephone, newspapers often copied items from other papers to widen their coverage of the news. Some of these accounts are on-the-spot eyewitness descriptions. Others are by writers who may, or may not, have been at the demonstration. One, at least, was not written by an eyewitness.

The laws which controlled demonstrations at that time stated that if a crowd did not disperse *within one hour* of the reading of the Riot Act by a magistrate, then they were guilty of a crime and could be arrested.

Source A

'Before 12 o'clock crowds began to assemble, each town or hamlet having a banner, and some a cap, with "Liberty" upon it: each party, as they came through the streets, kept in military order, with sticks shouldered. A banner was painted "Taxation and no Representation is tyrannical and unjust", and on the reverse "No Boroughmongering – Unite and be free – Equal representation or

Death". On another banner "Die like men, and not be sold like slaves". On a third, "Major Cartwright's Bill and no Corn Laws", on a fourth, "Unity and Fraternity" – "Strength and Liberty".

It was 20 minutes after one o'clock before Hunt appeared. "Gentlemen, I must entreat that you will be peaceable; a great deal depends upon that, and I trust all who hear me will remain quiet."'

The Courier

Source B

'The meeting was then addressed by the several orators, showing much menacing attitude, and the shouts seemed to rend the very air and shake the foundation of the ground. The constables were tauntingly insulted wherever they were observed to stand; sticks and hats always waving on every acclamation.

About half-past one the Magistrates deemed it expedient to read the Riot Act, and instantly after the platform was surrounded in a masterly manner. The manoeuvre would have taken place without bloodshed had not the mob assailed the military and civil authorities with every resistance in their power, and particularly with missiles. Consequently the cavalry charged in their own defence; not without first being witnesses to a pistol-shot from the multitude, against one of the gentlemen in our Yeomanry, who now lies in imminent danger.'

Letter in *The Courier*

Source C

'The troops dashed at full gallop amongst the people, actually hacking their way up to the hustings. Whether the Riot Act had been read, I am not enabled positively to say; but I affirm, from actual observation, that not the slightest breach of the peace had been committed.'

Letter in *The Star*

Source D

'Some 10 minutes had elapsed, all was certainly peaceable, when a body of cavalry rode up through the crowd, brandishing their drawn swords, surrounded the hustings, and seized Hunt. I was myself a spectator, and the conduct of the crowd was quite peaceable. It is not believed that the Magistrates read the Riot Act; if they did, at least, nobody was aware of it. There can hardly be a doubt, if the meeting had been permitted to take its course, it would have concluded as peaceably as they have always hitherto done; as it is, blood has been shed!'

Private letter

Source E

'The principal part of them were stout men, with sticks or clubs; but there were a few female Reformers. They marched in regular order, and in ranks of three or four each, and the word "Left, left," was repeated every time the left foot was put down. The word "Halt" was shouted and instantly obeyed. About a quarter past 1, Hunt arrived. At the corner of Quay-street, he waved his hat in a most insolent way to some officers.

The Magistrates were placed in a house near the hustings, with a line of special constables extending from them in order to report. After Hunt had spoken about 10 minutes, the Cavalry rode up to the hustings, and surrounded it. Instantly the mob assailed them with stones and sticks, and attempted to unhorse them. Mr. John Hulme was struck with a bottle, and then unhorsed and so wounded, as to be expected to die before morning.

The confusion then became dreadful, numbers were thrown down and trampled upon. The mob rallied at different points, and threw stones at the military. The cavalry then charged amongst them, and many were hurt with sabre cuts.'

Letter in The Courier

Source F

'Early in the morning the municipal authorities caused precautionary placards to be posted throughout the town.

"The boroughreeves and constables of Manchester and Salford most earnestly recommend the peaceable and well-disposed inhabitants of those towns, as much as possible, to remain in their own houses during the whole of this day, Monday, August 16, and to keep children and servants within doors."

Soon after 12 o'clock, the Magistrates repaired to the ground; and the Riot Act was read; but it did not appear to be much attended to by the crowd. We understand the travelling orator had begun to address the reformers, when an hour having expired, after the reading of the Riot Act, the warrants of the Magistrates were carried into effect.'

Manchester Herald

Source G

'A club of female Reformers, amounting in number, according to our calculation, to 156, came from Oldham; and bore a white silk banner, inscribed "Major Cartwright's Bill, Annual Parliaments, Universal Suffrage, and Vote by Ballot". The Reformers from Rochdale and Middleton marched to the sound of the bugle, marching in ordinary and double quick time, according as it pleased the fancy of their leaders to direct them.

A posse of 300 or 400 constables marched into the field about 12 o'clock. Not the slightest insult was offered to them.

The cavalry drew their swords, and brandished them fiercely in the air: upon which they rode into the mob which gave way before them. Not a brickbat was thrown at them – not a pistol was fired during this period: all was quiet and orderly. They wheeled round the waggons till they came in front of them.

As soon as Hunt and Johnson had jumped from the waggon (to surrender) a cry was made by the cavalry, "Have at their flags".

They immediately dashed not only at the flags which were in the wagon, but those which were posted among the crowd, cutting most indiscriminately to the right and left in order to get at them. This set the people running in all directions, and it was not till this act had been committed that any brick-bats were hurled at the military. From that moment the Manchester Yeomanry Cavalry lost all command of temper. A man within five yards of us had his nose completely taken off by a blow of a sabre.'

Special correspondent of *The Times*

The Times reporter, who was mistakenly arrested, was said to hold Hunt's views 'in as utter abhorrence as the most loyal subject of His Majesty'.

Source H

'Next came the odious instigators of the day's calamity, viz Hunt, Johnson, Knight. About half-past one they ascended the hustings. [After] some preliminary business, occupying about twenty minutes, the bugle sounded, and the cavalry advanced.'

Manchester Mercury

Study the extracts and look closely at the picture of the Massacre, comparing it with the reports.

1 *Make a list of all the statements for which there is at least one other opposing opinion. Is there any sign of bias in the picture? Can you detect bias in any of the extracts? Which sources put the blame for the disaster on Hunt and the Reformers? Which blame the other side, namely the Magistrates and the Yeomanry? Which version of events do you believe? Why?*

2 *Why was it called the Peterloo Massacre? What were the 'hustings'? Which extracts support the version of the Massacre drawn by the artist?*

3 *What did the demonstrators want? Make a list of their slogans. Group them together if you think they mean the same thing. Which slogans can be used as evidence to confirm the causes of unrest listed on page 234? What evidence is there of a women's movement at this time?*

4 *What evidence is there to suggest that some of the demonstrators may have had military training? Did they carry weapons? Is there any evidence that they were looking for trouble? Is this evidence from biased or unbiased sources?*

5 *How do we know the Magistrates were expecting trouble? How did they keep in touch with events at the demonstration?*

6 *What clues can you find to help you determine whether the writers were eyewitnesses at the demonstration, or not? Why do you think the versions given by the eyewitnesses differ? Why is it difficult to establish exactly what happened on an occasion like this?*

7 *Which statements are facts and which are opinions? Which statements seem to you unlikely to be deliberate falsehoods or distortions of the truth? Write your own account of the Peterloo Massacre, using these facts.*

8 *When did Hunt mount the hustings? Was the Riot Act read out by the magistrates and, if so, when? Are there any reliable eyewitness reports to this effect? When did the Yeomanry make their move to arrest Hunt? On this evidence, did the magistrates comply with the law?*

9 *Was the crowd 'peaceable' or not? Who do you think was responsible for the massacre? Imagine you are a wealthy landowner, like most of your fellow Members of Parliament in 1819. What is your reaction to the news you have read in* The Times *about the Peterloo Massacre? Draw up a list of recommendations you want to make to the Government, after first debating the issue with your friends.*

The Six Acts

In order to clear up the confusion about the conduct of public meetings **and** to curtail the freedom of working people to protest, the Government passed the Six Acts. These Six Acts of 1819:

(a) Made certain demonstrations illegal.

(b) Banned military training outside the army.

(c) Banned the printing of anything which might encourage people to riot.

(d) Made it quicker to bring rioters to justice in the courts.

(e) Gave local magistrates the right to search people's homes for weapons.

(f) Taxed newspapers, making them too costly for the working classes to buy. In this way the Government aimed to prevent radical writers spreading ideas which might lead to a revolution.

Look carefully at the Six Acts and at the sources which describe the Peterloo Massacre.

1 *Imagine you are a Member of Parliament in 1819. Quote evidence from* The Times *to justify each of the Six Acts above.*

THE EARLY TRADE UNIONS

The repeal of the Combination Acts

After the Napoleonic Wars, Francis Place, a Radical thinker and a tailor, joined with Joseph Hume, a Radical Member of Parliament, to take action to try to persuade Parliament to repeal the Combination Acts. Success came in 1824 and in 1825 (the first Act was thought too lenient). But the 1825 Act stipulated that:

> 'If any person shall by violence to the person or property, or by threats or intimidation, or by molesting or in any way obstructing another, force or endeavour to force, any journeyman, manufacturer, etc., to depart from his business, or to return his work before it is finished, or preventing any person from returning to his work, etc., every person so offending, or aiding, or assisting therein, shall be imprisoned for any period not exceeding three months.'

There was to be no punishment for those who just met together 'for the sole purpose of determining the wages' they required, or the hours which they were prepared to work.

---

1 *What did the Act prevent? Did it prevent strikes? Did it prevent peaceful picketing?*

2 *What is meant by 'intimidation' and by 'molesting'? If a picket stands at the entrance to a factory is that 'obstructing another'?*

3 *Why do you think trade unionists often found it difficult to know what they could, or could not, do within the law?*

During a dispute, nineteen years later, striking Northumberland miners sang a song with the words:

> 'They rub wet clay in a blackleg's face,
> And round the pitheaps they run a foot race
> To catch the blackleg miners.'

---

4 *Was this an offence under the 1825 Act? What is a blackleg? Is picketing legal today?*

On 17 July 1825, the following court case was reported in *The Age*, a London Sunday newspaper:

> 'All the men in the employment of Mr. Ashenden, a boot and shoemaker, at Hampstead, struck for wages about a fortnight ago.

Among them were Robert Ford and George Turner. The latter, however, was compelled by the rest to strike against his will; and when the whole party were assembled at a public house debating the matter, he said he was sorry he had left his work, and would return to it; upon which Ford, who was one of the most active promoters of the "strike" swore, that if he did he would drag him through a pond.

Ford, in defence, said he made use of no threat. The words he made use of were these:- "If you return to your work, you ought to be dragged through a pond".'

5 *Did Ford break the new law? Would you have found him guilty or not guilty?*

Caricature of a trade union meeting, from McLean's Monthly Sheet of Caricatures, *no. 53, c. 1830. What was the artist's opinion about trade unions and their aims?*

The need for unity

The repeal of the Combination Acts did allow many new unions to be formed, such as the Association of Colliers in the Rivers Tyne and Wear in 1825 with 4,000 members. By 1831, the Colliers' meetings were being attended by 10–20,000 people. The aim of the Association of Colliers was as follows:

'To make provision for themselves and families in cases of death, sickness, or other accidents or infirmities, and to unite in a firm manner, in order to obtain a more suitable recompense for, and to regulate the hours of labour.'

Annals of Coal Mining, Robert Galloway 1898

1 *Which of their aims were those of a friendly society?*
2 *Which of their aims were those of a trade union?*

As the name suggests, the Association of Colliers in the Rivers Tyne and Wear was still a regional rather than a national union. But when miners went on strike, there was nothing to stop employers bringing in non-union miners from other areas – apart from the violence offered them by the strikers.

The Colliers had a remarkable leader in Thomas Hepburn. In 1831, they had a notable success under his leadership, when they went on strike for seven weeks and gained a 30 per cent increase in wages and cut the hours worked by boys underground to 12 per day.

However, the pit owners were making plans. In 1832, when another miners' strike was called, they evicted strikers from their homes and brought in workers from other areas, such as Wales. Some of the black-legs were seriously injured, a local magistrate was killed and one of two miners responsible was later hanged. The strike broke up and the strikers were forced to leave the union.

The unions needed to find some way of co-operating with each other, otherwise similar strikes were also bound to fail. The owners could afford to wait for the strikers to come back to work, or could employ blackleg labour from other areas to do the jobs of striking workers.

Some movement towards unity had already been made. In 1830, John Doherty, leader of the Lancashire cotton spinners, organised a new union with members from cotton mills as well as from pottery works and other industries. It was called the National Association for the Protection of Labour but, like so many other unions at this time, it was basically weak and lasted only a matter of months.

The Grand National Consolidated Trades Union

In 1833, Robert Owen (see next page), an enlightened philanthropist, who had already made his name with his co-operative living scheme at New Lanark, persuaded some of the bigger unions to combine together to form the Grand National Consolidated Trades Union in February 1834. Almost immediately, the GNCTU was faced with a major crisis, when the Tolpuddle Martyrs were sent for trial in March 1834.

Robert Owen (1771–1858)

Robert Owen

Robert Owen was a self-made man. He was the son of a Welsh saddler, became the manager of a cotton mill before he was 20, and was the part-owner of the New Lanark cotton mills, near Glasgow, before he was 30. Here he tried to establish an ideal community, banishing dirt, crime, poverty, ignorance and conflict between employer and worker.

Owen refused to employ children under ten years of age. Instead he built a school and reduced the working hours of the older children. He provided his 1,800 workers with better housing than was then being built for factory workers and opened shops selling low-priced goods. So successful was New Lanark, that Owen showed it off to about 2,000 visitors a year. For example, *The Morning Chronicle* announced in September 1819 that:

> 'The guardians of the poor, acting for the township of Leeds, have appointed a deputation to visit Mr.Owen's establishment at New Lanark.'

Owen preached co-operation and wanted to establish communities where workers co-operated with each other to make goods, to buy and sell to each other and to run their own lives in harmony with one another. In many respects Owenism was a type of early socialism and in his day Owen was very influential. By 1830 there were well over 300 co-operative societies in Britain and attempts had been made, both in Britain and in America, to establish 'villages of co-operation', such as New Harmony in Indiana. But the only co-operative to survive was the highly successful shopping venture established by the Rochdale Pioneers in 1844, the founder of the modern co-operative society.

The Tolpuddle Martyrs

Six farm workers were prosecuted in 1834 when they tried to start a trade union in the Dorset village of Tolpuddle. They had been charged, not with joining a union, which was perfectly legal, but with swearing unlawful oaths. This law was an out-of-date relic from the legislation passed after the Spithead Mutiny in 1797. It related to the navy, not to trade unions, and should not have been used to try the Tolpuddle Martyrs.

Farm workers at that time lived on the poverty line and were hardly a major force. However, this was the time when the Captain Swing riots had alarmed landowners and farmers (see Chapter 1).

Working people were understandably shocked when the Tolpuddle Martyrs were sentenced to transportation to Australia.

Contemporary illustration of the procession by the Grand National Consolidated Trades Union in support of the Tolpuddle Martyrs, 1834

---

1 *Imagine you are a Member of Parliament in 1834. In what ways are you surprised by this procession of trade union members?*
2 *Compare this scene with the Luddite Riots (1811–12) and the Peterloo demonstration (1819). Which of these working-class protests was most likely to alarm the ruling classes?*

The case of the Tolpuddle Martyrs was a setback for the trade union movement, since it frightened off many workers who might otherwise have joined the new unions.

Public protest, not only that of the GNCTU and the working class, but also from Members of Parliament and influential members of the middle class, eventually succeeded in getting the sentences set aside, although it was not until 1838 that all the Martyrs returned to Britain.

Many workers lost confidence in trade unions after the Tolpuddle disaster, and after 1,500 workers at Derby were locked-out for being members of the Union. Soon afterwards the GNCTU collapsed.

Uneducated, illiterate workers, living at near-starvation levels, in squalid slums, were difficult to organise effectively, and too many blacklegs were prepared to take the jobs of strikers.

Inn sign in the village of Tolpuddle, Dorset. Is this sympathetic to the cause of farmer or farmworker?

> **3** *Why are strikes usually only successful in 'boom' years, when factories have full order books and can sell everything they make?*
>
> **4** *Conversely, why are strikes at times of recession or depression difficult for the workers to win?*
>
> **5** *Do any recent strikes confirm or refute these general principles?*

REFORM OF PARLIAMENT

In 1830 Parliament was failing to represent the people in many ways:

(a) Only a small fraction of the people had the vote – less than one person in every 50.

(b) Eligibility to vote depended on where you lived. In the counties (each entitled to send two Members of Parliament, no matter how small or how big they were) voters had to own freehold property, worth at least £2 a year in rent. In the boroughs there were differences in the eligibility of voters from town to town. But most involved the ownership of property in some form or other – usually as ratepayer or householder.

(c) In many cases the division of the country into constituencies dated back to much earlier times and bore little relation to the number of people living in them. One constituency in Wiltshire – Old Sarum – had two Members of Parliament. But there were no people actually living there, no houses even – only fields!

(d) Those people who were eligible to vote had to do so in public, by a show of hands. There was no secret ballot, so everyone knew who everyone else was voting for – such as their landlord, employer, or commanding officer. This meant that it was worth bribing people to vote for a candidate, since it was possible to check that people voted as they had been bribed.

Election scene in about 1740 by Hogarth

1 *What is the name given to the temporary wooden platform which you can see in this picture?*

2 *How is that name used today at election time, even though the platform has gone?*

3 *What evils of the old electoral system are shown in this picture? In what ways was an eighteenth-century election undemocratic?*

4 *What arguments are sometimes used to defend electoral systems where only the rich or powerful have a vote?*

Rotten boroughs

Constituencies such as Old Sarum were called 'rotten boroughs' – because a famous eighteenth-century politician had denounced them as being the 'rotten part of the constitution'. In every case their right to send two Members of Parliament to the House of Commons was based on tradition. By 1831 there were 56 of these rotten boroughs, many of them in Cornwall.

By contrast the 200,000 people who lived in Manchester had no Member of Parliament to represent them. Manchester had not been important in the Middle Ages; in 1831 it was a thriving industrial city. The need for reform was urgent. Hundreds of thousands of other people living in the rapidly growing industrial cities of Britain, such as Birmingham, Sheffield, Leeds and Bradford, were also unrepresented in Parliament.

Agitation to make fresh parliamentary constituencies went hand-in-hand with demands that the franchise be extended (to allow more people to vote). Manufacturers in the industrial towns were just as keen as their workers to see these changes. So too were liberal Members of Parliament, who understood how unjust the system was.

The passing of the Reform Act

The movement to reform Parliament gathered pace in the 1820s. Working people began to see that the only way they could change their living and working conditions was either through revolution or by exercising power in Parliament. Some would have preferred the former alternative but most pressed for the latter and sought an early reform of the voting system and an extension of the franchise, to enable all working men to vote.

The revolution in France convinced the Whig Party that danger lay ahead if the electoral system went unreformed. In 1831, they introduced the Reform Bill for the first time but it was later rejected by the House of Lords. By this time there were demonstrations, and even riots, among ordinary people who demanded that 'the Bill, the whole Bill, and nothing but the Bill' be passed. Nottingham Castle was set on fire and there were serious riots in Bristol (October 1831). Some provincial supporters of the Bill threatened to march on London, whilst people in the capital were urged to withdraw money from the Bank of England to upset the economy of the country.

In the face of massive public protest the Tory opposition agreed to let the Bill through. The Whigs persuaded King William IV to say he would create enough new peers (i.e. lords) from Whig supporters of the Bill to enable them to outvote the Bill's opponents in the House of Lords. The opposition collapsed and in June 1832 the Reform Bill became law.

Terms and results of the Reform Act

The Reform Act redistributed the constituencies, abolishing 56 rotten boroughs and giving their seats instead to the industrial cities. It also gave more seats to the counties with the largest populations.

In addition the rules specifying who was eligible to vote were changed. For the first time the law laid down that all voters had to be male, over

The House of Commons in 1834, from a contemporary print. In what ways is a meeting of the House of Commons today similar or dissimilar to the scene depicted in this picture?

21, and (in the towns) be the owners of property, or tenants of a house, with a rent of at least £10 per year. This was a substantial sum of money for those days – equivalent to a year's pay for a cook or maid. As a result, only the educated middle classes gained the vote.

The Reform Act had little effect on the voting ambitions of the working class – something that angered them when they realised the Act was not going to alter Parliament overnight. Altogether about another 300,000 people got the vote, making the proportion of voters in England and Wales about one person in every 30.

The Members of Parliament elected to the new industrial constituencies were manufacturers and industrialists **not** workers. The working classes were little better off after the passing of the Act than before. But there was one big difference. Parliament had at last overcome its resistance to changing the system which elected members of the House of Commons. Change would be much easier from that point on.

CHARTISM

In 1838 a group of men decided to press once again for electoral reform. Francis Place, the reformer who was largely responsible for getting the Combination Acts repealed, joined with William Lovett (Secretary of the London Working Men's Association) and John Roebuck (a Radical Member of Parliament) to draw up a People's Charter with a simple demand for six basic reforms. These were as follows:

The Six Points of the People's Charter

- **A vote for every adult male** – over 21, of sound mind, not a criminal. This is called adult male suffrage.
- **Secret ballot** – to protect the voter, so his employer could not influence the way he voted.
- **Annual parliaments** – to ensure that MPs did not go against the wishes of their constituents.
- **No property qualification for MPs** – so that poor men could also stand for Parliament as well as the rich.
- **Payment of a salary to MPs** – so that working men could afford to give up their jobs and stand for Parliament. (At that time only people with private incomes could afford to become MPs.)
- **Constituencies of equal size** – so that every constituency had the same number of voters.

Causes of the Chartist movement

Chartism owed its appeal to a number of factors.

(a) Anger at the exclusion of working-class voters from the new electoral system after 1832 – especially since working-class protests had helped to force the Reform Bill through Parliament.

(b) The decline of the trade unions after Tolpuddle and the collapse of the GNCTU. Without political power, many workers felt they could do little to improve working conditions in the factories.

(c) The passing of the Poor Law Amendment Act in 1834 (see Chapter 8) was seen as a vindictive and deliberate attack on the working classes – especially in the North. It meant that if unemployed workers wanted to apply for poor relief out of the rates, they had to go and live in the workhouse, where their families were split up. Moreover, Parliament had decided that life in the workhouse should be deliberately made as harsh and as unwelcoming as possible, to deter paupers who might otherwise seek the support of the parish rather than look for a job.

(d) It was a period of depression. Thousands of craftsmen were losing their jobs as more and more textile mills started to use steam-powered machinery (see Chapter 2). So the possibility of ending up in the workhouse was a very real threat for thousands of poor families.

Petitioning Parliament

People flocked to support the Chartists. It made sense to get the vote first and elect working-class Members of Parliament, who could then help to bring in the social reforms which people dreamed of. Representation in Parliament was the necessary first step.

The constitutional way to do this was to get Parliament to pass a law to that effect. But the Chartists had no power in Parliament. Place, Lovett and Roebuck shunned the idea of violence, so they persuaded their fellow Chartists to try to persuade Parliament by demonstrating the strength of public opinion with the aid of a monster petition, signed by thousands of people. This could then be taken to the House of Commons, with a demand that a new Reform Bill be brought in to implement the Charter.

Some Chartists felt that the petition was doomed to failure and some of the firebrands, such as Feargus O'Connor, advocated more open protest, although this still fell short of armed revolution. O'Connor gained his support in the North, where opposition to the Poor Law Amendment Act of 1834 (see Chapter 8) had reached fever pitch, with open defiance of the law and frequent demonstrations. At one stage, soldiers were even sent by train to the North, because the Government feared an armed Chartist uprising.

Chartism soon became an all-purpose political movement. Despite the Six Points of the Charter, most of its supporters wanted more than just electoral reform. Many workers joined the Chartist protests, hoping to improve working conditions in their factories or even to increase their wages. Others hoped to reform the Poor Law. It also attracted some middle-class people, who genuinely wanted to see Parliament reformed.

Lovett, like them, wanted to influence Parliament with words rather than deeds. No fewer than three petitions were eventually presented – in 1839, 1842 and 1848 – but to no effect. Opponents of the Chartists drew attention to the fact that amongst the signatures were names like the Duke of Wellington and Queen Victoria! At one time the Chartists contemplated a general strike, but this idea never came to fruition. The Chartists knew what they wanted but they did not know how to achieve it. Even in 1848, a year of revolutions in almost every European country, the Chartist meeting on 10 April passed off without major incident. This was how *The Illustrated London News* reported the meeting on London's Kennington Common.

> 'The van waiting for the delegates was inscribed on the right side with the motto, "The Charter. No surrender. Liberty is worth living for and worth dying for"; on the left, "The voice of the people is the voice of God"; while on the back of the car was inscribed, "Who would be a slave that could be free? Onward, we conquer; backward we fall". Banners were fixed (four on each side) to the car, inscribed, "The Charter", "No vote, no muskets", "Vote by ballot", "Annual Parliaments", "Universal suffrage", "No property qualification".'

The Government allowed the meeting to take place but banned the Chartists from marching through the streets of London with their

Contemporary print of the Chartist meeting in April 1848

petition. In addition they swore in 150,000 special constables and put the Duke of Wellington in charge, and the army on full alert. The Government feared an insurrection, like those which had alarmed Europe earlier in March. But their fears were groundless. Instead, the Chartists listened to the speeches and delegates took a monster petition to the House of Commons in a cab. The protest was over and Chartism soon fizzled out as an effective force in British politics.

1 *Which of the Six Points of the Charter are not highlighted in the account of the 1848 meeting?*
2 *What did the Chartists mean by 'Universal Suffrage'?*
3 *See if you can find out which of the Six Points of the Charter eventually became law. Did any of these reforms take place within the lifetime of an 80-year-old Chartist aged twenty in 1840? Which was the first of their Six Points to become law? Which was the last?*

Violent protest

Although Lovett advocated peaceful protest there were some violent incidents. The most serious outbreak of violence occurred in 1839, when a large group of many hundreds of Welsh miners, armed with clubs and other weapons, attempted to seize the town of Newport. But their plan misfired. Shots were exchanged with soldiers and the ringleaders were arrested.

In 1842 striking miners in Stoke-on-Trent listened to Thomas Cooper, a Chartist speaker, denouncing the oppressors of the poor. Afterwards they went on the rampage, breaking into shops and attacking any coal mines still at work. When an army officer faced the mob and asked what they wanted, back came the reply 'Our rights and liberties, the Charter, and more to eat'.

Later, three of the Chartist agitators were shot dead, others were injured, whilst the rioters burned down the Town Hall and other buildings.

The Newport uprising in 1839, from a contemporary engraving

In Stockport, Bolton and Huddersfield, workers demanded 'a fair day's wage for a fair day's work'. At many factories and mills, demonstrators disabled machinery by seizing the plugs in engine boilers. This is why the disturbances are sometimes called the 'Plug Riots'.

---

1 *In what ways did rioting harm the cause of Chartism?*
2 *Why was violence the very reverse of what the Chartists were hoping to achieve?*
3 *What action do you think might have persuaded the Government at that time to introduce further reform, since rioters were no match for a trained army and strike action had failed in the 1830s? Would you have supported Feargus O'Connor or William Lovett?*
4 *Set down the main points of a speech you might have made at the Chartist conference in Birmingham in 1839.*

Reasons for the failure of Chartism

The Chartist movement eventually failed for two basic reasons:

(a) The period of depression in industry and agriculture did not last. The Golden Age of Agriculture (see Chapter 1) was one of good harvests, so bread prices fell. It was also a time of prosperity in industry with the rapid growth in industrial production (see Chapter 2), which made Britain the 'Workshop of the World'. The advent of steam engines and machinery did not mean permanent unemployment. Wages began to rise in the 1850s and 1860s, at a time when bread prices were steadily dropping. Most working people now were better fed and less inclined to jeopardise their jobs and their higher standards of living for political protests.

(b) Chartism lacked effective leadership, split as it was between the fiery O'Connor with his appeal to violent protest and the peaceful Constitutional approach advocated by William Lovett. It also lacked effective middle-class support which could have provided the financial backing needed for a major reform movement of this kind.

THE REFORM ACT OF 1867

The demands of the Chartists were revived again, in 1865, with the formation of the Reform League. This time there were more receptive ears in Parliament, and Gladstone proposed, and Disraeli implemented in 1867, the enfranchisement (granting of the right to vote) of a substantial proportion of the working classes.

Reform League protest at Marble Arch, Victorian engraving

Riots and demonstrations played their part in persuading Disraeli to give the vote to all male householders living in urban areas. As a result most ordinary working men got the vote in the towns (not women, nor men living in the country), provided they were over 21, and either house-holders, or lodgers paying at least £10 a year in rent.

The 1867 Reform Act doubled the number of voters to about two million men. It was still far from representative of the people of Britain as a whole but it did give the working classes in the towns their first say in the choice of government. Working men in the countryside had to wait until 1884 for the vote. All remaining men over 21, and women over 30 were not granted the vote until 1918, and women over 21 not until 1928.

THE LATER TRADE UNIONS

The New Model Unions

Trade unions continued to function after the collapse of the GNCTU in 1834, but made little real progress in the following fifteen years. In the case of unions for unskilled workers, no real headway was made for 50 years. For skilled workers, however, a new type of trade union developed in the 1850s, with the emergence of the New Model Unions. The first to be formed was the Amalgamated Society of Engineers (ASE), in 1851, with a membership of 12,000 which grew rapidly to one of 33,000 by 1868.

The New Model Unions had the following features in common.

(a)   They were organised by a centralised executive council, or com-mittee, with paid officials based in a central headquarters, usually in London (like that of ASE). They were no longer regional or local unions. This was a direct outcome of the improvements in the railway system (see Chapter 3) and the introduction of the penny post (in 1840). It would have been impossible for working-class representatives to have organised such a method of trade union control in the days of the stage coach.

(b) Their members were skilled workers, such as the engineers and the shoemakers. Higher than average wages meant they could pay the high subscriptions required to run these new and efficient unions. Engineers had to pay 1s [5p] a week – as much as 5 per cent of their income.

(c) The unions offered substantial welfare benefits to their members, including sickness benefit, unemployment benefit and provision for old age.

(d) Their officials cultivated a middle-class image. The New Model Unions were respectable. Accordingly, their officials were more prepared to sit round the table and negotiate improvements in working conditions rather than try to force through higher wage claims with industrial action. When they did strike it was as a national union. Only official strikes were approved and financed (since the Union's funds were held at the headquarters). In any case, this was a period of a booming prosperous industry, when employers were usually much more inclined to settle a claim than lose potential profits during a prolonged strike.

The Junta

The secretaries of several of the New Model Unions formed a powerful but unofficial committee, later nicknamed the Junta. Its members included William Allan (Secretary of ASE), George Odger (from the Ladies' Shoemakers), Robert Applegarth (Secretary of the Amalgamated Society of Carpenters and Joiners), Edwin Coulson (London

Leaders of the New Model Unions: Robert Applegarth (Secretary of the Amalgamated Society of Carpenters and Joiners), William Allan (Secretary of ASE), George Odger (an official of the Ladies' Shoemakers)

Bricklayers' Union) and Daniel Guile (National Association of Iron-founders). They were a cautious, respectable group of men, whose middle-class appearance belied the fact that they spoke on behalf of the working classes.

They brought efficient business methods to the running of a trade union and utilised the newly developed railway system to good advantage. They were opposed by the older style of trade unionists 'who objected to all connection between the Government and the concerns of working men' and who sought confrontation rather than agreement.

The London Builders' Strike

Some of the trade disputes at this time were not so much about pay as about working conditions (see also Chapter 8). In 1858, the Amalgamated Society of Carpenters and Joiners of London asked the Master Builders who employed them 'to reduce the hours of labour from ten to nine hours per day, with the present rate of wages'. They were rebuffed and were soon joined in the dispute by the bricklayers, stone masons, painters and plasterers. In July 1859, the combined groups sent warning of a strike to four firms which had been drawn out of a hat.

A strike was called at one of these firms, whereupon all the Master Builders in London agreed to lock out their workers. In other words, they shut down all their works and building sites until all the workers agreed to return to work. The Masters demanded that in future all employees should sign a 'document' binding them not to become a member of a trade union. Over 20,000 workers were thrown out of work and by the end of the year a number of strikers were said to have died

Cartoon in Punch, *5 November 1859* Committee Man and General Talker *'What I say, my boy, is – Hold out! Hold out – and we'll soon bring the Masters to their senses!'* Worker *'Ah! It's all very well for you to hold out – you live at a Public House, and get plenty to eat and to drink – meantime, we are next to starving!'*

THE STRIKE, A SUBJECT FOR THE CONSIDERATION OF THE REAL WORKING MAN.

from starvation. In February 1860, the Masters agreed to a compromise; the 'document' would be withdrawn, but the men would continue to work a ten-hour day.

> 1 *To which strike does the cartoon opposite refer?*
> 2 *Who is the man in the frock coat on the left?*
> 3 *What is the significance of the piece of paper on the wall?*
> 4 *What was the attitude of* Punch *to the strike?*

The London Trades Council

The co-operation of the different unions during the London Builders' strike had one important result. The London Trades Council was formed as a local conference of trade unions from different industries. Trade union leaders, like William Allan and Robert Applegarth, recognised that the problems they wanted to solve were not specific to a particular trade or industry. There were many occasions when co-operation between the different unions was vital. Other regional trades councils were also formed, notably the Manchester and Salford Trades Council (which later took the initiative leading to the formation of the TUC).

The new image of the unions was beneficial in other respects, as well. Parliament passed the Friendly Societies Act in 1855, which the unions assumed protected their funds. In 1859, the Molestation of Workmen Act permitted peaceful picketing. The unions had every reason to believe that many of the legal hurdles barring the way for improving working conditions had been cleared. But two startling developments in quick succession threatened the very foundations on which the trade union movement then rested.

The Sheffield Outrages

'15 October 1866. Attempt made by agents of the Sawgrinders' Union in Sheffield to kill or maim one Fearnehough, who had withdrawn from their society. His house was blown up with gunpowder, but the inmates escaped with trifling injuries. The masters offered £1,000 reward, and the Government £100, for such information as would lead to a discovery of the perpetrators.'

Annals of Our Time, Joseph Irving 1869

Fearnehough had left the Sawgrinders' Union in 1865, and had been working during a strike of saw grinders and saw-handle makers. The strikers regarded him as a blackleg and attacked his house. Soon afterwards, in February 1867, the employers in the metal industries gave the Home Secretary a list of 200 other outrages allegedly committed by the trade unions in Sheffield.

A Special Commission was set up to investigate the outrages and heard members of the Sawgrinders' Union confess to a number of incidents, including the murder of a workman called Linley, who had broken the Union's rules. They also confessed to sending threatening letters to employers, and to several cases in which cans of gunpowder had been thrown down the chimneys of employers and workmen alike. Two other unions, the Saw-handle Makers and the Saw Makers, were both involved in the explosion at Fearnehough's house.

Saw grinders at work in Sheffield, The Illustrated London News, *6 January 1866*

The dispute in Sheffield was basically about the introduction of new machinery, which the unions claimed was unsafe. They wanted safe-guards, the employers refused them, and so the strike began in 1866. It was supported by the Junta. But the Junta members were as appalled as the rest of the public at the revelations concerning the action of the militants in Sheffield. One of the outcomes was that a Royal Com-mission was set up to 'inquire into the organisation and rules of Trades Unions' in general. It met at an opportune moment, since the judgement in the *Hornby* v. *Close* case (see the next section) meant that the legal position of the trade unions was far from clear.

The *Hornby* v. *Close* case

On 16 January 1867, the Lord Chief Justice confirmed the decision taken by Bradford Magistrates, in disallowing an action brought by the Bradford Boilermakers' Society against a former treasurer who had stolen £24 from the Society's funds (the *Hornby* v. *Close* case). The Court said that the objects of the Society, being partly those of a trade union, were not covered by the provisions of the Friendly Societies Act of 1855. This meant that the trade unions had no legal right to recover their funds if they were misused by an official. It also threw doubt on whether the unions were legal or not.

This was intolerable. The trade unions urged that the law be changed and took the opportunity presented by the holding of the Royal Commission inquiry into the organisation and rules of the trade unions to present a well-founded case for trade union reform. In particular they wanted the unions to have the same legal rights as other organisations. They impressed the politicians with their presentation of their case and effectively distanced themselves from the Sheffield Outrages.

---

1 *Why were the Sheffield Outrages a serious blow to the trade union movement in general and to the New Model Unions and the Junta, in particular?*

2 *What was the significance of the* Hornby v. Close *case? Why did the trade unions find this situation intolerable?*

3 *Why did they co-operate with the Royal Commission which was investigating the trade unions at this time? What did they stand to gain? What did they stand to lose?*

As the Unions prepared to give evidence to the Royal Commission, the Manchester and Salford Trades Council called a general trades union congress to enable members from all the unions in Britain to meet and co-ordinate efforts to try to persuade the Government to change the existing legislation on trade unions. They met to consider whether they should co-operate with the Royal Commission on Trades Unions, to consider matters of common interest and to decide whether to meet annually. Initially, the members of the Junta declined to join this Trades Union Congress, which met for the first time in May 1868, with 34 delegates representing 100,000 members.

In 1869, the Royal Commission presented two reports. The majority of the members of the Commission recommended that:

> 'With regard to the general question of the right of workmen to combine together for determining and stipulating with their employer the terms on which only they will consent to work for him, we think that, provided the combination be perfectly voluntary, and that full liberty to be left to all other workmen to undertake the work which the parties combining have refused, and that no obstruction be placed in the way of employers resorting elsewhere in search of a supply of labour, there is no ground of justice for withholding such a right from workmen.'

The other report was even more favourable to the trade unions, having been heavily influenced by the members of the Junta. The outcome of the Royal Commission was a new law, the Trade Union Act of 1871, giving the unions the legal recognition they wanted after the *Hornby* v. *Close* case. But the Criminal Law Amendment Act in the same year made picketing illegal – to be modified four years later, when the Conspiracy and Protection of Property Act of 1875 restored the right to peaceful picketing.

FURTHER QUESTIONS AND EXERCISES

1 *Look at the two extracts below and at the picture.*

Victorian illustration of the Rebecca riots, in South Wales, in 1843

'June 10, 1843. Disturbance at Carmarthen by "Rebecca and her Daughters". They marched through the town about 1,000 strong, took possession of the workhouse, and remained till the afternoon, when they were broken up by a troop of dragoons sent from Cardiff, and eighty of them taken prisoners. The following evening another mob assembled, Rebecca being on horseback in full attire. They set out for St. Clears'; there they demolished the turnpike-gate. This destruction of turnpike-gates by bands of disguised Rebeccaites continued for months to be an almost nightly occurrence in different parts of South Wales.'

'September 10, 1843. Rebecca and her followers murder an old woman, keeper of a tollgate. Government offer a reward of £500 for the discovery of the ringleaders, and afterwards appoint a Special Commission to inquire into the operation of the Turnpike Laws in Wales.'

Annals of Our Time, Joseph Irving 1869

'And they blessed Rebekah, and said unto her . . . and let thy seed possess the gate of those which hate them.'

Genesis 24:60

(a) Write two or three sentences to explain what is happening in the picture.
(b) Who was Rebecca? Do you think Rebecca was a man or a woman? Is the picture strictly accurate? Why do you think the rioters chose the name Rebecca? Why was it appropriate?
(c) Why did they occupy the workhouse? What was the main target of the daughters of Rebecca? Write a sentence to explain why they chose this method of protest, instead of trying to get the law changed. Did the protest appear to have any effect?

(d) What other political protests were being made in Britain at the time of the Rebecca riots?

2 What did the Chartists mean by the following terms, and why did they want:
(a) secret ballots,
(b) annual Parliaments,
(c) adult male suffrage,
(d) no property qualification?
Which other groups of reformers agitated for these reforms in the eighteenth and nineteenth centuries?

3 Write an explanatory account of the events leading up to the Peterloo Massacre. What were the results of the Massacre?

Cartoon from Punch, 1852

EFFECTS OF A STRIKE
UPON THE CAPITALIST   AND   UPON THE WORKING MAN.

4 Look at the cartoon from Punch, published in 1852. What was the point of this cartoon? How does it illustrate the difficulty which the trade unions faced in trying to improve working conditions before 1870?

5 Explain the importance of each of the following in the working-class movement before 1870:
(a) Francis Place
(b) The GNCTU
(c) The Sheffield Outrages
(d) The Combination Acts
(e) The New Model Unions
(f) Hornby v. Close
(g) Reform Bill of 1867
(h) Robert Owen

6 *Describe the electoral system before 1832. What were its principal defects? How were they remedied in:*
   (a) 1832,
   (b) 1867?
   In what ways was the electoral system still undemocratic in 1870?

7 *Imagine you are a Chartist in 1848. Write down the arguments you would use to try to convince one of the special constables on duty in London at the meeting on Kennington Common that you are right to make your protest.*

8 *To which events in working-class history do you think sources A and B refer? Write a paragraph setting out the background to each event and explain its significance and importance to the working-class movement.*

Source A

Evidence in court, 1834
'We were told to kiss the book, which looked like a little Bible. I then saw all the prisoners there. James Lovelace had on a white dress, it was not a smock-frock. They told us the rules, that we should have to pay 1s then, and a 1d a week afterwards, to support the men when they were standing out from their work.'

The Times 1834

Source B

THE DERBY, 1867. DIZZY WINS
WITH "REFORM BILL".

Punch cartoon, 25 May 1867

9 *What causes help to explain the origins of the Chartist movement? What were its principal objectives? Explain how and why most of them eventually became law.*

10 *Why did social and industrial change in Britain grow at a faster rate than political change in the early nineteenth century?*

Chapter Eight

Social Welfare and Reform

INTRODUCTION

Soup kitchen in London's East End, The Illustrated London News, *16 February 1867*

Look at this picture from *The Illustrated London News*, published at a time when many people in London's East End were suffering great hardship.

---

1 *What was a soup kitchen? Why did it serve soup? Who supplied the soup – the government or private charity?*
2 *Why were soup kitchens common in Victorian Britain?*
3 *How did the artist try to gain sympathy for the starving people of the East End? Do you think he succeeded?*

The welfare of working-class people was not of very great interest to influential people at the start of the eighteenth century. Ordinary people did not vote and most of them still lived and worked on the land. But from about 1790, the plight of landless farm labourers and the social problems caused by the rapid growth of towns and factories began to cause concern. Many well meaning people (called philanthropists) gave money to support good causes. Some (such as Lord Shaftesbury) devoted their lives to try to secure better working and living conditions for the poor. There were a number of reasons for this interest in social welfare.

(a)   One was a renewed faith in religion. The Methodists and Quakers had a deep interest in social problems. The Evangelical Movement in the Church of England stirred the conscience of wealthy people such as William Wilberforce (who was responsible for the abolition of slavery) and Lord Shaftesbury.

(b)   Enlightened manufacturers, like Robert Owen and Sir Titus Salt, showed what could be done.

(c)   The writings of philosophers and thinkers, such as the Utilitarian Jeremy Bentham (who believed that everything should have a use), influenced people like Edwin Chadwick.

(d)   Events such as the Peterloo Massacre, the French Revolution and the American Declaration of Independence, aroused passionate feelings among the reformers. Radical clubs and Reformist groups helped to spread new ideas.

(e)   New magazines and newspapers were published, many of them drawing attention to the need for reforms (as you can see in many of the pictures and extracts in this book). People could no longer say they did not know about these problems.

In this chapter you can see how some of the main social problems were tackled, many of them in the Age of Reform (between 1832 and 1855).

POVERTY AND ITS RELIEF

The old Poor Law

The problem of how the State can best assist those unable to help themselves (such as orphans, the elderly, the handicapped and the unemployed) is one of the most difficult for any government to solve. Under the Elizabethan Poor Laws of 1597–8 and 1601, which were still operating in the eighteenth century, every parish had to make some provision for paupers by levying a special poor rate to be paid by local inhabitants living in rateable properties. Local magistrates used this money to appoint an overseer of the poor, whose job it was to see that able-bodied paupers had work to do and that pauper children were apprenticed to a tradesman. Parishes could also erect a poorhouse (often called the workhouse) to be used as a home for paupers. If they lived in the poorhouse, this was called 'indoor relief'. If paupers stayed in their own homes, it was called 'outdoor relief'. Conditions in the workhouses were usually miserable. A report in 1770 said they were 'a real terror to all those who are ever likely to become the miserable inhabitants of them'.

In 1782, Gilbert's Act set up a special committee in each parish – the 'guardians of the poor' – whose responsibility it was to oversee the provision of Poor Relief and, in particular, to 'provide a suitable and convenient house' for the poor. This was only to be available for those who could not work for a living, such as people who were infirm through old age or sickness. The able-bodied poor were to be given work to do and the poor rates used to subsidise their wages, through the payment of allowances.

---

1 *Was it strictly accurate to call a poorhouse a workhouse in (a) 1723, (b) 1782?*
2 *What was the difference between 'indoor' and 'outdoor' relief?*
3 *What were the main drawbacks to the system?*

The Speenhamland System

In 1795, the continued rise in the price of bread (see Chapter 1) brought great poverty and distress to farm workers, whose miserly wages were insufficient to sustain their families. At that time, the wages of agricultural workers were determined by the local magistrates.

On Wednesday, 6 May 1795, the Berkshire magistrates met for this purpose at the Pelican Inn in Speenhamland, near Reading. But instead of raising wages, they merely urged farmers to do so. However, in order to alleviate the distress of the workers, they decided to supplement low wages out of the poor rate. They decided that:

> 'When the Gallon Loaf weighing 8lb 11oz [3.94 kg] shall cost 1s [5p], then every poor and industrious man shall have for his own support 3s [15p] weekly, either produced by his own or his family's labour, or an allowance from the poor rates, and for the support of his wife and every other of his family, 1s 6d [7.5p].'

The Magistrates also published a sliding scale which increased or decreased these allowances if the price of bread rose or fell – by 3d [1.25p] for the man and 1d [0.4p] for every other member of the family, for every 1d rise or fall in the price of the loaf. For example, if a loaf cost 1s 6d [7.5p] then the working man was to get 4s 6d [22.5p] and his wife and children 2s 0d [10p] each.

1 *How much do you think they got if the loaf cost 2s [10p]?*
2 *What allowance from the poor rates did a married man with a wife and ten children get, if he did the same work and was paid the same wage as a single man earning 3s [15p]? Was this fair?*
3 *Why did some critics say the Speenhamland System encouraged farm labourers to have large families? How did it discourage farmers from raising wages? Who paid the difference between the poor labourer's wages and the income he received? Was this fair?*

The magistrates in many rural counties in southern England introduced similar measures, but the Speenhamland System was not widely adopted in the industrial North since farm workers could often get jobs in mills and factories. Farmers there had to keep wages high in order to attract labour. Elsewhere the poor rate rose sharply, doubling the cost to ratepayers on average, between 1795 and 1834. In the village of Cholesbury in Buckinghamshire, tenant farmers even abandoned their farms, because the poor rate was so high.

4 *Was the Speenhamland System a sensible way to ensure a basic minimum income for workers, related to the cost of living?*

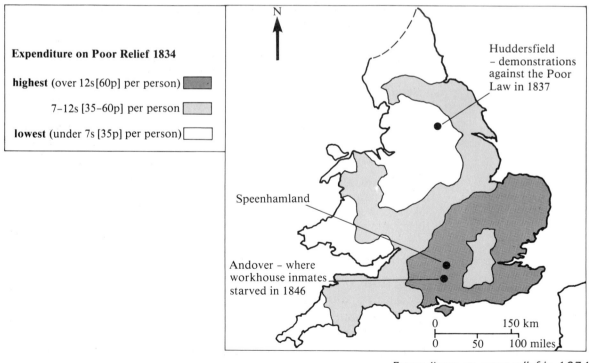

Expenditure on Poor Relief 1834

highest (over 12s[60p] per person)

7–12s [35–60p] per person

lowest (under 7s [35p] per person)

N

Huddersfield – demonstrations against the Poor Law in 1837

Speenhamland

Andover – where workhouse inmates starved in 1846

| 0 | | 150 km |
| 0 | 50 | 100 miles |

Expenditure on poor relief in 1834

5 *Write two or three sentences to describe the facts you can deduce from the map on the previous page.*

The Poor Law Commission

The Speenhamland System did little to encourage farmers to raise wages, and the great distress this caused in the rural counties helped to fuel the anger which sparked off the Captain Swing riots in about 1830 (see Chapter 1). The System was also wide open to abuse since it did little to encourage people to work.

The Government was aware of these problems and in 1832 set up a new type of fact-finding committee, called a Royal Commission, to examine the problem, collect evidence, hear witnesses and prepare a list of recommendations for a new Poor Law. This was largely the work of Edwin Chadwick (see page 224), whose administrative skill, drive and energy as a Commissioner, shaped its final recommendations. He later became Secretary to the Poor Law Commission, when it was established to implement the Poor Law Amendment Act of 1834.

In their Report, the Poor Law Commissioners were strongly influenced by the experience of a number of parishes in southern England, which had already tried to cut down the number of paupers in their districts. They had done this, by discouraging able-bodied workers from seeking help. The Poor Law Commisioners took the same line and made the following recommendations:

> 'That except as to medical attendance, all relief whatever to able-bodied persons or to their families, otherwise than in well-regulated workhouses, shall be declared unlawful. At least four classes are necessary: (1) The aged and really impotent; (2) The children; (3) The able-bodied females; (4) The able-bodied males. It appears to us that both the requisite classification and the requisite superintendence may be better obtained in separate buildings than under a single roof. Each class might thus receive appropriate treatment; the old might enjoy their indulgences without torment from the boisterous; the children be educated, and the able bodied subjected to such courses of labour and discipline as will repel the indolent and vicious.'

Report of the Poor Law Commission 1834

1 *How could you get support from the parish if you were an unemployed farm worker:*
(a) before 1834,
(b) after 1834?
2 *What happened to a family of ten (grandmother, mother, father, four sons, three daughters) if they sought poor relief after 1834?*

3 *Which provision in the Poor Law Amendment Act inspired this cartoon?*

THE "MILK" OF POOR-LAW "KINDNESS". *Cartoon from* Punch, *1843*

The Poor Law Amendment Act

Putting the Poor Law Amendment Act into effect meant creating a new system of local government. Parishes were grouped together in Unions under the control of elected Boards of Guardians. As before, the cost of operating the system was to be paid for out of local rates.

Responsibility for seeing that the Act was properly carried out was left in the hands of the new Poor Law Commission, with Chadwick as Secretary. The Commission was allowed to implement the Act in its own time, since it was recognised that it would take several years to divide the country into unions of parishes, elect Boards of Guardians, raise the necessary poor rates, build new workhouses and ensure a smooth transition from the old to the new system, which it was hoped would 'as far as may be practicable, be uniform throughout the country'.

In practice, there were many obstacles – particularly in the fast-growing industrial North, where the Speenhamland System was relatively unknown. Factory workers had little choice but to apply for poor relief when unemployed. It was not that they were idle or indolent, it was simply lack of a job. But under the new Poor Law Amendment Act they faced harsh discipline, petty rules, plain and inadequate food and the breaking up of their families into separate wards. This was intolerable and, not surprisingly, resulted in a mood of violent anger in many centres in the North.

In any case, the Union workhouses could not cope with the problems raised by sudden widespread unemployment. A slump in Nottingham in 1837 gave the Poor Law Commissioners no alternative but to permit outdoor relief in the city, although they did insist that the unemployed be set to work building a new road.

In Yorkshire, the officers of the Huddersfield Union were prevented from implementing the Act by a campaign of intimidation led by Richard Oastler (see also page 279). According to the Commission, he used 'violent and inflammatory language' at a demonstration designed to prevent the Board of Guardians from meeting. In the end, the Poor Law Commission had to concede that there were circumstances in which outdoor relief could be permitted.

The new workhouses after 1834

People who were really in need, such as the sick and elderly, and orphaned children, were often better cared for in the new workhouses than in the old poorhouses. But in order to 'repel the indolent and vicious', these new workhouses were told to provide living standards which would be below those enjoyed by 'independent labourers' outside the workhouse. The workhouse was to become the last resort of the pauper, not the first.

As the inmates of 'an uninviting place of wholesome restraint', paupers were sometimes treated as the prisoners of the master, written permission being required before leaving the building or entertaining visitors. There were restrictions on the consumption of beer and on smoking.

Penalties could be imposed, such as being put on bread and water, or having to wear special punishment clothes, for offences such as swearing, uttering insults or threats, uncleanliness, malingering, playing cards, misbehaving during prayers, or entering the women's ward (if a man). More severe penalties (such as imprisonment) were imposed for major offences such as drunkenness, acts of indecency, assault, mischievous damage, and wilful disobedience.

Compare the following accounts of visits to two workhouses in 1837 and 1866 with the aims of the Poor Law Commissioners.

Source A

'Having become weary of the abuse and praise alternately lavished on the workhouse system, a friend selected one about ten miles [16 km] from London; with the governor of this well-regulated establishment he became slightly acquainted, and without difficulty

obtained permission to inspect and overlook every thing. For two or
three days he became an amateur boarder, and although he slept
elsewhere, confined himself strictly to the fare or diet of the house.

I could myself board permanently in the house with comfort,
were I inclined or permitted to do so. The situation is splendid, and
commands a variety of the finest views imaginable. The women and
female children have what may well be called landscape gardens of
their own. The whole apartments are airy and roomy; everything is
kept as clean as a new shilling and wears an air of comfort.'

Dumfries and Galloway Courier 1837

Source B

'An adventurous gentleman tested the accommodation provided for the
houseless poor by passing a night with the casuals in Lambeth Workhouse.
He got himself up in a beggarly dress, his buttonless coat being tied with
twine. He was readily admitted and supplied with a thick slice of bread,
called in "casual" language "toke". The cold was severe. There were
neither bags of straw nor rugs for the entire number, so that shivering men
and boys were huddled together, sometimes four on one bag.

Imagine a space about 30 ft. by 30 ft. [9 metres square], a dingy
whitewashed wall, the fourth side of the shed boarded in; the remaining
space hung with flimsy canvas, with a gap at the top. This shed was paved
with stone, the flags thickly encrusted with filth. Half through the night
there was a tumult of cursing and telling obscene stories, whilst smoking
tobacco. At one o'clock, ten more men came in – great hulking ruffians,
and all madly swearing because there was no toke for them.'

Pall Mall Gazette 1866

---

1 *Why do you think two members of the middle class visited the
   workhouses and endured their discomforts? What do you think
   their motives were?*
2 *Do their motives have any bearing on whether we can treat their reports
   as being accurate accounts of what it was like to live in a workhouse?*
3 *Which of these two accounts do you think is more likely to give a
   realistic and unbiased picture of life in a workhouse? Write a
   paragraph to explain your choice.*
4 *Would either of these two reports have pleased the Poor Law
   Commissioners in 1834? Explain the reasons for your answer.*

Results of the new Poor Law

The cost of poor relief dropped sharply from £7 million in 1831 to £4
million in 1837. In individual parishes, the fall was much more notice-
able; the annual poor rate in Hitchin in Hertfordshire, for example, fell
from £1,716 to £496 after 1834.

At first the Poor Law Amendment Act caused much unnecessary hardship, breaking up families, treating destitute paupers little better than animals, maltreating them, even starving them. There was an appalling scandal, in 1846, when it was revealed that the semi-starving inmates of the Andover Union Workhouse had been fighting to get at the gristle left on bones, which they were supposed to be crushing as one of their jobs. One immediate consequence was the abolition of the Poor Law Commission and its replacement by the Poor Law Board in 1847.

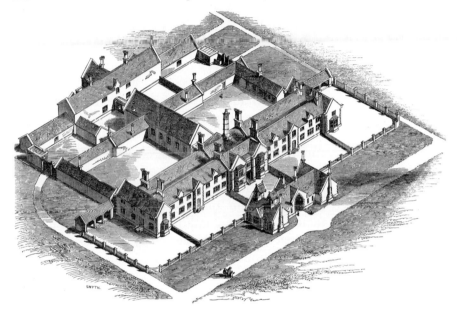

The Andover Union Workhouse, The Illustrated London News, 7 November 1846

---

1 *Write two or three sentences to describe the Andover Union Workhouse. Identify the four yards (for each of the four classes of inmate).*

2 *Do you think the Andover Union Workhouse was built before or after 1834?*

3 *In the article accompanying the picture, the writer concluded by saying that public opinion was against the erection of any further 'Bastilles'. Why do you think the new workhouses were given this name?*

On the credit side, the Poor Law Amendment Act did help to restore morale in the countryside, since it gave workers an incentive to seek employment rather than charity and it forced farmers to raise wages. In time the system softened and the rule about making relief conditional on entering the workhouse was ignored in many parts of the country.

Most of those seeking help, even the able-bodied labourers, received outdoor relief. As a result, a number of new roads, paved streets and drainage schemes were built with Poor Law labour. Some workhouse schools provided pauper children with a sound basic education – something other children did not get, as of right, until after 1870 (see Chapter 9). The Unions also appointed medical officers to take care of their old, handicapped and sick 'inmates'. As a result, paupers were sometimes better looked after than the 'independent' poor.

FACTORY WORKING CONDITIONS

The effects of mechanisation

The first industrial workers were employed in small workshops or worked at home in their own cottages. They were said to be ill-disciplined and highly independent, taking holidays at will. Factories could not be run like this. Employers, such as Richard Arkwright, made their employees work long shifts of 12 hours or more and wanted to keep their machines going night and day. They employed children as well as adults. A Birmingham manufacturer told the Commissioners looking into factory working conditions in the 1840s that without such employment children 'would be neglected by their parents, not sent to school, and left to stroll about the streets'. He argued that, if the law was to be changed, then compulsory schooling ought to be introduced at the same time.

Factory working conditions were under heavy attack in the early nineteenth century, but a lady visitor claimed, in 1844, on the strength of visits to two cotton mills near Bolton, that:

> 'The factory people are better clothed, better fed, and better conducted than many other classes of working-people.
>   I found the mill a large building, with a wide stone staircase, easy of ascent and very clean. The working rooms are spacious, well-ventilated, and lofty, kept at an equable temperature, and, like all parts of the factory, exceedingly clean. There are a number of windows in each room, indeed so many, that I wondered if they had any window-duty to pay. I observed that great care had been bestowed upon the "boxing-up" of dangerous machinery, and was told that accidents were very rare, and that when they did occur, they were the "result of the greatest stupidity or negligence".'
>
> *Chambers's Journal* 1844

In fact, this was not unusual. Many mills and factories were well run by efficient, progressive manufacturers, who, like Robert Owen, took part in the campaign to improve factory working conditions. The trouble lay with the bad employers, who could do what they liked, since there was little legal restriction on their activities as mill owners or mine owners.

Investigations in the 1830s and 1840s revealed many horrendous instances of cruelty, neglect, impossible working hours and appalling working conditions.

---

1 *What defects in the factory system was the lady visitor looking for when she toured the cotton mill in 1844?*

2 *What was wrong with her claim that the 'factory people are better clothed, better fed, and better conducted than many other classes of working-people'? What do you think her motives were for making such a statement?*

3 *Look at the table below, listing some of the poor working conditions found in factories and coal mines in the early nineteenth century. Find evidence in the Sources A-L (pages 275–285) to back up at least five of these statements.*

4 *Prepare your own report on factory working conditions, using the extracts and the pictures in this chapter as your only sources of information.*

Poor working conditions

(a) Unguarded machines – making accidents commonplace

(b) Long working hours – leading to fatigue and careless accidents

(c) Constant noise – clatter of looms and machinery

(d) Smells of oil, grease and unwashed bodies, made worse by poor ventilation

(e) Damp suffocating atmosphere

(f) Cruelty from harsh overseers – children beaten

(g) Infants employed to do dangerous jobs – such as crawling under machines

(h) Breathing in coal dust, cotton powder, iron filings, or other waste products – causing industrial diseases

---

Source A

Description of a Derbyshire cotton mill in 1797

'The people were coming out to dinner, for it was already one o'clock. From the glance I had of their appearance, the observations I made were these : They were pale, and their hats were covered with shreds of cotton. Apart from their want of exercise the light particles of cotton must be inhaled with their breath, and occasion pulmonary affections.'

Source B

Children in a textile mill in the 1800s, an early nineteenth-century engraving

Source C

Fork grinding

'Between 20 and 40 years of age, in this trade, 885 perish out of every 1000, while in England and Wales only 296.'

The Medical Times 1843

Source D

Visitor to a Birmingham metal works in 1844

'The process of pointing (sharpening pins on a grindstone) can scarcely fail, I should think, to affect the health of the operator; for although the brass dust flies away behind the stone into a wooden receptacle which covers it like a hood, a portion at least will reach the mouths and lungs of the grinder; yet he employs no precaution to avert any such injurious consequences.'

Chambers's Journal 1844

Source E

The Factory Child

'The racking noise of engines, the hell of sounds. The dragging, wearying monotony of the machine; the stifling heat; the unbroken noise; the necessity of constant action on the part of the workers; render the place and the employment all but intolerable.'

Douglas Jerrold 1840

Source F

Workshops in Wolverhampton

'In general the buildings are very old, and many of them are in a dilapidated, ruinous, and even dangerous condition. Nothing is more common than to find many of the windows broken. From defective construction all these old workshops are liable to become suffocatingly hot in summer (and also at night when the gas is lighted) and very cold in winter. Efficient ventilation is a thing unknown in these places.'

Treatment of children near Wolverhampton

'In Willenhall the children are shamefully and most cruelly beaten with a horsewhip, strap, stick, hammer, handle, file, or whatever tool is nearest at hand, or are struck with the clenched fist or kicked.'

Lace-making near Nottingham

'If the statement of the mother be correct, one of her children, four years of age, works twelve hours a-day with only an interval of a quarter of an hour for each meal at breakfast, dinner and tea, and never going out to play: and two more of her children, one six and the other eight years of age, work in summer from 6 A.M. till dusk, and in winter from seven in the morning till ten at night, fifteen hours.'

Second Report of the Children's Employment Commissioners 1843

Factory reformers

Conditions in the mills and coal mines came to the attention of the social reformers, notably Michael Sadler, Richard Oastler and Lord Shaftesbury (see below). They agitated for legislation to control factories and mines in general, and child and female labour in particular.

Lord Shaftesbury (1801–85)

Lord Ashley became a Member of Parliament in 1826, and succeeded to the title of Earl of Shaftesbury in 1851. He was probably the greatest and most successful of the many philanthropists of the nineteenth century, devoting his career to the relief of the oppressed.

He was a member of the Evangelical Movement and active in promoting missionary work at home and abroad. Like many other Victorian Christians, he placed a lot of emphasis on strong upright living, hard work and a strong sense of duty. He is probably best known for the work he did when he was Lord Ashley MP on behalf of the women and children whose appalling working conditions in mines and textile mills disturbed the conscience of the Victorians.

He also took an active interest in many other social reforms, such as the care of the mentally-disturbed, the plight of chimney climbing boys and the education of the poor. He was chairman of the Ragged School Union for forty years (see Chapter 9).

Although he took a deep and compassionate interest in the well-being of the working classes, he was no socialist and no radical. He opposed the extension of the vote to the working classes in 1867, fearing the effect this might have on property owners.

Lord Shaftesbury

THE FACTORY ACTS

The Health and Morals of Apprentices Act of 1802

In 1802, Sir Robert Peel (father of the Prime Minister of the 1840s) was instrumental in getting Parliament to pass an Act designed to prevent workhouse children from being exploited by mill owners in the cotton industry. The Act stated that, in future, they were to work for no more than twelve hours a day and they were to be given schooling.

However, laws are ineffective if no proper means are provided to see they are carried out. The provisions of this Act were supervised by local magistrates, many of them mill owners themselves. As a result, the Act had relatively little effect and it only applied to a small number of children anyway.

The Factory Act of 1819

Social reformers continued to agitate for improved factory working conditions. In 1819, Parliament approved a new Act banning the employment of children in cotton textile mills under the age of nine years, and restricting the working hours of children between nine and sixteen to twelve hours per day. But, like the 1802 Act, enforcement was still in the hands of local magistrates and therefore had little effect.

The Factory Act of 1833

The movement for factory reform quickened under the leadership of Richard Oastler, a Tory factory reformer, and Michael Sadler, a linen manufacturer and Member of Parliament. Sadler introduced a Ten-Hour Bill for all workers in textile factories in 1831 but although it was defeated, he was appointed chairman of a special House of Commons committee, set up to investigate child labour in factories. It was at this time that Oastler drew attention to 'Yorkshire slavery' in the worsted mills of Bradford. In a speech in 1832, he said:

> 'I have never ceased to use every legal means, for the purpose of emancipating these innocent slaves. On one occasion I was in the company of a West India slave master and three Bradford spinners; the spinners were obliged to be silent when the slave-owner said, "Well, I have always thought myself disgraced by being the owner of black slaves, but we never, in the West Indies thought it was possible for any human being to be so cruel as to require a child of 9 years old to work 12 hours a day; and that you acknowledge is your regular practice".'

Sadler's Report on child labour shocked Members of Parliament but he was defeated in the 1832 General Election and Lord Ashley took over as leader of the movement in Parliament to reform factory working conditions, whilst Oastler led the opposition outside. In a stirring speech to a huge crowd at Bradford, Oastler attacked hecklers with the cry:

> 'Silence ye hissers! I tell ye, ye cowards, and ye may go and tell the tyrants by whom ye are employed, that ye may do your worst – that the Bill is safe – that WE WILL HAVE IT – THAT IT SHALL PASS!'

In fact, the Ten-Hour Bill for all workers was not safe but the Government did agree to set up a Royal Commission to investigate working conditions in textile mills (Chadwick was one of its members) and on the basis of the Commission's Report, Parliament passed the Factory Act of 1833. It went much further than the Factory Act of 1819.

This Act prohibited the employment of children under nine years in all textile mills, not just cotton (but with the exception of those making lace and silk). In addition, children under thirteen were not to work for more than nine hours a day and not more than 48 hours in any one week. Similar restrictions – a twelve-hour day and 69-hour week – applied to young people under eighteen years. Children under eleven were to have two hours of education every day and no person under eighteen was to be employed at night.

The most important provision, however, was for the appointment of Government inspectors, with a legal right to enter factories. It was their job to ensure that the Act was carried out. This was not always easy. Compulsory registration of births was not made law until 1836 and people often worked shifts. The inspectors made reports on these visits and so provided official evidence which was later used to press the case for further factory reforms.

The 1833 Factory Act met with a lot of opposition, not only from mill owners forecasting ruin but also from many of the parents of child workers. Some opponents argued that hard work was good for children. Others argued that government interference, however well-meaning, ran counter to the spirit of *laissez-faire* (see Chapter 4). But Lord Ashley and his allies were not content and continued to demand a ten-hour day for all workers.

---

1 *What did the factory reformers originally want? What did they get?*

2 *Why did Oastler use the phrase 'Yorkshire slavery'?*

3 *Imagine you are a factory inspector in 1834. How would you find it difficult to enforce the following provisions of the 1833 Factory Act:*
  (a) the ban on the employment of children under nine years,
  (b) the restrictions on the length of the working week for young people under the age of eighteen?

4 *Why did people say that the Factory Act of 1833 was not in the spirit of* laissez-faire?

The Coal Mines Act of 1842

Lord Ashley was also deeply involved in the movement to improve working conditions in the coal mines. The *First Report of the Children's Employment Commissioners: Mines and Collieries*, 1842, complete with graphic illustrations, stirred public opinion with its vivid and horrifying descriptions of the conditions in which children and women were working in the mines.

Source G

Contemporary illustrations of conditions down a coal mine in 1842

Source H

The trapper

'The little trapper of eight years of age lies quiet in bed; between two or three in the morning his mother shakes him. He fills his tin bottle with coffee, and takes a loaf of bread, and sets out for the pit. All his work is to open the door and then allow the door to shut of itself. He sits alone and has no one to talk to. He has no light. His hours are passed in total darkness. He knows nothing of the sun.'

Near Halifax

'In many collieries in this district the children work all day long in water and mud, and in some the men actually hew the coals in water.'

Yorkshire coalfield

'In one case a child was regularly taken into the pit of his father at three years of age. It was made to follow him to the workings, there to hold the candle, and when exhausted with fatigue, was cradled upon the coals until his return at night.'

Lancashire coalfield

'Betty Harris, aged thirty-seven, drawer in a coal pit, Little Bolton: "I have a belt round my waist, and a chain passing between my legs, and I go on my hands and feet. The road is very steep, and we have to hold by a rope. It is very hard work for a woman. My cousin looks after my children in the day-time. I am very tired when I get home at night. I have drawn till I have had the skin off me".'

First Report of the Children's Employment Commissioners: Mines and Collieries 1842

Source 1

'In the West Riding of Yorkshire it is not uncommon for infants even of 5 years old to be sent to the pit. About Halifax girls from 5 years old and upwards regularly perform the same work as boys. Children are sometimes taken out of their beds at 4 o'clock. In Derbyshire the regular hours of a full day's labour are 14 and occasionally 16. In Oldham the ways are so low only little boys can work in them, which they do naked, and often in mud and water, dragging sledge-tubs by the girdle and chain.'

Speech by Lord Ashley in Parliament in 1842

On the basis of this evidence, the Government brought in the Coal Mines Act of 1842, in the face of opposition from the mine owners and even from John Bright and the Anti-Corn Law League (see Chapter 1). They were opposed to any Government interference in trade and industry because they believed in laissez-faire (see page 167), the policy of leaving things alone, of non-interference by the State. They applied this theory even to the regulation of mines and factory working conditions, especially since the Coal Mines Act, which was a major step forward in industrial reform, affected adults as well as children and brought in government safety regulations.

The new Act banned the employment underground of:
(a) boys under ten years,
(b) all women and girls, irrespective of age.

An Inspector of Mines was appointed to see that the Act was enforced. In addition there were new regulations regarding safety measures underground. In particular, no child under the age of fifteen was to be put in charge of machinery.

Source J

CAPITAL AND
LABOUR,
1843

This remarkable cartoon was published in *Punch* on 29 July 1843. The magazine said 'It is gratifying to know that though there is much misery in the coal mines, there is a great deal of luxury results from it.'

---

1 *What do you think the artist intended in this cartoon? Who suffered the misery? Who enjoyed the luxury?*

2 *What does this cartoon tell you about working conditions in the coal mines in 1843?*

3 *What do you think a mine owner thought about this cartoon? Write a short paragraph describing an imaginary meeting between Lord Ashley and a mine owner, in which this* Punch *cartoon is the only topic of conversation.*

The Factory Act of 1844

The pace of factory reform had begun to quicken and regulations concerning the employment of women were next applied to the textile industry. The 1844 Factory Act specified a twelve-hour working day on weekdays and a nine-hour Saturday for women and all young people under eighteen years of age, and a 'half-time' day for children under thirteen years. Their working day was cut to six and a half hours to give them time for three hours' compulsory education. In addition, the Act made it a legal requirement to screen dangerous machinery.

The Ten-Hour Act of 1847

Further legislation followed, and in 1847 the factory reformers finally got the Ten-Hour Bill through Parliament. After this all women, and boys under the age of eighteen in textile mills were to work a maximum of ten hours a day and no more than 58 hours in any one week. The reformers intended to reduce working hours for men at the same time, since they would no longer have the assistance of the women and children for more than ten hours. But the mill owners soon got round this, by putting women and children on shift work and as a result working hours for men were not reduced.

The Ten-Hour Act of 1850

In 1850 new legislation amended the Ten-Hour Act of 1847 from ten to ten and a half hours and specified that the working day for all workers in the textile mills should begin at either 06.00 or 07.00 and finish at either 18.00 or 19.00 – a total of twelve hours at work with one and a half hours allowed for meals. Saturday afternoons were to be half-holidays in addition to Sundays. The Ten-Hour Bill demanded by Sadler and Oastler in 1831–2 had been achieved.

Source K

Fork grinders in Sheffield, The Illustrated London News, *10 March 1866 (see also the picture of saw grinders on page 260)*

Up to this point the provisions of the Factory Acts only applied to textile mills, mines and collieries. But other industries employed workers under equally bad conditions, as you can see in this picture.

1 *What job is being done by the children? How old do you think they are?*

2 *How many of the workers in this picture are protected against flying sparks?*

3 *What other potential dangers can you see in this workshop? How well-lit is the working area?*

4 *Write a report on this workshop drawing attention to the hazards faced by the employees.*

The Factory Act of 1864

In 1864 regulations were made controlling industries other than textiles and mining. These were primarily concerned with safety measures in dangerous industries, such as those making gunpowder and matches. But the Government also took the opportunity to make the terms of the existing Factory Acts apply to these industries as well.

The Factories and Workshops Act of 1867

In 1867 the Factory Acts were applied to all works with more than 50 employees and other regulations were introduced to try to curb some of the evils which were commonplace in workshops employing fewer than 50 workers.

Source L

A tailor and his family at work in a gloomy attic in Bethnal Green, The Illustrated London News, *1863 (see page 208)*

1 *What work are the children in the picture on the previous page doing?*
2 *Write a description of the working conditions of these children.*
3 *Why were the Factory Acts powerless to come to their aid?*
4 *What other form of legislation could have done something to prevent the employment of young children during the daytime?*

LAW AND ORDER

Punishment

An execution at Tyburn in 1747

In the eighteenth century most people had little respect for the law, even though as many as 220 crimes could be punished with the death penalty, including the theft of goods valued at 5s [25p] or more and the crime of putting someone in 'Fear on the Highway'. In fact, only a relatively small number of executions were actually carried out. Judges and juries were reluctant to find prisoners guilty for such trivial offences. Crime was commonplace simply because most criminals were never caught. You can sense this if you look at the picture which Hogarth drew of a public execution in 1747.

1 *Does the crowd look afraid of the law? How did Hogarth show the brutality of the crowd?*
2 *Do you think Hogarth thought that public executions were an effective deterrent to crime? Give your reasons, quoting evidence from the picture.*

The alternative to the death penalty was transportation to America up until 1786 and to Australia from the 1790s onwards. Convicts were taken by ship, many of them dying on the voyage. On arrival, they were put to work on the estates of colonists.

Transportation was eventually abolished in the middle of the nineteenth century. By that time the Australian settlers had had enough – they wanted to encourage legitimate immigrants, not British convicts. As a result new prisons had to be built in Britain to accommodate the larger number of prisoners.

Policing the towns before 1830

In 1700, responsibility for law and order in the countryside was in the hands of local magistrates, with the assistance of unpaid constables, drawn from the inhabitants of each parish. But paid watchmen had been employed in some towns since 1663 (during the reign of Charles II) although most were elderly and incompetent.

> 'TRIAL OF WILLIAM RAVEN. 22 March 1733. Accused of stealing an iron rail worth 2s [10p] from Arabella Scattergood.
>
> First Watchman, 'I am Watchman in Cavendish Square. As I was standing in my Watchbox between 2 and 3 in the Morning, I heard the fall of an Iron Rail, and running out I saw the Prisoner with a Bar in his hand. I cried out "Stop Thief", he got past the first Watch, but was stopped by another Watch.'
>
> Second Watchman (Jonathan Dickenson), 'As I called Two o'Clock in Marlborough Street I thought there was some Roguery going forward; so I planted my lantern in the middle of Blenheim-street, that my Inhabitants might see I was upon my Duty.'
>
> Third Watchman, 'I heard a cry of "Stop Thief", and met the Prisoner running with his drawn Sword; I made a blow at him, but he put it by with his Sword; I called out to Jonathan Dickenson, who knocked him down.'
>
> The prisoner was found guilty and sentenced to be transported.'
>
> Extracts from Middlesex Sessions for 1732–3

---

1 Describe the watchman shown in the picture on page 204.
2 Which parts of the evidence given at the trial of William Raven tell you about the watchman's duties?
3 How would you have recognised a watchman in 1733? What did he carry at night? Where was he stationed? Why was he called a watchman?
4 Why do you think the watchmen were called Charleys? What sort of person is sometimes called a 'Charley' today?

5 *In 1733, Michael Allom was charged with stealing 43 pairs of stockings worth £3 10s [£3.50]. Why did the jury find him guilty of only stealing stockings to the value of 4s 10d [24p]?*

These early attempts at policing were largely unsuccessful. This can be seen from the frequency with which pickpockets, smugglers and highwaymen broke the law. Criminals could only be brought to justice if people caught them in the act, or if fellow criminals informed on their friends and accomplices in order to get a reward. Thief takers were paid £40 if they arrested a highwayman who was later convicted.

However, one or two attempts were made to create an effective method of bringing criminals to justice. In 1748, Henry Fielding, the Bow Street Magistrate, created a small force of constables, called the Bow Street Runners. In 1792, the idea was extended to other parts of London, and in 1798, a special police force was set up to patrol the banks of the Thames.

Peelers and policemen

The origins of the modern police force began in 1829, when Sir Robert Peel was Home Secretary. London had well over one million people by that time and, as Chapter 7 showed, the authorities had been seriously disturbed by the lawless behaviour of the mobs at Spa Fields in 1816, and at the time immediately before the Six Acts were introduced in 1819. At Peterloo, it was said that the unpaid constables on duty there lacked the discipline and training needed to face a crowd.

Sir Robert Peel was chairman of a committee which recommended the setting up of a civilian police force. Opponents said it would infringe people's freedom but, in 1829, he went ahead and brought in the Metropolitan Police Act. This created a police force for London (the Metropolis) under the ultimate control of the Home Secretary, but organised by Colonel Charles Rowan and a lawyer called Richard Mayne. They were the first two Commissioners of Police at their headquarters at Scotland Yard.

The new police force was organised into divisions and planned like an army, with superintendents, inspectors, sergeants and constables. All were paid a wage and wore blue coats and top hats (rather than military uniforms), to emphasise that they were civilians **not** soldiers. This is why they also carried wooden truncheons rather than guns. At first they were detested by judges, magistrates, juries, soldiers and Londoners alike, to say nothing of criminals. But good discipline, a soft but vigilant approach, good humour and a decline in the crime rate soon won them the respect and support they needed.

A Peeler, The Illustrated London News, *1844*

The Metropolitan Police Force was so effective it acted as a model for the other large towns, which were growing rapidly at this time. This is why the Municipal Corporations Act of 1835 (see Chapter 6) made it a requirement that each Borough should form its own police force, supervised by a watch committee. In 1839, the County Police Act authorised the formation of county constabularies which could also be financed out of the rates. But the Act only gave permission to do so – it did not make it a legal requirement.

By 1856 only half the counties had a properly trained police force. The County and Borough Police Act of that year made it compulsory for counties to form a County Police Force. This Act also gave local authorities an incentive to create an efficient force, by the payment of a Government grant to help subsidise the cost of running the police force. However, they only got this money if the force was deemed to be efficient by the Inspectors of Constabulary specially appointed for this purpose.

---

1 *Why were policemen called 'Peelers' at first? Why were the nicknames 'crusher', 'bobby' and 'copper' also used?*
2 *What is a 'watch committee' responsible for nowadays? Why is it called a 'watch' committee?*
3 *Refer back to the sources covering the Peterloo Massacre on pages 237–40. Who arrested 'Orator' Hunt? Who ordered his arrest? Who would have done so in London after 1829?*

Prisons and their reform

Before 1823, over 200 crimes carried the death sentence. Few people paid much attention to the plight of prisoners in gaol. Most of these people were debtors, since criminals were usually put in the stocks or pillory, or whipped, for minor offences, and transported or hanged for 'major' crimes. Some, the vagabonds and prostitutes, were put in the houses of correction (called bridewells) to undergo hard labour. Conditions in all of these prisons were unbelievably bad. Prisoners (some in shackles) were at the mercy of corrupt, unpaid gaolers and crowded into filthy, disease-ridden dungeons.

John Howard, the High Sheriff of Bedfordshire, had been deeply affected by his experiences as a prisoner of war in France, in 1756. In the 1770s, he visited gaols throughout Britain, and wrote *The State of Prisons in England and Wales* in 1777, drawing attention to the appalling conditions and suggesting remedies.

'Constant separation is desirable. The gaol will be kept cleaner and if the smallpox, or the gaol-fever [typhus], should infect one ward, the other at a distance may be free from it.

I wish to have many small rooms that each criminal may sleep alone. If it be difficult to prevent their being together in the daytime, they should by all means be separated at night. Solitude and silence are favourable to reflection, and may possibly lead them to repentance. The women-felons ward should be quite distinct from that of the men; and the young criminals from old and hardened offenders. Debtors and felons should have wards totally separate.'

1 *Which different groups of prisoner did he want to see kept apart? Why? What advantages did he think would come from keeping prisoners apart from one another?*

Bridewell Prison in about 1730

2 *What improvements would John Howard have wanted to make to Bridewell Prison, had he seen this engraving drawn by William Hogarth in about 1730? How can you tell it was a house of correction for minor offenders? What other forms of punishment can you see?*

Sir Robert Peel took the first positive steps to reform the penal system in 1823, when he abolished the death penalty for about 100 of the 200 capital offences at that time. Further crimes were taken off this list in the 1830s, and by 1838, the only crimes for which the death sentence could be given were murder, attempted murder and treason.

Peel also tried to improve prison conditions. As Home Secretary, he brought in some modest reforms in 1823, which provided for regular inspections and the payment of gaolers. He paved the way for the Prison Act of 1839, which laid down the basis for a more humane approach to the treatment of prisoners, giving them the right to exercise and to read books, whilst requiring that they be housed in their own cells and put to sensible, productive labour. Peel was influenced to a certain extent by the work of prison reformers such as John Howard and Sir Samuel Romilly (who was instrumental in abolishing the death penalty for some offences, such as stealing from a person) and also by a remarkable woman called Elizabeth Fry (see below).

Elizabeth Fry (1780–1845)

Elizabeth Fry reading to prisoners in Newgate Prison, from a painting by J. Barrett

Elizabeth Fry was a Quaker preacher and the daughter of a wealthy London banker. In 1813, she was invited to visit the women in Newgate Prison, where she was appalled to see the conditions in which they, and their children, were being held.

She was unable to help immediately, but in 1817 formed the Association for the Improvement of Female Prisoners in Newgate. Many women had to take their children to prison with them because there was no one else to look after them. Elizabeth Fry helped to teach the prisoners' children and some of the women prisoners themselves. She tried to bring Christianity into their lives and devoted the rest of her life to reforming prisoners and prisons. She wanted women prisoners to be segregated and properly looked after by women gaolers and this was achieved in some prisons under Peel's reforms of the 1820s.

FURTHER QUESTIONS AND EXERCISES

1   *Why was London a much safer city in which to live in 1850 than in 1700?*

2   *Explain briefly the contribution made by each of the following to social welfare and reform:*
(a) Elizabeth Fry,   (b) Robert Peel,   (c) Lord Shaftesbury.

3   *Imagine you are a Radical Member of Parliament. You have been visiting factories and mines in the north of England, in 1832. Write a short speech arguing the case for the new Factory Act of 1833.*

SPECIMENS FROM MR. PUNCH'S INDUSTRIAL
EXHIBITION OF 1850.
(TO BE IMPROVED IN 1851.)

4   *Look at the above cartoon from Punch. What was the point of the cartoon? To which Factory Act and to which other event does it refer? Why are different industrial workers on display? Write an explanatory caption for this picture.*

5   *In 1856 Dr Bence Jones said this about the St Pancras Workhouse:*

> *'Highly unsatisfactory. The arrangement for the administration of out-door relief is most defective. At half-past five o'clock as many as 150 still remain unrelieved. They had no food all day and many of them stated that they did not expect any until seven o'clock.'*

What did he mean when he said '150 still remain unrelieved'? Who, and what, was going to relieve them? What were the original intentions of the Poor Law Commissioners?

6 In what ways were working conditions unsatisfactory for women and children in textile mills (before 1844) and in coal mines (before 1842)? What steps were taken before 1850 to improve those working conditions? What prompted these reforms?

THE POOR MAN'S FRIEND.

7 Look at the above cartoon which appeared in Punch in 1845. Who was the poor man's friend? What type of building can be seen through the window, labelled 'UNION'? What was the point of the cartoon?

8 In 1835, Francis Place said that the habits of the lower orders had 'very greatly improved' since 1790. Crimes had decreased in proportion to the population. How do you account for the changes which had taken place?

9 What was the significance of the 1833 Factory Act? What were its main terms, why did it arouse opposition, and why was it ultimately unsatisfactory?

10 Write an essay on the Poor Law. Explain what provision had been made for the poor in the eighteenth century, how it functioned and why it was unable to cope with the distress of the 1790s. Explain how and why the Speenhamland System came into operation, how it worked, and what effect it had before 1834. Examine its weaknesses and show how and why it was replaced by the Poor Law Amendment Act after 1834.

Chapter Nine

Education

INTRODUCTION

National School (founded 1848) at Plaistow in London's dockland – for the education of the children of the working classes, The Illustrated London News, *27 June 1857*

The shed at Plaistow was about 9 metres long and 4.5 metres wide, with a rotten wooden roof covered with felt. The only windows were in this roof – broken panes of glass from an old greenhouse, which is why the mistress was 'obliged to keep school under an umbrella'. She was in charge of 120 pupils and was paid £35 a year.

1 *In 1857* The Illustrated London News *called this 'perhaps the cheapest National School in the kingdom'. Why?*
2 *Compare the National School at Plaistow with Charterhouse public school on page 296 (drawn in about 1860). What would your feelings have been, as a parent of one of the children seen outside the National School, if you could have compared it directly with Charterhouse at that time?*

The pictures illustrate the huge gulf in the nineteenth century, between the education available to a small minority of rich and influential people on the one hand, and that available to the large majority of the working classes on the other. They shared one common feature, in that both the National School and Charterhouse were supported by the Church of England. Religion played a big part in the growth of education in the eighteenth and nineteenth centuries.

In the early eighteenth century, education had little of the importance it was to have by 1870. The majority of children did not go to school in the 1700s. Many of those that did, went to the totally inadequate Dame Schools or to a small number of Charity Schools. Secondary education was confined to a small number of demoralised public schools and a larger number of decaying endowed grammar schools. Both taught the ancient classics to the exclusion of almost every other subject.

SECONDARY EDUCATION FOR THE RULING CLASSES

The endowed grammar schools

The endowed grammar schools largely owed their beginnings to old bequests made in the Middle Ages which specified what subjects should be taught in the schools. These subjects were largely irrelevant to the needs of pupils during the Industrial Revolution. The value of the original endowments had fallen and many schools had begun to charge fees, thus no longer accepting those who could not pay – the free scholars – for whom the grammar schools had originally been intended.

In 1805, a legal decision effectively prevented grammar schools from changing their curriculum – they had to teach 'grammar', if that was laid down in their endowment – and it was not until 1840 that the Grammar Schools Act allowed them to change. By that time the demand for better education from the middle classes had stimulated a revival in schools. Many endowed grammar schools expanded and improved and some went on to become public schools.

The public schools

Some grammar schools had already developed into public schools by the middle of the eighteenth century. They had become boarding schools for the sons of rich people from all over the country. But the standard of education was poor, and at the start of the nineteenth century they were as set in their ways as the endowed grammar schools, with which they shared many common features. The vicious use of the birch and the general air of lawlessness and needless cruelty in these schools even led pupils to riot (such as the Great Rebellion of boys at Rugby School, in 1797).

Charterhouse (founded 1611) – one of the great English public schools, The
Illustrated London News, *1 March 1862*

Most public schools taught classics to the exclusion of every other
subject. Lord John Russell (Prime Minister 1846–52) said that when he
was at Westminster School, the teaching had consisted entirely of Latin.
On half holidays, he and other boys had had to go to an outside teacher
to be taught arithmetic and writing.

In the early nineteenth century, schools such as Westminster held their
lessons in one huge school room. The boys sat on benches (or forms) with
a desk in front of them. (This is why each group of boys, under an usher
or assistant master, was known by the form it occupied – First Form,
Second Form, and so on.)

By 1870, many new public schools had been founded and others had
expanded. There were a number of reasons for this:

(a)   The newly rich middle classes wanted their sons to be educated
      as young gentlemen; and they had the money to pay for it.

(b)   The railways made it feasible for boarding schools to cater for
      pupils from all over the country.

(c)   There were still relatively few good day schools which could
      provide a similar education.

(d)   Communal life in a boarding school was praised for its own
      sake, irrespective of the quality of the school.

(e)   Enterprising headmasters, like Dr Butler of Shrewsbury (who
      started the prefect system) and Dr Thring of Uppingham (who
      introduced music and organised games), radically altered the
      type and quality of the education offered by their schools.

Dr Thomas Arnold of Rugby School was probably the most famous
and the most influential of these Victorian headmasters. He made

Christianity and the Chapel the focus of school life and placed great emphasis on character-building through sport and the development of the prefect system. But he still emphasised the classics rather than the sciences and placed his trust in the birch rather than the carrot.

---

1 *How did the Industrial and Transport Revolutions affect the development of the public schools?*
2 *What influence has the nineteenth-century public school system had on the state system of education today?*

ELEMENTARY EDUCATION FOR THE WORKING CLASSES

Charity Schools

At the end of the seventeenth century, Charity Schools had been founded for 'the Education of Poor Children in the Knowledge and Practice of the Christian Religion as professed and taught in the Church of England; and for teaching them such other things as are most suitable to their condition'.

These schools flourished in the early eighteenth century and were financed out of donations made by wealthy people for this purpose. The children learned to read and write, the boys going on to learn 'Arithmetick to fit them for Services or Apprenticeships' and the girls 'generally to knit their Stockings and Gloves, to Mark, Sew, Make and Mend their Cloaths'.

Dame Schools

The children of most poor parents did not go to school. They lacked money to pay the fees and the incentive to do so (since children could get a job). Parents who were prepared to spend a few pence each week could send their young children to a Dame School. These were small private schools which were run to make a profit for the teacher – a woman who was not always as old or as forbidding as her title suggests. The Dame was rarely qualified to be a teacher. Her school was sparsely furnished, equipped with the inevitable birch rod and the children learned the three Rs (Reading, Writing, Arithmetic) by rote (from memory) using horn-books. These were pages of text mounted on a wooden bat and covered with a thin transparent sheet of cattle horn – rather like a modern workcard! Similar schools were run by schoolmasters. They flourished in the eighteenth and early nineteenth centuries.

The Sunday School movement

It was Robert Raikes who first tackled the problem of education for the very poor. In 1780, he saw children 'wretchedly ragged, at play in the streets' of Gloucester, spending their Sundays in an atmosphere of gambling, 'noise and riot, and cursing and swearing'. Raikes and his supporters paid a Dame School teacher to run a Sunday School. The children were divided into classes and taught to read the alphabet first of all, then short sentences, before being taught to read from a children's hymn book and ultimately from the Bible.

> 1 *Why did Raikes teach the children to read and write, first of all, at a Sunday School dedicated to religious education?*
> 2 *What was the main reason for the Sunday School Movement – education or religion?*

By 1783, there were over 250 pupils in the Gloucester Sunday Schools. Similar Sunday Schools were started in other parts of Britain in the following twenty years.

The Bell and Lancaster Monitorial system

The Sunday School movement spread rapidly because there was a very real need for schools for the poor. But there was a problem in meeting that need on the other six days of the week. Poor people could not afford to pay the fees required by qualified teachers nor those in the Dame Schools. In about 1800, Andrew Bell (an Anglican) and Joseph Lancaster (a Quaker) both thought they had found the answer. They devised somewhat similar methods, independently of each other, enabling one teacher to educate a large number of pupils at the same time.

Joseph Lancaster (1778–1838) opened his school in Borough Road, London, in 1801. The best scholars were made monitors, and each was put in charge of a small number of pupils. Lancaster taught the monitors at the start of each day, before the other children arrived. Later on, the monitors taught the pupils in their different groups. Lancaster claimed he could teach a thousand children in this way and described his system in a book called *Improvements in Education*, first published in 1803.

'The whole school is arranged in classes; a monitor is appointed to each, who is responsible for the cleanliness, order, and improvement of every boy in it. The proportion of boys who teach, either in reading, writing, or arithmetic, is one in ten.'

The classes were grouped according to ability. The lowest form was called the sand class because the children printed letters of the alphabet with their fingers in the sand. Besides the teaching monitors there was a monitor in charge of ruling the writing books, inspecting monitors to see that children successfully learned their lessons, a monitor of slates, a monitor of absentees and a monitor-general.

Pupils who did well were given Merit Badges in reading and spelling and when they gained a set number of badges were able to choose a prize from the toys, bats, balls and kites hanging up in the school room. But there were punishments as well – a wooden log worn round the neck, like a pillory, shackles on the legs, suspension from the ceiling in a basket, notices displaying the nature of the offence, and when a boy came to school with dirty face or hands 'a girl is appointed to wash his face in the sight of the whole school'.

The children were expected to pay a few pence each week for their education but children of the very poor were admitted free of charge. Charitable organisations and private individuals later helped to finance many other schools which were founded on the same principles.

Lancaster's Monitorial School in Borough Road, London, contemporary print, c. 1805

1 *Why was there only one large classroom?*
2 *What can you see hanging from the ceiling of the schoolroom? What educational purpose did they serve?*
3 *In what ways did the Monitorial System resemble the factories which were then spreading rapidly in Britain?*

Andrew Bell (1753–1832) had developed a very similar system to Lancaster's in Madras in India, with the aid of pupils he called tutors. When he returned to England, he published *An Experiment in Education*, in 1797, setting out his system. He later put it into practice in a school in London's Aldgate.

Bell claimed that a single master 'if able and diligent, could, without difficulty, conduct ten neighbouring schools, each consisting of a thousand scholars'.

Like Lancaster, he placed great emphasis on praise and rewards, and was opposed to corporal punishment. Detention was the last resort, but the extra hours kept back at school gave the pupil an opportunity to learn his lessons properly – something corporal punishment failed to do.

However, Bell and Lancaster were of different religious denominations. Bell was an Anglican (Church of England) and Lancaster was a Quaker (Nonconformist). Their respective supporters soon began to argue with each other, after a Mrs Trimmer wrote a booklet, claiming that Bell, not Lancaster, had invented the monitorial system.

The Voluntary Schools

The disagreement between Bell's and Lancaster's supporters led to the formation of two church voluntary societies, both formed with the intention of founding more schools for the working classes along similar lines.

(a) 'The National Society for Promoting the Education of the Poor in the Principles of the Established Church' was founded in 1811 and was based on Andrew Bell's methods. It was to be a national education founded on the national religion, and its schools were called National Schools.

(b) The British and Foreign Schools Society ('The Institution for Promoting the Education of the Labouring and Manufacturing Classes of Society of every Religious Persuasion') was founded in 1814 and based on Joseph Lancaster's methods. Reading lessons were to be taken from the Bible but no denominational religion was to be taught in the Society's schools, although children were to be encouraged to go to 'the place of worship to which its parents belong'. The schools were usually called British Schools.

This educational division on religious grounds was to plague British education for the rest of the nineteenth century!

Although most people thought the Monitorial System provided an excellent, cheap and effective way of educating the working classes, it did have its critics. At Robert Owen's school in New Lanark (see pages 245 and 301), the children were often taught out of doors and were given instruction in music and dancing as well as in the basic subjects. Owen employed 10 or 11 teachers to teach his 700 pupils and claimed that the Monitorial System tried 'to educate a great number without proper assistance'.

Contemporary picture of Robert Owen's School at New Lanark in about 1820

1 Write a detailed description of the classroom in Robert Owen's school. In what ways does it resemble a modern school? What would this lesson be called on a modern timetable?

2 Write a paragraph comparing this school with Joseph Lancaster's Monitorial school (shown on page 299).

3 What would you say were the main defects of the Bell and Lancaster Monitorial System? What were the main advantages?

Study sources A and B carefully.

Source A

'A BAZAAR in aid of the Fund for the Erection of the NEW BRITISH SCHOOLS, NORTHAMPTON, will be held at the GEORGE HOTEL, on the 21st and 22nd of April. The Schools will be open to all, without respect of sect or party, and the system of education will be conducted on the principles of the British and Foreign Schools Society.'

Advert in *The Northampton Herald* 1846

Source B

National Schools in 1861

'The school-buildings in general are large and commodious, well warmed and ventilated. Convenient playgrounds are in many cases attached to them, and fitted up with swings, vaulting-poles, and other game apparatus. Others have gardens cultivated by the boys, or workshops where a little carpentering is done.

The internal fittings of the school are in almost every case good; the floor, the seats, the desks, must all be such as shall from year to year satisfy the Privy Council on Education; and the text books are ample and cheap, being partly supplied by grant from Government, and partly by purchase of the school-managers. Black-boards for oral teaching are in sufficient numbers; and the walls are adorned with the best maps.'

Cornhill Magazine 1861

---

4 *How do the extracts suggest the British and National Schools were financed (apart from the few pence a week paid by each pupil)? How did a British School differ from a National School?*

5 *How had schools for working-class children changed in the fifty years since the Bell and Lancaster schools of the 1800s?*

6 *What evidence is there of Government involvement in elementary education by 1861?*

7 *Look at the picture of the National School at Plaistow in 1857 (shown at the beginning of this chapter). Write a short comparison with the National School described in the 1861 extract above. What do you think a typical National School was like? In which direction and in what ways might the 1861 description be biased?*

Ragged schools

Brook Street Ragged and Industrial School, The Illustrated London News, *17 December 1853*

The children of the very poor were sometimes excluded from the voluntary schools. But in some towns they could attend Ragged schools. These were founded in the middle years of the nineteenth century and in 1844 the Ragged School Union was started with Lord Ashley (later the Earl of Shaftesbury) as its chairman.

'A ragged school is a Sunday school, established by private charity in a city district of the meanest kind, where every house is worn-out and crazy, and almost every tenant a beggar, or, perhaps, something worse. A school, moreover, in which no children are to be found who would be admitted into any other school; for ragged, diseased, and crime-worn, their very appearance would scare away the children of well-conducted parents; and hence, if they were not educated there, they would receive no education at all.'

Chambers's Journal 1845

At Brook Street Ragged School pupils were given practical instruction as well as basic education. The school had a workshop where at one stage they learned shoe-making.

---

1 *What was a Ragged School?*
2 *Why was the Ragged School the only chance of an education for some children? What does this tell you about the voluntary system of education?*
3 *Look at the picture and write a short paragraph describing the teaching methods in use at Brook Street Ragged School.*

TOWARDS A STATE SYSTEM OF EDUCATION

The first government grants

In 1833, J. A. Roebuck introduced a proposal in the House of Commons, which would have given Britain a compulsory national system of education for all children between the ages of six and twelve. Instead Parliament approved a measure proposed by Lord Althorp granting £20,000 a year to be spent on new school buildings 'in aid of Private Subscriptions for the Erection of School Houses'. This was under £1 million by today's values – a minute sum to spend on a nation's schools. The £20,000 was to be spent on new school buildings by the British and National School Societies provided that half the cost of building was met from private sources.

The Committee of the Privy Council for Education

In 1839, the grant for education was increased to £30,000 a year and Government inspectors were appointed, to ensure that the government grant was being spent properly in the schools. The Government set up the Committee of the Privy Council to be responsible for education, under its Secretary, Dr (later Sir) James Kay-Shuttleworth. He soon identified one major weakness – the shortage of qualified teachers, and encouraged the voluntary societies to do something about this, by starting teacher training colleges.

Kay-Shuttleworth had a low opinion of the Monitorial System and wanted to improve the quality of teaching in the schools aided by the Committee. So in 1846 the Committee set up a training scheme for pupil-teachers. The following extract shows how it operated in 1861.

> 'The pupil-teachers are selected from the school, on account of their character, attainments, and special aptitude for the office of school-master; and beside the practical training in school work which they receive in school hours, a minimum of one hour and a half is fixed by the Privy Council Office for special instruction in subjects defined for each year of their apprenticeship.
>
> An examination is held annually by the inspector of the district to ascertain whether these subjects have been thoroughly taught; if they pass, each pupil-teacher receives from the Council Office his yearly stipend (e.g. £10 in year 1, £20 in year 5), and the master his fee (£5 for the first pupil-teacher, £4 for the second, £3 after that). Supposing the pupil-teacher passes at least five examinations, he may then present himself as a candidate for a Queen's scholarship.'
>
> *Cornhill Magazine* 1861

On reaching a suitable standard, the pupil-teacher went to training college at the age of 18 for one to three years, took the college exams and if successful was then conditionally granted a certificate of merit. After teaching satisfactorily for a further two years, the teacher was at last regarded as fully trained and entitled to a salary plus a government grant.

---

1 *How old do you think you had to be before you could start on your first year as a pupil-teacher in school? How many years did it take to become a fully certificated teacher?*

2 *What were the advantages and disadvantages of the pupil-teacher system compared with the Monitorial System? In what ways were the two methods similar?*

In 1846, the Committee of the Privy Council also authorised the payment of a grant 'in aid of the salary of every schoolmaster appointed to a school under their inspection'. The annual grant varied according to the years spent by the teacher at a training college – £15 or £20 for one year's training, rising to £25 or £30 for three years in college.

The Revised Code

In 1858, the Government set up a Royal Commission under the Duke of Newcastle, with a view to seeing whether the government grant for education was being well spent. The members of the Commission took a very limited view of the value of education – one member thought that

Government Inspector testing pupils in school, Punch, *21 December 1872*

the most a working-class pupil could aim for was the ability to spell simple words, read a newspaper and add up a grocer's bill. Since many children were already leaving school without this basic ability, the Commission decided to recommend a system of payment to teachers based on results to improve the standard of achievement. Robert Lowe, the Minister responsible, introduced his Revised Code of 1862 with the promise 'If it is not cheap, it shall be efficient; if it is not efficient, it shall be cheap'.

After this the government grant to teachers was only made after an official inspection each year. Individual grants to teachers (see page 304) were abolished. In future the government grant was paid in a lump sum to the managers of the schools. So although the Revised Code generally had a bad effect on education, it did mean that in future teachers were paid by the local managers and not by the State. In this way control of education was retained by the local authorities and not directly by the Government. A school received 6s 6d [32.5p] for each child under six years, provided the Inspector was satisfied with their general performance. The other children were divided into Standards I to VI and at each Standard were tested in Reading, Writing and Arithmetic. In this way each child could obtain a total of three passes. The school was paid 2s 8d [13p] per child for each pass plus 4s [20p] if the attendance of the child had been satisfactory – making a maximum grant of 12s [60p] per child.

The test for Standard III, for example, specified that scholars passing the three subjects had to read a short paragraph from 'an elementary reading book used in the school', write out a sentence to be dictated from the same paragraph and do a basic sum. However, the most celebrated Government Inspector in Britain, the poet Matthew Arnold, wrote in 1867:

> 'I feel sure that our present system of grants does harm to schools and their instruction by resting its grants too exclusively upon individual examination, prescribed in all its details by the Central Office, and necessarily mechanical.'

From the point of view of the Treasury, the Revised Code was highly successful. The government grant fell by about £175,000 in three years and there was a marked improvement in attendance.

The defects of this system of grant were many and obvious. Teachers trained children hard to pass the three Rs, ignoring other subjects such as history, geography, art, music and science. It was not too difficult to get the children to learn their reading books off by heart! They were bullied into coming to school on the day of the inspection, even though they may have been ill. There were even false entries in attendance registers and cheating during the inspection. The Code was later amended, in 1867 and in 1875, to widen the number of subjects tested to include those such as history and geography.

---

1 Why were teachers so anxious to get children to school on the day of the inspection? Why did some teachers falsify the attendance registers?

2 What did Matthew Arnold mean by 'prescribed in all its details'? Why was the examination 'necessarily mechanical'? Give examples.

3 What do you think was the effect of the Revised Code on teaching in schools? How would it have affected the National Schools described in the extract on page 301?

The 1870 Education Act

In the next ten years, pressure for a national system of compulsory education came from interested organisations, such as the Manchester Education Aid Society (which was founded in 1864), despite the Newcastle Commission's opinion that it was 'neither attainable nor desirable'. The Commission was satisfied with the existing system and thought that religious differences would make State education unattainable. The Birmingham Education League and other Nonconformist groups, for example, wanted free compulsory undenominational education, whilst the National Education Union composed of Anglicans wanted Church teaching to continue. The bickering between the two sides over the role of religious education in schooling delayed the passing of the Education Bill, but it was eventually passed in 1870.

The new Act established school boards elected by local people. They had to build new schools, out of the rates, if the voluntary societies were

THE THREE R's; OR, BETTER LATE THAN NEVER.

Look at the above cartoon, published in Punch in March 1870.

1 What were the 'Three Rs'?

2 Write a reasoned account explaining why the cartoon was called 'BETTER LATE THAN NEVER'.

unable or unwilling to provide adequate schools. Education was not to be free. The children would continue to pay up to 9d [4p] a week and the government grants would also continue (see page 305). School boards could offer free education to the poor and make school attendance compulsory if they wished (usually for children aged five to ten).

Religious instruction in the new rate-supported Board Schools had to be taught in such a way that it could not be said to follow the creed of a particular Church. The Cowper Temple clause in the Act read as follows: 'No religious catechism or religious formulary, which is distinctive of any particular denomination shall be taught in the school.' A Conscience Clause ensured that children who attended Church Schools could opt out of religious education if their parents wrote a letter to that effect.

The 1870 Education Act was a great milestone in social welfare. For the first time it created a state system of education. In 1860, only 25 per cent of the children had gone to school. By 1880, the proportion had risen to over 80 per cent. At last, in 1880, attendance at school was made compulsory for all children between five and ten years (and raised to twelve years by 1899). After 1891 it was also free.

FURTHER QUESTIONS AND EXERCISES

THE PATRON OF EDUCATION
AND FRIEND OF THE POOR.

Contemporary engraving

1 *What type of school is shown in this picture? Write a brief description of the teaching method used in these schools, explaining how this system of education differed from that provided by an endowed grammar school or public school at that time.*

2 *Choose any three of the following types of school. For each one, explain how and why it was started, and what type of education it provided at the time given:*
   (a) *Charity School (1710),*   (d) *Boys' Public School (1800),*
   (b) *Sunday School (1780),*   (e) *Ragged School (1850),*
   (c) *Dame School (1800),*   (f) *National School (1860).*

3 *Describe briefly the contribution to English education of,*
   (a) *Dr Thomas Arnold,*   (d) *Andrew Bell,*
   (b) *Sir James Kay-Shuttleworth,*   (e) *Joseph Lancaster.*
   (c) *Robert Raikes,*

4 *What were the main advantages and disadvantages of the Monitorial System?*

5 *What do you notice about the graph opposite showing the number of children at school and government expenditure on education in the middle of the nineteenth century? Explain fully why the two trend lines differ in the period 1860–70.*

6 *What was the role played by:*
   (a) *religion,*
   (b) *government,*
   in the development of English education before 1870?

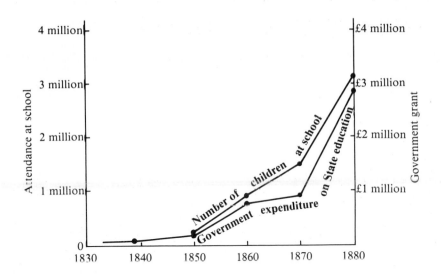

Numbers of children attending school and the amount of government money spent on education between 1833 and 1880

'That men unable to sign their own names should be engaged in business involving large capital, seems to us unaccountable. What have the educated and learned classes of England been thinking of for the last three centuries, that they have allowed the common people to grow up in masses around them without the least tincture of education?'

Chambers's Journal 1837

7 What had 'the educated and learned classes of England been thinking of'? How did they improve matters in the period after 1837?

8 Write an essay describing and explaining the history of elementary education from 1700 to 1870. Your essay should mention the Charity Schools, the Sunday Schools, Dame Schools, the Bell and Lancaster system, Government grants, the British and National Schools, the Committee of the Privy Council, the pupil-teacher system, the Revised Code and the 1870 Education Act.

Chapter Ten

Medicine and Surgery

INTRODUCTION

Bethlehem Hospital for the mentally ill in 1735 – as seen through the eyes of William Hogarth

> 1 How can you tell from this picture that people who were mentally ill were treated as if they were criminals?
> 2 In the early eighteenth century people could pay an entrance fee of one penny to visit the Bethlehem Hospital (known as Bedlam) to laugh at the antics of the 'lunatics' (as they called them). Was Hogarth aware of this practice?
> 3 Compare this picture with that of the men's ward in 1860, on page 316. That too shows Bethlehem Hospital for the mentally ill. What changes took place between 1735 and 1860?

In the early eighteenth century the medical knowledge of most doctors and surgeons was extremely limited and most of it unsound. For one thing, they did not know how to distinguish between many diseases, such as the different types of fever. As a result they had little idea what it was that caused people to be ill. As Chapter 6 showed, many diseases were attributed to miasmas (noxious vapours) in the air. Inevitably, doctors were unable to suggest cures or effective courses of treatment. They did not know why people became mentally ill; so they had no remedy to offer them.

ADVANCES IN SURGERY

Surgery before 1847

Surgeons were no more successful than doctors and no better informed. They were often powerless to take action, even if they were able to locate the diseased part of the body which experience told them ought to be removed. Surgery was still in its infancy.

It owed a lot in the eighteenth century, however, to the work of John Hunter, a Scotsman, who threw new light on the anatomy of the human body, a subject he pursued with the aid of a huge collection of specimens. Hunter gave surgeons a more precise and more detailed knowledge of the organs of the body and their functions.

Before 1847, patients who underwent an operation in a hospital did so as a last resort, since their chances of survival were very low. At that time there were no anaesthetics to dull or deaden the pain of an operation. Patients had to be restrained whilst the surgeon operated. This is why they were sometimes given a bottle of brandy to drink to make them insensible. The skill of the surgeon lay in his ability to operate as rapidly as possible in order to minimise the ordeal of the patient, but many patients died from the shock of the operation.

However, a number of discoveries were made in the nineteenth century which paved the way for the use of anaesthetics. Sir Humphry Davy studied nitrous oxide (laughing gas) in 1799 and noted its effects, but surgeons did not appreciate its potential as a general anaesthetic until 1844, when an American dentist, Horace Wells, used it to extract a tooth. Michael Faraday knew in 1818 that ether could put people to sleep, but again it was not used as an anaesthetic until 1842 (by C. W. Long in a surgical operation in America). It did not come into more general use until after 1846, when W. T. G. Morton in Boston (America) and Robert Liston in London proved its value for conducting surgical operations. However, ether was an irritant and made people choke and cough during operations and at that time surgeons found it difficult to control.

Use of anaesthetics

Inhaling chloroform in the 1850s, contemporary illustration

One of the first medical men to welcome ether as an anaesthetic in Britain was an Edinburgh professor of midwifery, called James Young Simpson (1811-70). You can read about his experiments with ether and chloroform in the following extracts, written by two of his relatives in 1897. They were recalling the excitement of discoveries he made fifty years earlier in 1847.

Source A

'We think of the night on February 28th, 1847, at the foot of Blackford Hill, when, on arriving too late, he said to our mother, "I'm so sorry, but you will never have to suffer such pain again; this would have put you to sleep" – as he held up a bottle of ether – "and made it painless".'

Mrs A. R. Simpson 1897

Source B

'Constantly during 1847 he tried various decoctions on himself. None beat ether, but some went near to killing him. His assistants at the time were Doctors George Keith and Matthews Duncan. The experimenters in their months of labour tried all sorts of compounds, often rendering themselves ill.

In conversation with Mr. Waldie, a chemist, perchloride of formyle (as chloroform was then called) was suggested. It had been first compounded about 1830 for internal, if any, use. Mr. Waldie promised to send a sample. It did not arrive, so Duncan and Flockart's in Edinburgh, made some at Dr. Simpson's request. It looked unvolatile (not easily vapourised) and smelt foully sweet. The doctor put it aside on his desk, where it was speedily buried under an accumulation of papers.

On the evening of November 4th, 1847, the trio as usual took an appetiser of experiments (i.e. before they had supper). It was drawing near midnight when the Professor rose, hunted among his papers on the side table, and said, "This will be our last try to-night." He dropped a few drops of chloroform into three tumblers for himself and his henchmen. The onlookers, well accustomed to these ventures, heeded little when three heads were bent over the newly-charged glasses, inhaling the heavy odour. "In a trice," wrote the Professor, "we were all under the mahogany." Never were three men so soundly asleep on that floor before. When Dr. Simpson looked round, he said, "This is something better than ether." Matthews Duncan lay snoring heavily. Dr. Keith stared wildly at the alarmed audience.'

Eve Blantyre Simpson 1897

Professor Simpson lost no time in putting his discovery about chloroform to good use. Within a fortnight he had used chloroform to ease the delivery of a baby and had tested it, in public, during three operations performed in Edinburgh Infirmary on 15 November 1847.

1 *When did Professor Simpson first use an anaesthetic? Which anaesthetic was it? For what purpose did he first use it?*

2 *What methods did he use, and how long did it take him to find an alternative to ether for use as a general anaesthetic? Why was an alternative needed at that time?*

3 *What do you think he meant by 'we were all under the mahogany'? How did he know that chloroform was the anaesthetic he had been looking for? What convinced him?*

4 *What tragic consequences might have occurred during this time? Would his testing method have satisfied modern doctors?*

5 *How do these sources differ from eyewitness accounts? Is there any evidence that they were based on what was seen, heard or experienced at the time? Are they primary or secondary sources? In what respects might they be unreliable? Are they likely to be biased? Do you think they show bias in any way? Are they of any value to a historian?*

At first, there was considerable opposition to Simpson's use of chloroform as an anaesthetic, particularly during childbirth. Opponents said it was unnatural and critics (men) even quoted the Bible at him, 'in sorrow shall she bring forth'. But Simpson knew the Bible and told them that the correct translation read 'in labour shall she bring forth'. But it was only when Queen Victoria herself used it at the birth of Prince Leopold, in 1853, that its use became widespread.

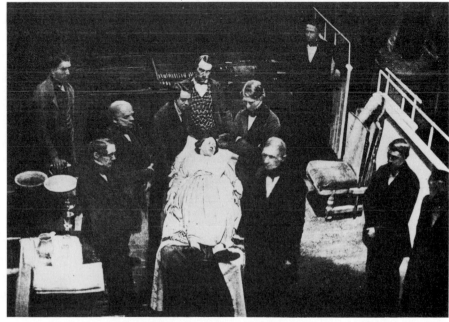

Hospital operation in 1847 – one of the first to use an anaesthetic on a patient. Make a list of the differences between this scene and what you would expect to see in a modern operating theatre.

By using anaesthetics surgeons no longer had to work rapidly and inaccurately in order to save the patient extended agony. Careful and precise surgery was possible at last. Complicated, deep-seated operations were feasible, which would have been impossible with a conscious patient.

But there was still a problem. Many patients lived through an operation only to die later, when poison got into the operation wound causing it to putrefy. Joseph Lister (1827–1912), Professor of Surgery at Glasgow University, said this was due to harmful germs; but Simpson thought this was nonsense!

Antiseptic surgery

Since anaesthetics had made it much easier for surgeons to operate, there were far more operations from the middle of the nineteenth century. But as a result more patients than ever died in the surgical wards. Surgeons could not understand this. They used the same scalpels and surgical instruments as before. They operated in the same old frock coats, stained as always with blood from earlier operations. What had gone wrong?

Joseph Lister tried to discover the reasons for this disturbingly high mortality rate. Like most doctors he thought that some form of poison in the air was making the operation wounds putrefy. He insisted on cleanliness in the treatment of wounds but without any obvious effect on the survival rate of his patients.

Luckily, Dr Thomas Anderson, Chemistry Professor at Glasgow, drew his attention to the work of the great French scientist, Louis Pasteur, who proved that germs are present in the atmosphere and that injured tissue does not become infected if protected from them. It seemed clear to Lister that the 'hospital fever' in his surgical patients was caused by germs infecting the body both during and after the operation, causing poisoning (sepsis) and eventual death. This is what Lister wrote in 1867:

> 'When it had been shown by the researches of Pasteur that the septic property of the atmosphere depended, not on any gaseous constituent but on minute organisms suspended in it, it occurred to me that decomposition in the injured part might be avoided by applying as a dressing some material capable of destroying the life of the floating particles.'

1 What did he mean by the 'septic property of the atmosphere'?
2 How had Pasteur's researches shown that the theory of miasmas (noxious vapours) was wrong? Which phrase in the extract means the same as miasma?
3 What deduction did Lister make as a result of his reading of Pasteur's work?

> **4** *Lister wanted 'some material capable of destroying' the 'septic' (poisonous) organisms. What do we call such a material?*

He decided to use carbolic acid, a new by-product from coal, because it had been successfully used in Carlisle during an epidemic. Carbolic has a peculiarly pungent smell, which was why it had been poured into Carlisle's sewers to drive away the noxious fumes or 'miasma' thought to be infecting the drains. It did so of course, because it was an antiseptic and it destroyed the different bacteria and other micro-organisms which caused the smells and spread diseases.

Lister began to experiment, using carbolic acid applied to a surgical dressing. After successful trials with patients suffering from compound fractures (where the bone breaks through the skin) he started to use it as an antiseptic during operations. Sprays disinfected the operating theatre as he worked. Dilute carbolic acid sterilised his surgical instruments and his own hands before the operation. He cleansed the patient's skin with antiseptic before making an incision and continued to dress the wounds with carbolic dressings.

Remarkably, many more of his patients began to survive his operations than had done so before. In 1864–6, the survival rate had only been 55 per cent of all his patients undergoing surgery. In 1867–9, the proportion of survivors increased to 85 per cent – a truly remarkable improvement.

But despite this convincing evidence, many surgeons refused to accept his findings and even Florence Nightingale rejected the theory, because she had never seen any germs! However, Lister triumphed in the end, saving countless lives with his revolutionary methods and becoming accepted as one of the greatest surgeons in the history of medicine. He was made Lord Lister in 1897.

HOSPITALS

The eighteenth century saw a great increase in the number of hospitals built in Britain, especially in London, where several new hospitals, including Thomas Guy's (1722–4), were founded at that time. By 1825 over 150 hospitals and places for dispensing medicine had been founded by voluntary organisations, many of them as 'lying-in' hospitals (i.e. maternity hospitals). Better water supplies, better food, improved drainage, cotton bandages, use of antiseptics and greater emphasis on cleanliness all contributed to the better nursing care of patients in the middle of the nineteenth century.

As the picture shows, the standard of care in some hospitals had reached a high standard by 1860, thanks in part to the work of a remarkable woman – Florence Nightingale (see over).

Hospital Ward, Illustrated Times, *2 June 1860*

1 *In what ways is this hospital ward similar to a modern hospital ward? What privacy did the patients have when seen by a doctor? How was the ward lit?*

2 *What improvements would be needed to bring this ward up to the standard of a modern hospital ward?*

Florence Nightingale (1820–1910)

Florence Nightingale was born in Florence in Italy. She trained as a nurse in Germany and France and was in Britain, in 1854, when news of the sufferings of the soldiers in the Crimean War horrified public opinion. A war correspondent, wrote:

> 'Are there no devoted women among us able and willing to go forth to minister to the sick and suffering soldiers of the East in the hospitals of Scutari?'

Many nurses took up the challenge, including Florence Nightingale, although by coincidence a letter was already on its way from her friend Sidney Herbert, Secretary of State for War, asking her to take charge of the nursing party. They arrived at the main British Army hospital at Scutari, near Constantinople, on the eve of the bloody battle of Inkerman. The thought of women nurses in a hospital filled with wounded men shocked many strait-laced Victorians.

When the nurses arrived at Scutari, a forbidding barracks of a building, housing 10,000 sick men, they found dirt and filth throughout the hospital. Patients were lying in the corridors as well as in the wards, many of them suffering from typhoid fever and cholera, as well as from wounds sustained in battle.

Florence Nightingale and her team of 38 nurses scrubbed the hospital clean; washed the sheets, blankets and towels; cleaned the hospital's kitchens and prepared better, wholesome food for the patients. Most important of all, Florence Nightingale got army engineers to repair the hospital's drains and improve its supply of pure drinking water. As a result the survival rate at Scutari rose sharply.

Newspapers and magazines sang her praises. On her return to England, in 1856, she devoted her life to the training of nurses, with the aid of a fund of £50,000, which had been subscribed by a grateful public.

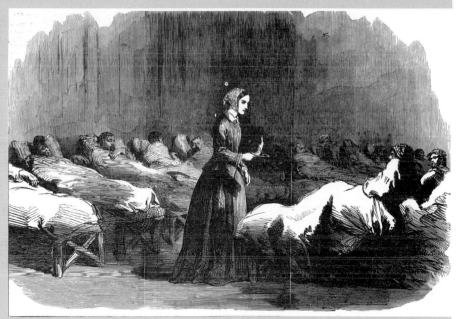

Florence Nightingale in the hospital at Scutari, The Illustrated London News, *24 February 1855*

3 *Do you think Florence Nightingale's clothes were suitable for use by a nurse?*

4 *What differences are there between this ward and the hospital ward in 1860? How do you account for this?*

5 *What do you think were Florence Nightingale's most important achievements?*

ADVANCES IN PUBLIC HEALTH

As Chapter 6 showed in the section on public health (pages 212–20), Edwin Chadwick, Dr Southwood Smith, Dr John Snow and others led the way in the 1840s and 1850s, in drawing attention to, and in condemning the poor living conditions which helped to spread epidemic diseases, such as cholera and typhus. But one epidemic disease had already been brought under control by the middle of the nineteenth century. This was smallpox, one of the great scourges of the eighteenth century.

The Turkish practice of variolation (a form of inoculation), by scratching the skin with fluid taken from the blisters of someone suffering a mild attack of smallpox, had been used since the early 1700s when it was introduced into Britain by Lady Mary Wortley Montagu. But it was risky and some of those inoculated with smallpox in this way had died, or been the cause of a minor epidemic of the disease spreading through a town. This is why variolation was banned by Parliament in 1840.

Edward Jenner (1749–1823), a doctor practising in Gloucestershire and a former student of John Hunter, was fascinated by the traditional country belief that anyone who caught cowpox (a relatively mild and harmless disease) thereby gained immunity from smallpox. It was a commonly observed fact that dairymaids, in constant contact with cows, rarely caught smallpox.

Jenner decided to put this theory to the test. On 14 May 1796, he took some fluid from the hand of Sarah Nelones, who was suffering from cowpox, and inserted the fluid into two slight scratches on the arms of James Phipps, a healthy boy of eight years of age. In the following July (1797), the boy was deliberately brought into contact with a smallpox victim but failed to catch the disease. Jenner had proved his point.

As with almost every other major discovery in medicine, he was immediately attacked by opponents from every quarter. A cartoonist even published a cartoon showing people looking like cattle after vaccination with cowpox serum! The Anti-vaccinarian Society called it 'the cruel despotic tyranny of forcing cow-pox misery on the innocent babes of the poor – a gross violation of religion, morality, law and humanity'.

Jenner's great achievement was eventually rewarded both with fame and money, and, more importantly, with a sharp reduction in the number of cases of smallpox – from an estimated 3,000 deaths per 1 million people per year in England in the late eighteenth century, to less than 500 deaths per 1 million people per year by 1840.

In 1853 the Government brought in a compulsory vaccination programme for all children within four months of birth, to an outcry from critics who said it was an interference in personal liberties.

Vaccination in London's East End in 1871, a contemporary print by E. Buckman. Why were poor people more likely to catch smallpox than the well-to-do?

1 What was the main argument of the Anti-vaccinarian Society? Do you think they were justified in their opposition to vaccination?
2 Write a dialogue between a supporter of the Society and Edward Jenner, putting forward the arguments for and against vaccination.
3 What arguments are still used today by opponents of vaccination and immunisation programmes?
4 In what ways have recent governments 'interfered' with personal liberties in the interest of better health? Do you think they are right or wrong to do this?

FURTHER QUESTIONS AND EXERCISES

1 Describe the contribution of the following to the advance of medicine, or surgery, in the eighteenth and nineteenth centuries:
   (a) Edward Jenner,
   (b) James Young Simpson,
   (c) Florence Nightingale,
   (d) Joseph Lister.
2 Imagine you are either James Young Simpson, Joseph Lister, or Edward Jenner. Explain to an awkward patient what you are going to do and the benefits to be expected from the action you are about to take. Reassure the patient with an anecdote or description to show how successful this new method is, compared to the old.

3   Read the following extract.

> 'There were no vessels for water or utensils of any kind; no soap,
> towels, or clothes, no hospital clothes; the men lying in their
> uniforms, stiff with gore and covered with filth to a degree and of a
> kind no one could write about; their persons covered with vermin.'

To what is the writer referring? Explain fully the circumstances which
provoked this outburst and say by whom, why, when and how these
deficiencies were rectified.

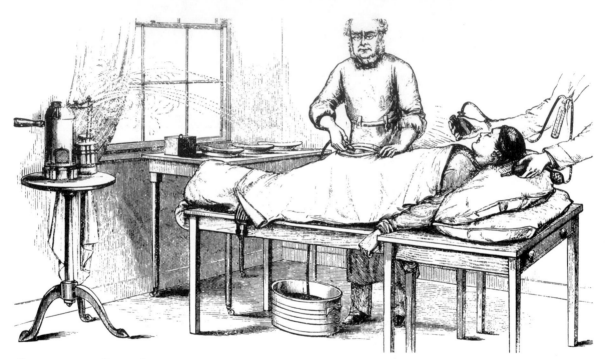

Contemporary illustration

4   Write a short essay commenting on this picture. Explain the events
which led up to the two major developments in surgery which it
illustrates.

5   What were the different methods used by doctors and scientists to
develop new surgical and medical techniques in the eighteenth and
nineteenth centuries? To what extent were their discoveries luck and to
what extent were they the fruits of careful and intelligent observation?
In what respects might some of their methods be condemned today?

6   How did the Industrial and Transport Revolutions help to facilitate the
work of doctors, surgeons and nurses in the eighteenth and nineteenth
centuries?

Time Chart

	Working-class movements	(Chapter 7)
1691–1730	Some workers 'combine' to improve working conditions	
1731–70	**Formation of Friendly Societies and Trade Clubs** 1736 Porteous Riot	
1771–90	**French Revolution inspires Reformers**	
1791–1810	**Reformist groups active; Robert Owen at New Lanark** 1792 London Corresponding Society 1799 First Combination Act 1800 Second Combination Act	
1811–30	**Demonstrations and riots; government clampdown on freedom to protest** 1811 Luddite riots begin 1816 Spa Fields meeting 1819 Peterloo Massacre; Six Acts 1825 Repeal of Combination Acts	
1831–50	**Early trade unions; agitation for electoral reform; Chartism** 1831 Colliers' strike in north-east England 1832 Great Reform Bill 1834 Grand National Consolidated Trades Union; Tolpuddle Martyrs 1839 Newport uprising 1842 Plug riots 1843 Rebecca riots 1848 Last great Chartist meeting	
1851–70	**New Model Unions** 1851 First of the New Model Unions founded 1859 London Builders' Strike 1866 Sheffield Outrages 1867 *Hornby* v. *Close* decision; Royal Commission on trades unions 1868 First meeting of Trades Union Congress	

Agriculture and Industry   (Chapters 1, 2, 4)

1691–1730	**Domestic industry; open fields in much of England** 1694 Bank of England founded 1709 Darby smelts iron ore with coke 1712 Newcomen steam engine 1720 South Sea Bubble
1731–70	**Jethro Tull; 'Turnip' Townshend; increase in number of Enclosure Acts; growing industries** 1733 Kay's flying shuttle 1740 Huntsman's crucible steel process 1760 Rotherham plough 1767 Hargreaves's spinning jenny 1769 Wedgwood opens Etruria Pottery Works
1771–90	**Adam Smith; Arthur Young; Robert Bakewell; Thomas Coke; water-powered textile machinery; steam engines in factories** 1771 Arkwright's water frame at Cromford Mill 1776 Boulton-Watt steam engine 1779 Crompton's mule 1782 Watt's double-acting steam engine 1784 Cort's puddling furnace 1789 Cartwright's steam power-loom
1791–1810	**Pace of enclosure quickens; factory system expands** 1799 Income Tax introduced
1811–30	**Agricultural distress; growth of factory towns** 1815 Corn Laws; Davy safety lamp for miners 1823 Reciprocity of Duties Act 1827 Bell's reaping machine 1828 Neilson's hot blast iron furnace 1830 Captain Swing riots
1831–50	**New fertilisers; rapid increase in use of farm machinery; decline of handloom weaving; rapid growth of all types of industry** 1839 Nasmyth's steam hammer; Anti-Corn Law League 1842 Phosphates factory at Deptford 1844 Bank Charter Act 1846 Repeal of the Corn Laws
1851–70	**Golden Age of Agriculture; 'Workshop of the World'** 1851 The Great Exhibition 1853 Saltaire Model Factory opens 1856 Bessemer Converter 1861 Siemens's open-hearth furnace

Transport (Chapter 3)

1691–1730	**Atrocious roads; navigable rivers; Turnpike Trusts**
1731–70	**Stage coach services expand; Canal Age begins** 1757 Sankey Navigation opens 1761 Brindley completes Duke of Bridgewater's canal
1771–90	**'Blind Jack' Metcalf; wagonways on coalfields** 1777 Trent and Mersey Canal completed 1784 First mail coach service begins
1791–1810	**Canal mania; steam engines used for transport** 1801 Steamship *Charlotte Dundas* launched 1803 Trevithick's first steam locomotive
1811–30	**Thomas Telford; John McAdam; George Stephenson; first railways; Golden Age of Coaching** 1812 Bell's *Comet* on Clyde 1825 Stockton and Darlington Railway opens 1829 Rainhill Trials 1830 Liverpool and Manchester Railway opens
1831–50	**Isambard Brunel; George Hudson; Railway Age begins; decline of coaching and turnpikes; steamships and ironclads at sea** 1841 Great Western Railway opens 1843 Launch of Brunel's *Great Britain* 1844 Parliamentary Train Railway Act 1846 Railway mania reaches peak; Broad Gauge Act
1851–70	**Decline of canals; steady growth of railways; steamships overtake sailing ships** 1858 Launch of Brunel's *Great Eastern*

Social problems and reform (Chapters 5, 6, 8, 9, 10)

1691–1730	**Charity Schools: high death rate; high infant mortality rate** 1701 England & Wales 5.8 million
1731–70	**Death rate begins to decline** 1748 Bow Street Runners formed in London 1751 England & Wales 6.4 million; curb on gin drinking
1771–90	**Position of paupers improves; some social reforms** 1777 John Howard's *The State of Prisons in England and Wales* 1780 Robert Raikes starts Sunday Schools Movement 1782 Gilbert's Poor Law Act
1791–1810	**Monitorial system; rapid rise in population** 1795 Speenhamland System 1797 Jenner uses vaccination 1801 First Census; England & Wales 8.9 million 1802 Health and Morals of Apprentices Act 1807 Abolition of slave trade
1811–30	**National and British Schools; rapid rise in cost of the Poor Law; population still rising rapidly** 1813 Elizabeth Fry visits Newgate Prison 1819 Factory Act 1829 Metropolitan Police formed
1831–50	**Robert Owen; Lord Shaftesbury; Richard Oastler; Edwin Chadwick; New Poor Law; Factory Acts; emigration; famine in Ireland; cholera epidemics** 1833 First government grant for education 1834 Poor Law Amendment Act 1835 Municipal Corporations Act 1836 Registration of births, deaths, marriages 1839 County Police Act; Committee of Privy Council for Education 1842 Coal Mines Act; Chadwick's Report on Towns 1844 Co-op in Rochdale; Factory Act 1846 Pupil-teacher system; public parks 1847 Simpson uses chloroform; Ten-Hour Act 1848 Public Health Act 1850 Free public libraries; Ten-Hour Act
1851–70	**Improvements in nursing, surgery, educational provision for working classes, living conditions in towns; further Factory Acts** 1854 Florence Nightingale at Scutari 1856 County and Borough Police Act 1858 Newcastle Commission on Education 1859 London Mains Drainage scheme 1862 Revised Code 1867 Lister pioneers antiseptic surgery 1870 Education Act

Index